GONER

The final travels of UG Krishnamurti

Louis Brawley

NON-DUALITY PRESS

This book is possible thanks to Mukunda, Balaji, Mahesh, Anirban, the Guhas, Roger, Nancy, Aiden, Jesse and, of course, UG.

GONER

First edition published May 2011 by NON-DUALITY PRESS
Revised edition June 2013

© Louis Brawley 2011
© Non-Duality Press 2011

NON-DUALITY PRESS | PO Box 2228 | Salisbury | SP2 2GZ
United Kingdom

ISBN: 978-0-9566432-7-8
www.non-dualitypress.com

You are trying to present me as a religious man, which I am not. You are failing to comprehend the most important thing that I am emphasizing. There is no religious content, no mystical overtones at all, in what I am saying. Man has to be saved from the saviors of mankind! The religious people—they kidded themselves and fooled the whole of mankind. Throw them out! That is courage itself, because of the courage there; not the courage you practice.

goner [ˈgɒnə]

n

Slang a person or thing beyond help or recovery, esp a
person who is dead or about to die

Collins English Dictionary—Complete and Unabridged
HarperCollins Publishers 1991, 1994, 1998, 2000, 2003

UG often professed a liking for American underground slang.
More than once he told the story that while he was down and
out in London with his 'head missing' he would sit in the British
Library in the chair where Karl Marx wrote *Das Kapital*. He
spent hours reading a tome called the Dictionary of American
Underground Slang to pass the time. *Goner* was one of his
favorite words to describe the people who 'hung around' him.

CHAPTER 1

March 13, 2007

On March 13, 2007 I walked out the door to what we called his 'cave' knowing it was the last time I would see him alive. A life of constant travel with a sage was coming to an end and I was so exhausted I couldn't think. After spending day and night with him for almost eight weeks the door clicked shut behind me and a five-year encounter with oblivion ended, or so it seemed at the time. The curtains were pulled against the fresh smell of the garden where the grass was glistening with dew and the scents of a lush Italian garden. The two-hundred-year-old palm tree in the middle of the garden threw a long cool shadow across the sparkling green lawn where for eight weeks UG Krishnamurti spent his final days sitting up long enough to shout at us, collapsing after increasingly shorter bursts of invective against everything mankind thought, felt and believed.

He monitored his own death with indifferent curiosity.

"How am I doing, doc?" he would ask any one of his medical friends.

Yet, unlike the recovery after his last fall, he grew gradually weaker each day. He seemed incapable of or uninterested in doing anything that might 'prolong the misery'; that was his assessment of the usual medical treatment we seek in order to sustain life in a constant battle of ideas verses the natural order. Seeking medical help in any form was out of the question, so it took a while to realize that he might actually die, because of his indifference to the outcome of his situation. To the end of

1

his days there was a wild card up his sleeve. He'd come close to dying more than once in his life already. The fact is, by all accounts he'd already died and been re-born years before, not spiritually, but literally, physically.

Our last meeting was silent. He allowed me to come on the condition there would be no talking. For days I'd been thinking I should thank him, tell him what he meant to me, how lucky I was to have met him, but the timing never seemed right. Old friends were professing their love, giving heartfelt testimony about the gratitude they felt, asking for final blessings or just saying goodbye, yet I'd been in there with him every night and day for weeks and I knew that he knew everything I was thinking and feeling. It was unnecessary.

Suddenly I was out in the garden, swept into a new life on a fierce current. That was it. The human tornado that had been blowing through my life was gone.

Mahesh was waiting for me in the driveway. It seems fitting that a Bollywood director was taking over for the final days of 'packing him up'. Everything about the most obscure man in the universe was a contradiction that made perfect non-sense.

"Well?"

"That's it. He gave me everything I need; asking for more would be ridiculous."

"I know it doesn't look like it now, but when you look back on this day it will be the most important day of your life."

I wasn't so sure about that, but after Mahesh's pep talk, walking across the garden to the apartment, a warm fear wormed right up my spine. It felt like I was walking off a cliff.

I knew I was already lucky to have met, let alone spent so much time with a man like him. It was a stroke of dumb luck in an otherwise ordinary life. He had everything I wanted, or so I thought as long as I was sitting in front of him. He was a human wilderness, fearless and unpredictable. The first day I met him he confirmed my darkest suspicions about the bullshit world surrounding me; at the same time he was an affirmation of life at every turn. His words were simple and baffling, hilarious, repetitive and boring at times, but his actions were clear as a bell ringing in a forest.

When I left his side that day, I carried the words inside me where he left them like gifts to be opened later. His company was a teaching. He was so alive there was no room for understanding. He was too quick for that sort of crap.

I sensed all this more than I understood it from the first encounter with him. Very soon after meeting him I knew I'd stumbled into something like a cosmic lottery win. As my misery intensified, I stuck it out, knowing damn well that whatever happened to me as long as I was around him would be for the best. For a bunch of crazy reasons I was able to get close to him almost immediately and from then on my life raced in unforeseen directions like a log broken loose from a jam and thrown over a waterfall.

What can I say? Hanging around with him was just like that.

CHAPTER 2

My background is worthless: it can't be a model for anybody,
because your background is unique in its own way. Your
conditions, your environment, your background—the whole
thing is different. Every event in your life is different.

I was born and brought up in small-town America at the height
of the cold war and the explosion of capitalist pop culture. Being
Catholic in my family meant attending church every Sunday
which was more than enough to turn me off religion as a kid.
Parochial school and the sadistic nuns who went along with
it the rest of the week sealed the deal. By the time I escaped
the clutches of that school I had lost any interest in religion
or god, at least for the time being. Public high school was a
relief from the force-fed religion my mother took more to heart
than my father, for whom being Catholic was a matter of pride.
My father was also proud of being Irish like the Kennedys and
wore Brooks Brothers' suits and spit-shine wing-tip shoes. Being
middle class in any country is like being sandwiched between
a tortured urge to be rich and the terror of being perceived as
poor. My response to my father's bullshit ambitions was juve-
nile delinquent behavior. Heavy drinking, drug consumption
and shoplifting were my remedies for being habitually annoyed
by adults and chronically short of cash.

Chapter heading and other quotations from UG Krishnamurti are taken
from *The Mystique of Enlightenment* which is freely available without
copyright from sources including: http://www.well.com/user/jct/ and
http://en.wikisource.org/wiki/The_Mystique_of_Enlightenment

Yet among other things (like a talent for excessive drinking), I inherited my father's obsession with reading. As a teenager I read Herman Hesse novels, Carlos Castaneda's mystical trickster books, and Aldous Huxley's *Doors of Perception*. It was the same stuff a lot of teenagers were reading back then. I also spent a lot of time at the school library poring over art catalogues and at an exclusive local art museum where I got the idea of being an artist. Maybe you're just born with that ridiculous idea. At the time I was mainly interested in anything other than what my parents were interested in. My father wanted me to be a lawyer or a golf pro. Safe to say I was heading in the opposite direction from those professions.

During my last year of college an art professor handed me a book by a man named Jiddu Krishnamurti. Having escaped the Catholic church, the last thing I wanted to do was get involved with a guru, but I read the book out of respect for her. The book surprised me. Here was a so-called spiritual man stressing that doubt was an essential tool for approaching life, truth, and so-called spirituality. His manner and expression gave me the impression that he'd had a spiritual transformation of consciousness. It sounded like what I'd read about enlightenment, an idea that seemed unusual to come across in modern times. He didn't quote other people when he spoke, and there *was* a certain quality to what he had to say. Could there actually be a man like Siddhartha out there?

> *Religion is the skeptical enquiry into the whole of our existence, which is our consciousness. If there is fear your meditation is utterly meaningless. A free mind is essential for enquiry and when there is fear there is no freedom.*[1]

The tone appealed to me, he was taking a new approach to the whole issue of religion that bothered me. I mean, there must be something to religion, but what? The references to his experiences with some kind of 'immensity' were interesting in the sense they sounded like something real and reasonable. "Don't accept a thing the speaker is saying," he repeatedly emphasized, encouraging real enquiry, which was something I never encountered in the Catholicism of my youth; any questions I had about religion were met with stock answers, so unconvincing I dismissed them out of hand.

While reading a dialogue in one of J. Krishnamurti's books with a physicist named David Bohm, I felt as if someone had reached into my brain and twisted things in a new direction. There was an eerie sensation that someone was watching me which made me freeze in my chair. The world was suddenly irreversibly different in every way, but what that was I had no idea.

> No time. Then what takes place? What is happening? Not to me, not to my brain. What is happening? We have said that when one denies time there is nothing. After this long talk, nothing means everything. Everything is energy. And we have stopped there. But that isn't the end.[2]

Reading the careful dissection of the mechanics of time and thought, the unusual precision and insight of their exchange had a profound effect on me. I'll never forget the shabby little kitchen table where I sat reading that book. Until that moment, spirituality had been just a theory: suddenly it was frighteningly real. I was gripped by the sensation as if someone I couldn't see was staring at me from somewhere in the room. I couldn't explain these feelings, let alone ask someone about them. As a result of that experience I turned a corner and there was no way back; despite myself, I set off down that pathless path Jiddu Krishnamurti was talking about, just as blind as could be.

At the first opportunity I went to see the impeccably dressed elderly Indian man give a talk. He emerged from behind a huge curtain in Madison Square Garden looking slightly lost, took a seat on a simple folding chair in front of a packed hall and placed his shaking hands neatly under his thighs. Scanning the audience with a slightly stiff neck, he sat quietly for a few minutes until the audience began to applaud at which point he became visibly annoyed:

"Why are you clapping, sirs? This is not an entertainment!"

Then again, closing his eyes and gathering himself, he hesitantly, slowly, began to speak:

"Can we take a journey, like two friends, walking together?"

For the next hour and a half you could have heard a pin drop. In a very proper sounding British accent with a faint Indian lilt to it, he engaged the audience with carefully chosen words, encouraging us to see if they rang true for us. Addressing the troubles of mankind and the search for freedom, happiness, and truth, he urged the listeners to look into these things with him, using great attention as we did. He proceeded word by word urging us to be 'choicelessly aware' of our reactions to what he was saying.

> *Do you know what it means to learn? When you are really learning you are learning throughout your life and there is no one special teacher to learn from. Then everything teaches you—a dead leaf, a bird in flight, a smell, a tear, the rich and the poor, those who are crying, the smile of a woman, the haughtiness of a man. You learn from everything, therefore there is no guide, no philosopher, no guru. Life itself is your teacher, and you are in a state of constant learning.*[3]

"See for yourself, sirs! Don't take my word for it!"

It was the same message contained in his books, but listening to the man, whose story was by then familiar, had a certain excitement to it. He was a rare individual who had the guts to walk out of a worldwide organization, the Theosophical Society, just as he was about to take over as the world teacher.

After seeing him in person, I convinced the art professor to come with me to his talks in Ojai. We camped in the mountains nearby. It was my first encounter with the Rocky Mountains. The hills were full of lavender and the road signs were full of bullets. At the talks it was disconcerting to enter a huge parking lot and stand in line after paying for the privilege of witnessing the former world teacher speak to his 'friends'.

If you examine the nature of organized religion you will see that all religions are essentially alike, whether Hinduism, Buddhism, Mohammedanism, Christianity—or communism, which is another form of religion, the very latest. The moment you understand the prison, which is to perceive all the implications of belief, of rituals and priests, you will never again belong to any religion; because only the man who is free of belief can discover that which lies beyond all belief, that which is immeasurable.[4]

While we were there, rumors were circulating about a rift between J.Krishnamurti, and Rajagopal, his former manager, who still lived on the grounds. What I didn't know at the time was that I was carrying on with an affair in much the same way this non-guru turned out to have carried on with his manager's wife for 28 years. Unbeknownst to me, there were striking similarities between our situations at some point in time, but back then I was in the first flush of an infatuation with a 'godly' man.

As before, he sat on a slightly raised platform, his hands trembling with Parkinson's Disease, occasionally wiping rheumy tears from big soulful eyes with a neatly folded white handkerchief. A slight breeze blew through the oak grove as a packed crowd listened to his every word. He started more or less the same way.

In listening to the speaker, if you merely interpret the words according to your personal like and dislike, without being aware of your own tendencies of interpretation, then the word becomes a prison in which most of us, unfortunately, are caught. But if one is aware of the meaning of the word and of what lies behind the word, then communication becomes possible. Communication implies not only a verbal comprehension, but also going together, examining together, sharing together, creating together.[5]

He was a master performer, commanding attention from the huge crowd, but I was disturbed. The fact is I was bored and distracted.

Now, what has happened to the mind, to the brain, that has listened to all this—not merely heard a few words, but actually listened, shared, communicated, learnt? What has happened to your mind that has listened with tremendous attention to the complexity of the problem, with awareness of its own fears, and has seen how thought breeds and sustains fear as well as pleasure? What has happened to the quality of the mind that has so listened? Is the quality of this mind entirely different from the moment when we began this morning, or is it the same repetitive mind, caught in pleasure and fear?[6]

It was even hard to concentrate while thinking about what I must be missing. The notion that he was beyond all that only made me feel worse. When I left the talks I was depressed at my lack of moral fiber. By this point I'd given up drinking and drugs, but I had the distinct impression that he was a more pure human being than I could ever be. The idea of applying for a position in one of his schools, or leading a celibate life, occurred to me but that would have meant dropping my ambitions as an artist and leaving the woman who had introduced me to him. The idea of becoming a celibate was a convenient excuse to distance myself from her, but her tears were all it took for me to drop both ideas.

My life went on as usual, but changed. I was young, insecure, poor and unaccomplished. I was lost.

Eventually J.Krishnamurti's books started gathering dust on my bookshelf. I occasionally dipped into them, trying to 'get it', maybe from another angle, maybe after a month, or a year, or two years.

If you have not given your attention, everything you have, to find out what thinking is, you will never be able to find out if it is possible to observe without the 'me'. If you cannot observe without the 'me' the problems will go on—one problem opposing another. [7]

No matter how much I tried, in the end it was like playing a game of hide-and-seek with the unknown. Shaking myself loose from the grips of that man once and for all took another twenty years and another Krishnamurti.

---

1. Lutyens, M. 1988. *Krishnamurti: The Open Door.* London, John Murray Publishers Ltd. p 37.

2. Krishnamurti, J. and Bohm, D. 1985. *Ending of Time.* New York, Harper and Row

3. Krishnamurti, J. 1989. *Think on These Things.* New York: HarperOne. p 10.

4. Ibid p149.

5. Krishnamurti, J. 1972. *The Impossible Question.* London: Victor Gollancz, p32

6. Ibid p 36

7. Ibid p 29

CHAPTER 3

*I was just telling the people here: the worship of the bull
there in the temple, and the worship of Shiva—you know
that yoni and lingam business—has come down from the
original man: to him sex was the highest kind of pleasure that
he knew. Later on man experienced the bliss, the beatitude,
and all that moved over; but, originally, sex was the most
important thing. Even the cross is a phallic symbol.*

Despite all my attempts to escape my troubles over the years
the story of my life was strung together by one reaction after
another to people, for things I imagined they had done to make
me miserable. It hadn't occurred to me that what I was doing to
myself was far worse. Once the relationship with the professor
fell apart I moved through a string of others, unable to commit.
It seemed the end was in sight even as I entered them. I don't
know whether I was unable to afford the trappings of marriage
or unwilling to, but it always felt like a trap to be avoided. It
wasn't the women I felt trapped by, so much as the social pressure to participate in all the things I was running from.

After languishing in Philadelphia, painting pictures no one
ever saw for too long, I moved to New York to pursue a career
as an artist. I got a masters degree in fine arts and continued to
seek girlfriends and therapy as solutions to my personal problems. Frustrated with the endless navel gazing uselessness of
therapy I discovered that a Twelve Step program helped with
the nuts and bolts anxiety of life, but the persistent current
running underneath everything in life seemed to elude me. I

tried meditation for eight years, read endless books about spirituality, spiritual people and philosophy in search of something
that seemed missing.

After attending a second Zen retreat upstate that reminded
me of Catholic school, I finally went back to Jiddu Krishnamurti
(JK) in search of answers. He seemed to be the one man who
lived what he spoke. Unfortunately, or fortunately as the case
may be, not only was he long since dead, the story of his sex
scandal came to my attention for the first time. I had to laugh.
It was old news to the folks in the JK discussion group I was
attending. The foundation even admitted the stories were true,
but I brushed all that aside. After all, his lover was a close
friend, even if she was the wife of his manager. I rationalized all
this with the idea that he never said sex was wrong. After all he
never spoke highly of marriage so why not? It was even a relief
to realize he was human after all; a man with real drives, almost
like me. Despite this evidence that he had not been living the
'celibate life' he pretended to be when he said things like, "The
thought of sex never even enters my mind." He was too elevated
in my mind to fall from the pedestal I didn't quite realize I had
placed him on.

Once again I spent hours poring over his books at home, at
work or on long subway rides. I ordered audiotapes, listening
as 'K' went 'slowly, sanely, logically, step by step' over word
after word. I hung on each phrase, sure that with the proper
attention I could grasp the '...possibility of transforming that
which is', as he put it in his talks. When I look at them now I'm
amazed that I could stand it.

I attended an annual celebration of his birthday in Ojai. It
was strange to revisit this place after so many years. The professor was now long dead, JK was dead, my life was different, yet
some things remained naggingly the same. Hope had not died,
but the once bustling compound around the Oak Grove was
a dusty remnant of its former glory. The mire of institutional

power struggles in the schools and organization established 'to preserve the teachings in their pristine purity' had overgrown the place like weeds.

I met people who had moved to Ojai to be with the great teacher and stayed on long after he died. They expressed bitterness and disappointment with him, with the school, with the teachings. How could that happen? One of his old houses was turned into a study center that smelled like a church retreat. His personal papers were stored in a climate-controlled vault that sounded like a power station buzzing away behind the hedges of manicured lawns.

Despite this lifeless dead end, I decided to go to India to see what was happening in the schools he'd started there. Maybe they held some clue to the real heart of the teaching. I mentioned this in the chat room (where I spent most of my work hours stealing corporate time at the office), and a former teacher from a JK school said they were full of rich brats who only went at the insistence of their parents. There was something wrong with the picture.

I just couldn't put my finger on it.

CHAPTER 4

*You see that is the trouble: you dare not question that
basic thing, because that is going to destroy something there
which is very precious to you: the continuity of yourself
as you know yourself and as you experience yourself.*

The day before I was supposed to leave on my first trip to Asia
I checked the weather in India online. Temperatures in Delhi
were soaring into the hundred-degree range. I felt panicky. I
was going halfway around the globe out of curiosity and the
Krishnamurti scene was on increasingly flimsy ground. The discussion group I had been attending in the west village was full
of members of what he called the 60-year club and the occasional nut-job. The JK chat room was full of self-congratulatory
'understandings' springing up like weeds and clogging the hours
of office boredom with another kind of boredom. This news
about the weather in Delhi was the final straw that inspired me
to abort the trip. I cancelled, lost $100 and felt relieved.

Weeks later I was still browsing the JK site when I found a
UG Krishnamurti listed in a website just beneath his. I wondered if it was a relative riding on the coat tails of his famous
spiritual uncle. Spiritual imitators are a dime a dozen, yet sheer
mental suffocation forced me toward this window of entertainment opportunity. I opened the link with no idea and little
hope of what lay beyond.

The site featured photographs and quotes and I recall my
acute disappointment with the fey appearance of a man sitting
with his legs gathered to one side in a long flowing garment. I

learned that UG Krishnamurti was at one time a follower of J Krishnamurti, not a relative. Krishnamurti was a name as common as Smith in India. People on the JK chat dismissed him as 'an imitator' and after glancing through the site I posted my own sarcastic note about the UG site on the JK chat. I'd read nothing.

A message came back from someone who knew both men and said JK used to ask him each time he visited UG, "What is he saying?" I was impressed to have connected with a person who actually knew JK well enough to have spoken to him face to face. This was already a glimpse into the inner circle so to speak, deeper by far in a few words than I'd gotten in months, maybe ever.

There was another site linked to the first, posting his books on line for free. I'd spent ungodly sums of money on JK material that year already so this was a break. Unlike JK, I noted that UG didn't write the books and took no money from sales of them. They consisted of recorded conversations with no mention of a foundation, schools, seminars, or retreats. The only thing written by the subject of the book was a disclaimer on the opening page in the first book called *The Mystique of Enlightenment*.

My teaching, if that is the word you want to use, has no copyright. You are free to reproduce, distribute, interpret, misinterpret, distort, garble, do what you like, even claim authorship, without my consent or the permission of anybody.

The next page got right to business.

People call me an 'enlightened man'—I detest that term— they can't find any other word to describe the way I'm functioning. At the same time, I point out that there is no such thing as enlightenment at all. I say that because all my life I've searched and wanted to be an enlightened man, and

*I discovered that there is no such thing as enlightenment
at all, and so the question whether a particular person is
enlightened or not doesn't arise. I don't give a hoot for a
sixth century BC Buddha, let alone all the other claimants
we have in our midst. They are a bunch of exploiters, thriving on the gullibility of the people. There is no power outside
of man. Man has created God out of fear. So the problem is
fear and not God.*

I don't think I've ever opened a book about spirituality where
the person dismissed the idea of enlightenment without sneak-
ily replacing it with some transparently newfangled word for
the same thing. I read on in search of the carrot. What I didn't
realize until much later was how well I had been prepared
for what was about to come at me in this man's words. JK's
approach to spirituality was a radical departure for me from the
previous definitions of either spirituality or philosophy, since
he spoke directly to his audience without reference to other
texts or practices. His life story impressed me as much as his
words. Since his death, the story of his affair had put a dent
in my image of him but the content of what he was saying was
still impressive.

What I encountered in UG's words was a step further, more
like a quantum leap that was so subtle at first I didn't realize
what it implied about JK's teachings. One thing that troubled
me in JK's early career was his poetry full of mushy Victorian-
sounding phrases about the beloved and the otherness. There
was something suspiciously sentimental about these beginnings,
but that style had been eliminated as he matured, presumably a
result of the 'process' whereby some kind of influence referred
to in still mystical terms, but mostly privately, continued to
'prepare the mind' for the teaching.

In the opening pages of *Mystique* a fresh voice came across in
a tone of dismissal that cut through any hope of mystification,

with no patience for the sentimental meanderings of spiritual poetry like those still lingering in Krishnamurti's published journals, for example. Where Jiddu Krishnamurti radicalized spirituality, UG was a man wiping the slate clean of the word spirituality.

When pressed to comment on such things UG drew attention to the uselessness of careworn spiritual terms, which have always been a pet peeve of mine. It's so easy to throw words around, but if there was anything to something like enlightenment, how could it be contained in a word? All I'd been fed so far was words. So far there was nothing in direct contradiction to JK's approach, but there were differences in the implications of his comments that left JK in the dust.

At some point, of course, I wanted the prize, to be enlightened. Even if it was just an idea I'd picked up, the idea that someone could teach a thing like that seemed inconsistent with what it meant, no matter how many books I read. UG stated the origins of seeking in a totally new and simple light: "I didn't want to want what they wanted me to want." JK never promised enlightenment, that's for sure; in fact the more I read, the less likely it seemed to be possible, but the hope of it lingered between the lines of his talk. While he never promised anybody anything, he spoke of going together like friends, which implied leading you by the hand to a 'pathless land' to an unspoken reward that remained undelivered. UG dismissed the possibility that he could help at all.

UG Krishnamurti grew up in a religious home with wealthy grandparents who took care of him after his mother died in his infancy and his father left and remarried. As a child he practiced meditation and yoga, and had numerous mystical experiences between the ages of fourteen and twenty-one, dismissing them as he witnessed the hypocrisy of each of his spiritual teachers and saw the blueprint for his experiences in books he'd read. Second-hand experiences were not good enough for him. The models being held up to him were leading him nowhere and he didn't take other people's word for the reason why.

Everybody says, "Don't get angry"—I am angry all the time. I am full of brutal activities inside, so that is false. What these people are telling me I should be like is something false, and because it is false it will falsify me. I don't want to live the life of a false person. I am greedy, and non-greed is what they are talking about. There is something wrong somewhere.

He spoke with rare simplicity of a life of frustration in the search for truth.

I am a brute, I am a monster, I am full of violence—this is reality. I am full of desire.

As a young man he met a famous saint in South India named Ramana Maharshi, who he said was the last 'holy man' he saw. A friend dragged him there and he asked a question:

"What you have, can you give it to me?"

"I can give it, but can you take it?"

He later said, and then denied, that this reply helped him to formulate the question that would percolate in him for the next 29 years: "What is that state these people are in?"

He never went back to see that man because he said his answer was too traditional. Given that he'd been brought up in the environment of the Theosophical Society, it's not surprising that Maharshi struck him as a traditionalist. Jiddu Krishnamurti was a stylish western-educated character with great charisma whose influence on UG I would not grasp for years to come.

When he realized that none of his spiritual practice could tame his sex drive, he married, and began a career as a public lecturer for the Theosophical Society. It was a natural career trajectory for a wealthy young man of his inclinations. The story of his encounters with JK was riveting for me, and if he said Ramana Maharshi was the last holy man he ever saw then what, I wondered, was JK to him?

In *The Mystique of Enlightenment* he explained:

I inherited the Theosophical Society, J.Krishnamurti, and a lot of money from my grandfather.

As it turned out, he was able to confront the man who had lured me into the seeking game at a time of his greatest vitality. He spent seven years participating in small private discussions and one-on-one conversation with JK. His young family seemed to have been favored with the man's attentions. At some point there was a frustration, a break with the older man, and UG's life started to fall apart in the wake of his intense scrutiny of the teachings. The price he paid for his inquiry spoke volumes compared to the armchair speculations and comfortable whimsy many people apply to these perennial questions. By the time of his 'calamity' UG's life had been, to all intents and purposes, destroyed. When people asked JK if anyone understood anything he was saying the answer was a resounding "No!" So what happened to UG? Was he staking a claim with his critique? Could this be a way of putting some distance between his own and the older man's business so he could open his personal chain of spiritual restaurants? On the subject of J Krishnamurti he said:

He spoke of no teaching, no teacher, no taught, and then went around setting up schools and foundations to preserve the teachings in their pristine purity for posterity.

It was an obvious point that never occurred to me. As I read on, it seemed someone had finally 'torn apart' the teachings that baffled me for years. Preserving the teachings for posterity was so obviously the key to establishing a religion that I felt as though UG had only pointed out what was staring me in the face the whole time.

So what was UG doing?

CHAPTER 5

The whole chemistry of the body changes, so it begins to function in its own natural way. That means everything that is poisoned (I deliberately use that word) and contaminated by the culture is thrown out of the system. It is thrown out of your system and then that consciousness of life (or whatever you want to call it) expresses itself and functions in a very natural way. The whole thing has to be thrown out of your system; otherwise, if you don't believe in God, you become an atheist and you teach, preach and proselytize atheism. But this individual is neither a theist, nor an atheist, nor an agnostic; he is what he is.

UG Krishnamurti followed the teachings of Jiddu Krishnamurti (JK) for decades and was highly critical of the world teacher. Had someone finally succeeded and 'torn apart' the teachings as JK implored his listeners to? His words shed light on a previously impenetrable chamber of confusion. Beneath the familiar words and phrases was something raw and crystal clear, quite unlike JK's hopeful leading methods of choiceless awareness.

UG spoke of his personal search with blunt, ruthless honesty. While JK often claimed memory loss about his early life after the 'process' took over, UG spelled out the steps of his disillusionment with spiritual concepts. The 'process' JK talked about in private was a heavily guarded secret, something he never discussed in public, let alone in a talk. UG spoke of having had a significant 'experience' in a Paris burlesque show whereas JK's 'process' involved fainting spells in the laps of beautiful women with whom he was intimately involved, at least as friends.

UG spoke of a fiery confrontation with the teachings of JK, something I had a keen interest in:

Then (July 1967), there arrived another phase. Krishnamurti was again there in Saanen giving talks. My friends dragged me there and said, "Now at least it is a free business. Why don't you come and listen?" I said, "All right, I'll come and listen." When I listened to him, something funny happened to me—a peculiar kind of feeling that he was describing my state and not his state. Why did I want to know his state? He was describing something, some movements, some awareness, some silence—"In that silence there is no mind; there is action"—all these kinds of things. So, I am in that state. What the hell have I been doing all these years, listening to all these people and struggling, wanting to understand his state or the state of somebody else, Buddha or Jesus? I am in that state. Now I am in that state. So, then I walked out of the tent and never looked back.

Then—very strange—that question "What is that state?" transformed itself into another question, "How do I know that I am in that state, the state of Buddha, the state I very much wanted and demanded from everybody? I am in that state but how do I know?"

The next day (UG's 49th birthday) I was sitting on a bench under a tree overlooking one of the most beautiful spots in the whole world, the seven hills and seven valleys (of Saanenland). I was sitting there. Not that the question was there; the whole of my being was that question: "How do I know that I am in that state? There is some kind of peculiar division inside of me: there is somebody who knows that he is in that state. The knowledge of that state—what I have read, what I have experienced, what they have talked about—it is this knowledge that is looking at that state, so it is only this knowledge that has projected that state." I said to myself "Look here, old chap, after forty years you have not moved one step; you are there in square number one. It is the same knowledge that projected your mind there when you asked this question. You are in the same situation asking the same question How do I know? because it is this knowledge, the description of this state by those people, that has created this state for you. You are kidding yourself. You are a damned fool". So, nothing. But still there was some kind of a peculiar feeling that this was the state.

The second question, "How do I know that this is the state?"—I didn't have any answer for that question—it was like a question in a whirlpool—it went on and on and on. Then suddenly the question disappeared. Nothing happened; the question just disappeared. I didn't say to myself, "Oh, my God! Now I have found the answer." Even that state disappeared—the state I thought I was in, the state of Buddha, Jesus—even that has disappeared. The question has disappeared. The whole thing is finished for me, and that's all, you see. It is not emptiness, it is not blankness, it is not the void, it is not any of those things; the question disappeared suddenly and that is all.

This non-event caused a sudden explosion inside, blasting, as it were, every cell, every nerve and every gland in my body. And with that 'explosion', the illusion that there is continuity of thought, that there is a center, an 'I' linking up the thoughts, was not there anymore.

The simplicity of UG's depiction of the problems with JK's teachings were easily overlooked. He refused to give up his search until it was impossible to continue. His assessment of the situation one faces as a seeker was unlike anything I'd read before. His testimony spoke to his own shortcomings in the futile search.

Clearly I had fallen for the image of a man who was supposed to be living a life of celibate purity. That was one thing I deliberately overlooked. The Foundation maintained this image after his death until the scandal with his manager's wife made it embarrassing to do so. UG made no attempt to paint a pretty picture of himself, instead he highlighted a one-night stand and a tendency to jealousy and violence. This was startlingly blunt material which read like a fire racing along out of control. It was mesmerizing.

In a private conversation JK implored him: "The house is on fire, sir! What will you do?"

UG's retort: "Pour more gasoline on it and burn the whole thing down!"

JK was a perfect set-up to UG, a perfect one-two punch to my solar plexus. It was unraveling so fast there was no choice but to read on. UG insisted there was no mystical or spiritual content in the physical changes that had occurred in his body as a result of the 'calamity'. It was not related to any practice, not even JK's 'choiceless awareness', a method he now went so far as to mock. UG took the position of no position to an absolute terminus. When he pointed out the fact that nothing he had done could have caused what happened to him, this in itself was a blow to the ideas of attentiveness and awareness I'd been hanging on to consciously or not. All his attempts at understanding merely blocked the natural functioning of his body. In light of that, anything anyone said that promised a spiritual awakening was necessarily a lie. Awakening itself was a lie, an idea cooked up to promote teachers who 'thrive on the gullibility and credulity of the people'.

Until the sales pitch of enlightenment is thrown out of your system by the simple confrontation with its futility, it will continually mislead you, and once it is kicked out, you will see there is no need for it. What was baffling about his case as clearly as he articulated this, was that it appeared to have fallen away without his volition. He didn't know how it happened that he gave up. In this line he was not far from JK, who said the thought we were using to approach the problem was the problem itself and we were in danger of sharpening the very instrument that was the trap. Yet in life, JK's actions were another matter and in his talks there was always some shred of hope dangling; he never really pared it down to the brutal hopelessness UG went right to the heart of. JK spoke dismissively of gurus yet went on to establish schools in his name. UG established nothing but an irascible attitude that was highly appealing, refusing to soften the blows in order to give false hope.

What you are looking for does not exist. You would rather tread an enchanted ground with beatific visions of a radical transformation of that non-existent self of yours into a state of being which is conjured up by some bewitching phrases.

In the opening pages of his first book, *The Mystique of Enlightenment*, UG Krishnamurti blew up the elusive frustration I'd been grappling with for years. He later said the 'old man', as he would sometimes refer to JK, had implied that if such a thing happened it would devastate one down to every nerve, every cell in the body, which is precisely what happened to him. The state JK was in is anybody's guess; his talk of 'the beloved' and 'the otherness', describing the beauty of watching a solitary tree, listening to the river and watching the clouds, sound like the musings of a very high mystic.

UG's response to these aesthetically pleasing sentiments was severe:

For the man who is expecting something like what they have described, this is a calamity!

He said you couldn't even see the tree and if you did see it for once in your life, you'd drop dead.

JK was an expert at exploring the workings of the mind,

revealing the limits of thought with stunning clarity. UG was blunt, fierce and down to earth, but the effect was deeper, cleaner and subtler than I realized at the time. I thought I'd seen the limits of thought but UG made such obvious points about the futility of JK's approach that it was embarrassing to admit to myself I could have been so gullible. There was no poetry in what he was saying, rather he was going out of his way to demystify everything he could get his hands on.

That is one of the reasons why I express it in pure and simple physical and physiological terms. It has no psychological content at all, it has no mystical content, it has no religious overtone at all, as I see it. I am bound to say that, and I don't care whether you accept it or not; it is of no importance to me.

I was impressed but it was a daunting feeling, like having the rug pulled and tossed from underfoot. There were passages when he seemed just plain bleak. I have yet to come across a teacher, philosopher or guru who so boldly denied the tools of what I still assumed was his own trade. His indifference to ancient systems, scriptures and the value system of spiritual practice was a slap in the face.

JK hinted at a similar direction but went slowly, carefully, holding your hand in a way that later struck me as manipulative. UG raced along like a maniac with no regard for anything, no foothold, no reassurance except in the naked loneliness of a physical existence stripped of the trappings of comforting magical phrases.

There is nothing to understand—that understanding somehow is there, and how it came about nobody knows, and there is no way at all of making you see this, and you ask "Why do you talk?" You come here. (that is why.)

My encounter with JK had given me the sensation that a finite 'me' could perhaps touch something infinite, giving the distinct impression that he was in touch with this infinite all the time. A lot of his teaching was designed to lead seeker-lemmings hand in hand off this cliff of self-inquiry into the void of 'choiceless awareness', a labyrinth with Escher-like self-contained frustrations.

UG denied the existence of a 'self' as anything other than a grammatical form:

> *There is only the first person singular pronoun! I don't see any 'I' there!*

Reading UG Krishnamurti produced sensations in me from elation to a cold sweat. He highlighted the prison of 'self' with a terrifyingly claustrophobic clarity. As far as he was concerned whatever happened to him proved to him that the whole religious and spiritual pursuit was the cause of human suffering, not the solution.

Jiddu Krishnamurti was beginning to look like a hypocrite and so, with one monkey being knocked off my back, I had no idea of the scope of the three-hundred-pound gorilla about to grab me by my short hairs and yank me into the world.

CHAPTER 6

The question of being useful doesn't arise?
It doesn't at all. He doesn't think that he is chosen, chosen
by some power to reform the world. He doesn't think that
he is a savior or a free man or an enlightened man.

Having discovered something unexpected, something I'd given up hoping to find, the first thing I wanted to do was find out how to see this man. I got in touch with the technical designer of the UG website who sent me a phone number in California. After a few calls a woman finally picked up:

"Hello."

"Hello, I'm calling about UG Krishnamurti."

"Yes, would you like to talk to him?"

That was the last thing I expected to hear.

"Well is he available?"

There was another voice in the background.

"Who is it? What do they want?"

Could it be that the voice was his?

"What is it you want? He would like to know…"

Thinking fast, I just stated the obvious:

"Well, just read all his books online and feel very relieved for some reason. I just wanted to thank him."

There was a muffled conversation on the other end of the line and the next thing I knew Mr UG Krishnamurti was on the line:

"Hello, UG here. Who are you?"

"Well, sir, I just read all your books online. I used to be a

JK freak as you call us, and I feel so relieved. I don't know why exactly but I wanted to thank you!"

I didn't know what to expect but he laughed. He had a reputation for being pretty rough on people but over the phone he was quite charming.

"Don't think about it!"

Not knowing what else to say, I asked if he had any plans to come to New York. He said his plans were uncertain and left it that he would be passing through New York again on his way to Europe. This gave me the feeling that one day soon I might actually meet him.

For years I'd been reading and obsessing about Jiddu Krishnamurti with no hope of ever meeting him. That much was clear from the beginning. The one other teacher I had met was the Zen master upstate. In that instance I was ceremonially introduced and had to ask permission to seek his wisdom. With UG, I made a phone call and chatted without as much as a reservation. I was more amazed by the ease of this first encounter than I'd been by seeing JK live. There was something so real about it.

When I put down the phone I was elated. I sat back, let out a long sigh, and smiled.

CHAPTER 7

But those men who have 'made it'—they live
amongst the people—you can see them there.

On October 16, 2001 I looked up a woman in New York who
had known UG for years. Years later I found the entry in one of
the many books I carry around 'making notes' about practically
everything, god knows why:

> *Called X this morning out of the phone book about see-*
> *ing UG's tapes. She called back. He may be coming. I will*
> *go up there next Monday. All sounded very low key. It's*
> *interesting that... what? Nothing, just making a note of this.*
> *How will I respond to being around someone like that? "You*
> *wouldn't want this." Of course the 'me' is why I am not free.*
> *Freedom means no me.*

I was welcome to stop by any time, so I fixed a date and showed
up at her door within a day. The New Yorker was some fifteen
years my senior, yet her energy was youthful, bohemian and
welcoming. I never felt a shred of hesitation when she opened
the door to her apartment. The interior betrayed bohemian sen-
sibilities and deep pockets. White fabrics covered the furniture,
a white grand piano stood in the corner of the spacious living
room. UG spent forty days and nights in a tiny room behind the
kitchen. It was the smallest room in the apartment. We sat at
a small desk in his room, watching a video of him talking with
friends in houses around the world. After a couple of hours of

conversation, I went on my way loaded with books and videos about UG.

During my second visit there was a woman sitting on the floor when I came into the living room. She was photographing her artwork - delicate looking etchings with tendril shapes in vaguely fleshy colors. She was so quiet I could barely make out her voice when she spoke. A trip to Europe to visit UG on 9/11 had obviously been cancelled and since that time she had been waiting around for him to come back. The peculiar way she spoke, in a high soft voice, sounded like she was pining for the man as if he was her boyfriend. A former dancer and an artist, who taught and practiced yoga, she sounded like Marilyn Monroe and looked like Ingrid Bergman, it was a lot to take in. I was relieved to hear she was married. In any case Yogini was unmistakably beautiful.

In February the New Yorker finally called to say UG was in town. I immediately went to the hotel where he was staying. Looking back, it occurred to me that it just happened to be right across the street from Madison Square Garden where I'd seen Jiddu Krishnamurti speak for the first time years before. The door to room 2107 was slightly ajar, but I knocked anyway.

Someone inside said, "Come in, it's not locked!"

I was dressed for winter weather and it was cold outside but the room was noticeably overheated. The New Yorker and Yogini looked up, smiled and said hello when I walked in, leaving my leather jacket and boots inside the entryway.

The man I had come to meet was sitting on the couch in the living room of the hotel suite talking to a handful of people. He was small, elderly, thin and quick with a full head of white hair parted in the middle covering his ears. I couldn't say whether he looked Indian exactly; his manner of speech was slightly Indian with English overtones, hard to place. It was not unlike JK's voice at times when he affected a British accent. The trimmed collar of his shirt was sticking up around a sinewy neck from beneath a slightly darker sweater. His bare feet dangled and shifted beneath his creased brown slacks. The tan colors of his outfit complemented his skin tone.

The New Yorker introduced me.

"Why have you come here?" he asked politely, taking me in with grey eyes that seemed neither friendly nor hostile.

I didn't mention our conversation on the phone.

"I wanted to meet you after reading your books."

Leaning forward he said:

"The fact that you are here after reading the books means they have not done the job."

Having said that, he leaned back into the couch again. I didn't know what to say so I kept my mouth shut.

"How did you find out about me?"

"I read about you on the website."

"I see. Well anyway, now that you have come I think you should go away, you are not going to get anything here. I have nothing to offer anybody and I don't need to tell you, you will find out for yourself that you have no need to get anything from anybody in this world."

Despite the idle threat, I didn't feel unwelcome, so maybe he didn't really mean the part about going away. As for the rest of what he said he was adamant. With a decisive sweep of his arm, he brushed aside the possibility of getting anything from him in one movement. I felt a jolt in my stomach. Uncertain what to do, I stood for a minute until someone offered me an ottoman to sit on in front of him, and he went back to talking.

"Yes, yes, please make yourself comfortable."

Sitting in front of him, it seemed as if he was talking to everyone and to no one in particular. The others were assessing the first impact of UG on the stranger in their midst. There were so few people I felt relaxed, almost too relaxed. It was a little like a casual visit to a relative; no ceremony, just a bunch of people sitting around chatting. Well, one of them was chatting anyway.

I couldn't quite get what he was talking about, or why he was saying what he was saying at all for that matter. He went back to some talk about Indian history.

"That bastard Gandhi was the worst thing that ever happened to India. I don't even want to touch the Indian Rupees. Why they have to put his filthy picture on every note? I want to know! That book he wrote he should have called *My Experiments with Food*, not *My Experiments with Truth*. If he were here right now I would kick him in his pants. I said to his face when I met him: 'One day they will put a teeny veenie bullet in you and that will be the end of you.'"

It was entertaining, but what he had against Gandhi wasn't clear to me. His comments were funny to listen to. I got the feeling he knew it, yet he was so emphatic at the same time.

"Then that Nehru went in for partition because he was sleeping with Mountbatten's wife Edwina. That bitch talked him into it. She was a real bitch."

It was interesting that he'd met Gandhi and I'd certainly never heard this about Nehru. Of course, with my background, what I knew about Indian history could be summed up in about one paragraph. He was chatting away about these events as if they were the most important thing in the world.

For the time being, I watched the way he moved. His hands danced in unison with his words, sweeping and pointing, grasping and tossing things here and there as he shifted his legs around with unusual agility for a man his age. He was as relaxed as he appeared in the videos, but much older looking. His face was wrinkled but not slack; with regular yet harmonious features and steel grey eyes. The eyes were definitely vacant. Even though he looked at things he never seemed to focus for long. He had a high, well-formed forehead with an unmistakable rise in the middle of it shaped like a leaf, the point of which touched a mole between the eyebrows, where traditionally a person's third eye is located. His hands and feet were well formed and slender, as quick as his talk. The hands seemed larger because of the amount of action he was putting them to and the feet moved with nearly the same agility as the hands.

Yogini was sitting in front of him with her legs twisted around into a graceful yogic contortion. There was a stuffed chair in the middle of the room occupied by a woman with dark curly hair, named Ellen Chrystal, who was introduced as the person responsible for editing one of the books of his talks called *The Courage to Stand Alone*. The New Yorker introduced me to an Indian couple named Lakshmi and Guha. Sabyasachi was the first name but UG immediately started calling him Guha, which means 'cave' in Bengali. She'd already told me a little about them. They had been deeply affected by UG and sat at his feet with a contented sense of purpose.

For most of the time, the New Yorker was seated at a desk opposite him, writing on her laptop or talking on her cell phone, occupied with this or that while the others sat quietly around the room, taking in the main event with a kind of passive awe that was at the same time good-humored and casual.

At one point he addressed me, acknowledging my previous interest in J. Krishnamurti:

"You know, the name Jiddu means grease in our language. Uppaluri means rock salt. That is the name of the place where they mine it. I like to say this salt is needed to remove that grease!" referring to his name, Uppaluri Gopala. And he laughed at this.

I had to laugh along with him. It was the perfect explanation of what had just happened to me. He laughed along with me with a glint in his eye, while pointing to the non-existent presence of the 'grease' in the room.

The window opposite the couch had a view to the north up Seventh Avenue. Now and then he would comment on the fact that he always took the same room in the hotel, with a preference for the number 7 and multiples of it; he liked having that corner room number 2107. At one point he started talking about the Buddha and what an idiot he was. That was a new one.

"I call him a 'bud-hu', which means 'idiot' in Hindi."

Then he got the idea to share something with me:

"Hey! I want to show you something!"

Lightly touching my arm, he jumped up from the couch with an impish grin and disappeared into the bedroom. His touch was like air, cool and fleeting. While he was out of the room I looked around at the others, who were smiling at some unspoken joke. Soon he was back, standing full in front of me with a thin folder. Selecting a paper from the folder, he presented me with a most colorful computer printout.

"Look! This is the mother of that Buddha!"

It was an image collaged together from various sources, and not too artistically at that. There was a homely Asian woman's face plastered on the body of a porn star with her legs up in the air, engaging in bestial sex with a white elephant no doubt ripped from a nature magazine. It was so crude and left nothing to the imagination. UG was standing in front of me, searching my face for a reaction with gleefully vacant eyes. All I could do was smile and laugh at the absurdity of the whole thing. He reminded me of a school kid in the playground, so pleased with his naughty picture. I was so happy in a way, since I have never really bought into the cult of the Dalai Lama.

"This I sent to the Dalai Lama on the birthday of that bastard Buddha. It's a picture of his mother being entered by a white elephant! That is the legend of that bastard's mother so I sent it to the Dalai Lama on his birthday! His personal secretary is a very good friend of mine."

With the enthusiasm of a twelve-year-old he bragged,

"That bastard doesn't like me!"

"No wonder!" I couldn't help saying.

It wasn't so much the picture that shocked me, as the fact that of all things to do on a first visit, he was showing me this absurdly offensive thing so proudly. Apparently he had adopted outrageous ways of dealing with people of late. In his books he equated logic with fascism so his methods matched his words; that much was clear. I was about to learn the difference between a teacher and a person like him, but I was still poised for something to sink my brain-teeth into. I sat for a few more hours enjoying the absurdist prattle, patiently waiting for an opportunity to jump in and ask him something meaningful. Hours went by and it was impossible to interrupt the cascade of words so I finally launched a question into the rapids, or at least tried to:

"UG, you are obviously in another…"

Before I got the whole sentence out he cut me off mid-stream, "No sir!"

He suddenly looked very irritated.

"… state, but I…"

He was already crouching forward with his hand upraised:

"Nothing to it! All empty words and empty phrases!"

"But…"

He severed the line immediately with more words as if he'd been waiting for this nonsense to come out of hiding in the brush…

"That is not your question! Do you know how many people have crossed the threshold of my doors over the years asking the same questions?"

I was hit, and things were going downstream fast…

"… but your state… that natural state…"

Just forget it, I was lost…

"The only state I am in is New York State!"

He went on smothering me with words, leaving me sitting like a fool in the dust with my aborted question.

Something told me, *Relax! This might take a while.* Talking to the guy was like reaching into water to grab a reflection. Impossible.

GONER

Finally, as it grew dark outside, I sensed the time had come to say goodbye. I thanked him, he graciously thanked me for the visit, and I left.

My head was spinning.

CHAPTER 8

July 2002

My talking to people is incidental—I mean it—otherwise I would get up on a platform. What is the point in getting up on a platform? I am not interested. I have no message to give.

I couldn't believe I was finally going to the place where JK had spoken all those years before, to see UG Krishnamurti. I also couldn't believe how beautiful Switzerland was. It took about three hours to get to Gstaad by train and car. UG was staying next door to Saanen where he had listened to that talk by JK in 1967. The train ride was like moving through a postcard fantasy.

The New Yorker and Guha picked me up in a nearby village and drove me to the chalet where UG was meeting people next to an open field with a barn full of Swiss cows.

Stepping out of the car under a clear blue summer sky, puffy clouds wandering across it over the Alps, I followed them to a twisting cement stairway leading under the chalet. The door opened into a large basement room full of people sitting around on miscellaneous furniture. UG was seated against the far wall talking to the room.

He shouted when we walked in:

"What? You? What are you doing here?"

I felt his words on me.

"Just stopped in for a visit."

"Don't say the age for miracles is over!"

Dressed in creamy white shirt and neatly creased slacks,

GONER

with his bare feet up on some kind of ottoman, he threw up his hands with feigned surprise.

"What is wrong with you? Why have you come all-ll the way?

"Hello!"

"How are you, sir?"

"Couldn't be better! I am just talking to some people. What is the matter with you?"

I had nothing to say about that.

"Well, come in anyway, we are just talking some nonsense."

Yogini was in a chair in front of UG with a tall man sitting on the arm of it. I noted his arm around the back of it. She waved and, returning the wave, I quickly averted my eyes back to UG.

The others looked up briefly and went right back to the main attraction. I found a spot in the back of the room of people gathered like moths to UG's flame. The curtain behind his chair covered water pipes running down the wall. When a faucet ran or a toilet flushed on the upper floors, a little burst of water music filled the room. There was a couch next to his chair under the only window in the basement. During the day a tiny shaft of light moved across the couch like a sundial. People went through contortions trying to get fresh air into the basement while blocking the light at the same time. The reason for their caution was his commentary on fresh *anything*:

"Fresh air is a sensual pleasure! This body doesn't need fresh air. You are all addicted to ideas about health and fresh air. Fresh air, fresh food; all ideas put in there by those bastards! You all want to be healthy. You eat ideas and wear labels! I eat only canned food and for a vegetarian I never eat vegetables! I'm not like you people! Look at me! I am 85 years old by the Indian calendar; 'running' 86 is how they say it. You people all want to think you are yo-ung!" (pronounced 'e-eng').

His dispute about the disparity between Indian, Tibetan

39

and 'filthy Western' calendars was comical. The way he talked, you could jump in at any point. He spoke in complete statements with no need for build-up or background. He told the story of a man who came all the way from Brazil to see him who was profoundly disappointed when UG talked about economics all day. Leaving in a rage (UG was fond of telling us about those who 'walked out in a rage'), he came back the next day and extended his stay for weeks despite his initial 'rage' at UG for addressing worldly-wise non-spiritual issues.

It was just like the New York visit and at times I wondered indeed why I had come all that way, as he'd said, but pretty soon I found it hypnotizing, energizing, boring and intriguing all over again.

His audience in Switzerland was a varied collection of men and women, mostly European from the looks of it. There was a large middle-aged guy with dark circles under his eyes sitting on the couch in front of him next to a woman with a faraway look in her eyes. The Americans looked like they were drowning in his presence. Ray and Sharon were running a new age church in the Midwest, spending enormous sums of money on trips to see him whenever they could. Sharon's daughter, Cindy, sat transfixed in his presence just as much as they clearly were.

That afternoon he talked about his arch nemesis, JK. To this day I don't know who arrived in that valley first, UG or JK.

"I never saw that filthy bastard after our last meeting in Wimbledon in 1960! He invited me to come, that bastard. He had the nerve to ask me, 'Why have you de-tached yourself from your family sir?'" UG threw in an exaggerated British accent, imitating the old man. "I didn't even want to see him! He was the one who told me to come. He was sitting there petting a cat. You know he liked pets. He asked me, 'Do you like pets, sir?' and I told him 'I don't even like human pets!' Can you imagine?"

Everyone laughed.

GONER

"Nawwo, sir!" The Reverend Ray uttered, slumped in the overstuffed couch, staring into UG's eyes as if digging for gold, his leg jiggling in what appeared to be a euphoric spasm.

Addressing him UG carried on:

"I said 'I never want to see you again!' and I walked out. You know what he did? He tried to hug me! I didn't ask him at that time but now I would have said to him, 'Krishnaji, do you have any homosexual tendencies?' Can you imagine? That bastard!"

"Myeahh!"

This theatre about Jiddu was especially fun for me. I felt an unmistakable wonderment at finding myself in that valley I'd read about so long ago. It was once an unimaginable paradise and now I was hanging around with a man who'd known Jiddu and seemed to have ingested his essence and spat out the rest. I knew all the stories he was referring to.

I'd been sitting next to Narendra, a young Indian man from the hotel in New York. When Narendra split to town for emailing, UG picked me out of the back of the room.

"Where is your friend?"

I was pleased to be noticed.

"He went to email in town."

"Oh. I see."

While Narendra was away I talked to a French couple sitting close by. They seemed a bit dismayed with what was going on, or not going on. This was the first I heard of people saying UG was no longer 'talking'. It seems according to them that he had given up discussing things with people in favor of a lot of nonsense chatter about money to an audience who would listen to anything. Having read his books, I knew he was capable of 'serious' talk, and couldn't imagine that a person like him could ever 'lose it', whatever 'it' was.

Meanwhile, you could get the impression from the way he was chattering away up there that he didn't even know you existed. Most of the time he appeared to be absorbed in the

41

stories, yet there was something disconnected about the sound of his voice. I soon realized that he kept close track of the people coming and going from the room. If I was away and ran into Narendra coming from the room, he would tell me, "He was looking for you."

It was flattering. As if it mattered to him that you weren't there.

There was some discussion of the phrase 'spiritual coma' coined by a young woman who seemed to be with the American couple sitting in front of him. People appeared to be falling asleep around him, while others sat staring at him with expressions of kind of a blank, glowing ecstasy.

"Don't call it energy! Spiritual coma!" he'd say, indicating someone in the room who appeared to be napping. The 'spiritual coma' was something he would only refer to as a joke, but it must have been that quality I noticed that caused people to look somehow younger and calmer in his presence. I noticed, when we were out of the room, that the people who looked so serene and peaceful, nearly floating while sitting in his presence, looked distinctly earth-bound by contrast when they were outside. Meanwhile he was hell-bent on claiming, quite to the contrary, that there was nothing at all extraordinary going on around him.

"There is no such thing as spirit. Spirit is a Latin word that means *breath*. That's all. There is nothing to your spiritual nonsense! Not one genuine article, I'm telling you! They were all *criminals*. They fooled themselves and fooled you all. Don't talk of meditation to me! I have done all that kind of a thing. *Nothing to it!* Kick all those bastards and kill all those bastards."

This comment was usually followed by a warning: "Anyone who has meditated seriously will end up in the funny farm singing Looney Tunes and Merrie Melodies, or commit suicide. That happened to some of those holy men!"

I liked his reference to the cartoons. It reminded me of his description of one sensation he noticed after the calamity where, as he lay in bed, his body was to him like the Tom and Jerry cartoons where a character is flattened by a steam-roller. As with so many of his comments, it was misleading to think you understood what he meant by what he said, like when he talked of sending people away, not wanting to talk, etc. In this sense you were always on alert by default. If you left the room, he wanted to know where you were going, what you were doing and why.

Then when you returned: "Where did you go? What did you see?" he would ask pleasantly with a wave of the hand.

I discovered that one way of leaving the room unnoticed was to exit while his attention was occupied elsewhere. He was so absorbed in what he was looking at, irrespective of the content, that if a person got up on one side of the room while he was absorbed in the movement on the other side, he would miss the movement. The next thing you knew, he'd look up with a look of wonder, like a child that has misplaced a toy,

"Where is that fellow?"

Somehow someone always knew who he was talking about.

"Oh, I think he left."

"Where did he go?"

That summer was the first time UG allowed so many people to take meals together in his company. He repeatedly said he abhorred the idea of an ashram, which presumably included so many people eating together in his company. In earlier years he met people from 10 am to noon and again from 4 pm to 6 pm. Now he was available all day long, from 6 am to 8 or 9 pm. In the afternoons there was a coffee break at around three, which he referred to as 'high tea'.

Aside from a smattering of 'JK widows', there were quite a few of what he called 'Rajneesh widows' in the crowd. JK was the 'greatest fraud of the twentieth century' while UG liked to describe the former guru named Rajneesh as 'the greatest pimp of the twentieth century', explaining:

"He took money from the boys and the girls and kept it all-ll for himself!"

UG had nasty things to say about almost everyone in the spiritual business. Inspired by Rajneesh, aka Osho, his line about holy people changing their names was repeated often that day: "Only criminals and holy men change their names. I would rather be a con-man than a God-man!"

There was a peculiar distance in him that made it impossible to feel you were intimate, even though he seemed disarmingly familiar. People were friendly, but it was obvious they were fully occupied with him. He talked to a particular individual as if talking through them to the rest of the room. His vacancy created a vacuum effect where you felt attracted by his movements and the glance of those pale grey eyes that seemed to go on forever in no direction.

The crowd was a constantly shifting microcosm of the world population with European, Middle Eastern, Asian, South American and Russian. There were Muslims, Jews, Hindus of all varieties, Buddhists, Christians of all varieties, and of course former followers of the recent religious teachers and gurus. It seemed like everyone had a history with one or the other of these teachers: Rajneesh aka Osho, Sai Baba, Da Free John, Andrew Cohen, and of course Jiddu Krishnamurti. Various professions were represented, as well as everyone from the unemployed to the wealthy, with a wide range of age groups.

Over the years he maintained close friendships with heterosexuals, homosexuals, bisexuals and transsexuals. He seemed truly oblivious to sexual preferences, a subject he addressed with a quote from Christine Jorgensen, the first sex-change celebrity:

"Gender is in your head, not your body! Don't get me wrong! I'm not against it!"

He pronounced "agana-st' in a charming way. Continuing, he would point out:

"Sex and war spring from the same source. There is nothing

to your 'I love you darling deary!' When you don't get what you want out of that relationship what happens? It turns to hate. Love is a four-letter word!"

Then, if that didn't make the point,

"All my relationships are based on one thing: what do I get out of it?"

Which pretty much put the last nail in the coffin of romance.

He made an unforgettable assessment of the physical aspects of love:

"All holes are the same. They may be tight in the beginning but they will loosen up in due course."

Very sentimental.

Of course the fact that, for us, love needs two, means anything that springs from separation means conflict. I had plenty of first-hand experience with that observation.

The fact that people who came to see him had already been involved with some kind of spiritual practice was significant. It is highly unlikely that anyone would hang around him without having done what he called their 'homework', meaning some kind of spiritual *sadhana*, or practice, and those who had done it seriously could not 'brush him aside'. The things he was talking about were not so absurd if you'd poked around in the spiritual theatre.

The thing that brought people to him was the quality of his company. The way he used language made him impossible to sell. He went out of his way to see to that, dismissing the idea that one could teach what had happened to him. It was an event without a cause. This is extremely difficult to explain since it was a means of functioning for him, but an idea for anyone who functioned otherwise.

Here he would use the example of a classic Indian philosophical argument that says: "Where there is smoke there must be fire", asking: "Why do they have to link them up? Each event is an independent event."

The unspoken element here was that through observation of the man and how he moved among people, how he behaved, you could learn a lot; maybe what there was to learn came from this alone. The reason he sounded so absurd was that he exposed logic as fascism and operated so directly that language was action. He used to describe how sound follows image in film. Similarly, his action preceded his words. One of his favorite lines for a driver was: "Look with your eyes, not your head!" A functional camera lens simply transmits an image it has no need to label.

"You people are afraid to face the fact that you are a machine, that's all."

The implications of his claim that his image-making structure had been destroyed by the calamity were difficult to grasp. My profession depended on image making and the exploitation of it. I understood that after the calamity his words came only as needed in response to a situation, they no longer formed images in him the way they did in us. That may have been why he was so hard to follow. There was something so transparent about his presence; it was like running water, you couldn't help being hypnotized by his movement, but you couldn't hold it. His actions spilled through your senses.

CHAPTER 9

You have no way of knowing anything about your death, now or at the end of your so-called life. Unless knowledge, the continuity of knowledge, comes to an end, death cannot take place.

UG had a habit of repeating certain passages he picked up somewhere:

"Christianity shows us the strength of suffering, Hinduism reveals profound spiritual possibilities and Islam and Judaism teach us to be zealously devoted to God and faithful in action!"

For the longest time I thought he was saying *jealously* devoted because of his accent.

His constant blasting of certain figures from religious and political life was also curious. No matter what he said about Sri Ramakrishna, I knew it had nothing to do with the man. The constant mention of Ramana Maharshi, whom I had never heard of, inspired me to read a book of his dialogues. While reading, it occurred to me that such a book was not something I could say I had willed myself to be interested in. Had I willed myself to be born into a personality that would take an interest in these matters? Why the interest in these people? It certainly wasn't something I picked up around the house as a kid. I never gave much thought to the concept of free will until I read Maharshi's dialogues. It was while reading them that I realized the amount of control I exercise in my life over most things is negligible.

On the second day in Switzerland, UG invited me into his car on a drive up Le Diableret mountain pass. We went up the curved mountain roads with spectacular mountain walls across the valley and pine forests spilling dark cool greens into the valley below. As we drove, I asked UG:

"Is there anything to free will?"

"Nothing to it, sir," he said quietly.

Like many other instances, it was that reading that inspired the question and I had the sense that he knew this and was speaking to it.

After the drive that day, we had dinner at a local pizza restaurant. I saw UG standing at the edge of the parking lot outside the restaurant throwing out the mushroom soup he'd just eaten. It was the first time I'd seen him 'throwing out'. Despite the fact that you would call it vomiting, it just didn't look like that. It was strangely graceful. He was bent slightly forward and with a smooth gesture of the hand he introduced the contents of his mouth to the elements, spewing a stream of liquid into the brush. He did this a couple of times, then neatly wiped his mouth casually with a paper towel and returned to the waiting car. In the early years following the calamity doctors thought UG may have had cancer. He had himself tested but there was no cancer. Later it was determined that his condition was achalasia, or cardiospasm, a problem with the esophagus.

I was lying in the dark of my little hotel room, staring at the full moon through the hotel window. A sensation of energy being sucked out of my chest cavity like a vacuum cleaner started. Sitting up, I gathered myself, backing away from the frightening sensation. A cold sweat trickled down my back. The feeling subsided as I listened to the calming sound of cows munching grass across the road, the bells around their necks tinkling in the dark. Eventually I relaxed and fell back to sleep.

It was absurd, the hope I entertained that summer that something would happen while I was hanging around. The barest hint of something uncertain happening immediately brought terror to the door. As soon as my little world was shaken, that 'parallel thinking' he talked about jumped in to save my ass from oblivion. I was chasing shadows, harmless ideas based on the image of him I was already building in my head. What I did with his words, the conclusions I came to about what he meant, were obstacles. He gave the analogy of a child running to get away from its shadow to describe the attempt to free yourself from thought.

Another afternoon while sitting in the basement with him, I had the feeling of being completely vacant as if my head were a charred stick of wood. When I told Narendra and Andre, a Dutch man, about it on the walk back to the hotel that night, they had a good laugh.

It was beginning to occur to me that these are the sorts of sensations that the big success stories in the spiritual business make millions on. The only requirement is that you *want* to believe in this nonsense. I wish I could say UG crushed the possibility of fooling myself about it from then on. In the simplest terms, the only way out of this is death—a simple truth he was putting across, which cut through the comforts offered by the usual gurus and teachers and guaranteed him a tiny following. He wasn't talking about suicide, but he harped on this death business all the time.

"You are going to be a marvelous human being tomorrow! If anything is going to happen it has to happen now!"

He saw everything coming and swatted it away like a bug.

Two days before leaving town, Yogini and I went for a stroll into the alpine meadows. We had a little picnic in an idyllic setting and went back to her apartment for a nap. She invited me to share her bed and we wrestled like teenagers in the sheets. The scene unfolded like a dream happening in the wrong place at the wrong time. I remember looking out the window of the chalet thinking it was all so perfect, but perfect like that scene at the end of *Blue Velvet* with the toy bird singing in a shaft of Hollywood sunlight. By the time we got back to the room my stomach was churning just slightly.

Sitting at the airport on the way home, an icy feeling washed over me. Everything looked and felt as insubstantial as glass. I felt like a ghost beyond reach of my surroundings. It was a pleasantly disturbing feeling, and very strong.

The feeling was gone by the time I reached New York.

CHAPTER 10

I have no right to say anything against anybody
in India, because I am not working here.

It was a hot September night in 2002 when I arrived in Mumbai. Monstrous palm tree shadows were tossed around overhead in the darkness like a mushy Soutine landscape. The odors in the air were completely unfamiliar, a combination of mold, dust, shit, spice and perspiration. Eager taxi wallahs swarmed toward me as soon as I stepped off the sidewalk. Struggling against the fatigue and dizziness of a long flight, I picked a driver to take me to a hotel I'd already reserved online. We started off on a highway and eventually turned into a mass of tangled dirt roads alternating with wide crowded avenues. From the open sides of the cramped three-wheeled rickshaw, dilapidated buildings soared up on either side. After some sweating and mumbling the driver found the hotel on a dirt backroad in the heart of the city. Being lost took on a new meaning when I arrived at a place where they were expecting me with absolutely no idea where I was.

Waking up in India, that peculiar smell now included disinfectant mingled with the smoke. I was not eager to face the heat and swarming masses I knew were out there in the streets. After a passable breakfast I hung around as long as I could stand it in the air-conditioned room with a cable TV that showed nothing but Hindi movies with increasingly irritating songs and cricket matches I didn't understand. Finally I was driven into the bleached heat outside.

I had two days to kill before UG arrived.

Wandering into a web of streets, I made my way in what I thought was the direction of the train station; my way was quickly swallowed in dusty curves, alleys, ending up at a dead end road running parallel to a highway. The other side of the road looked ominously like the wrong way. Not wanting to turn back, I trudged on in the heat, determined to keep moving. Stopping was impossible. There was no relief from the sun, nowhere to sit. It seemed like stopping would make matters worse, I might begin to attract a crowd or just melt in the heat.

To my left as I walked, there were endless little shacks; some were walls with no roof, men in threadbare shirts and knee high ragged pants, were banging on metal, shaving wood furniture with the most elemental tools, or tinkering with ancient objects that looked like they were on their second or third incarnation as usable junk. What was remarkable was that these people could be so industrious with such meager bits. Recycling in India is not so much an environmentalist concession as an economic necessity.

None of them looked up at the sweat-soaked Western fool wandering alongside the road. The long thin muscles of a life sentence of labor strained against tools; banging sounds rang out in the blank heat as dogs scrambled by, or lounged in and around the scrappy bits of shade provided here and there among corrugated metal sheets and crumbling concrete walls. The same, pale brown, worried looking mutts were everywhere.

I had no idea where the hell I was or where I was going. Turning to a road with a bridge offering shade in the dark piss stench of its shadow I moved in the direction of some trees offering the hope of cleaner shade. The broken reflections of a white-skinned fool bumbling through the wrong scene glittered off a dusty pane of glass here and there.

Finally there was a sign for MG Road, a main artery that would carry me back to something like relief from this destitute place. Sure enough, the useless map that had gotten me lost in the first place indicated some familiar names and I found the train station a little further on.

Having achieved the milestone of wandering for a couple of hours in this mess, I felt justified in going back to the hotel to cool off in the safety and relative cleanliness of my room. As dusk fell I went back out and wandered over to the Juhu Beach area, supposed to be an upscale neighborhood. No matter, a walk in an upscale Mumbai neighborhood wasn't the same as a walk in an upscale New York neighborhood.

A slight detour down a ragged lane carried me into a huge dusty field where people lived in tents and shacks to either side. Eyes were on me more distinctly here as darkness fell and I dreaded having to ask directions, trying to look as if I knew where the hell I was going. Soon shop lights transformed the neighborhood into unrecognizable new puzzles and patterns of streets and alleyways. I was amazed when I finally found my way back to the hotel after dark. The main thing at that point was to find some food that wouldn't make me sick and call it a day.

Jetlag got me into the streets before the sun was up the next morning. A welcoming cool silence lay in the sparsely populated streets with those worried brown mutts wandering here and there like ghostly sentinels, with the occasional cow munching on a trash pile. Like coyotes, the dogs were a rough and tumble bunch, too busy with their subterranean survival to bother with the human race. They were a far cry from the average American dog living in the lap of luxury, a national symbol of friendliness and domestic bliss. These poor bastards barely survived in the urban chaos. Cows, monkeys and goats also mingled in the streets maintaining a parallel flow.

Growing up, if we spotted a real cow or a horse, not to mention a goat or a pig, we were thrilled. We'd pull over in the car and take a picture. We ate them every day, but we never saw the living animal. In the West everything is assigned a place, with

LOUIS BRAWLEY

the poorest driven from sight, animals carefully leashed, cor-
ralled or killed off for the comfort or consumption of humans
(aside, of course, from the rats and cockroaches living under the
cement and in the walls where we can't see them; a society even
more heavily populated and possibly more orderly in its own
way than the human one).

In the silent hours before the sun began cooking the world,
brightly colored festival lights strung up everywhere spot-illu-
minated gnarled trees and gloomy buildings with yellow, pink
and orange gates called Ganesh Chaturthi pandals. The frames
stood at the entry to smaller streets, the cheery glow throwing a festive explosion of color over the squalid surroundings
signaling a religious festival. Crudely hand-painted advertisements for movies, health clubs, soaps and pots and pans covered
crusty little walls everywhere. The advertisements for products
named after the various Hindu gods were mixed up with actual
religious figures and symbols. It was a collage of cultural confusion and I savored the richness and novelty of it.

The building where UG would be staying was several blocks
away from the train station, through a maze of streets on the
other side of the tracks from my hotel. It was directly across the
street from a children's school, a concrete affair with deeply
worn cement stairways painted a fading earthy pink with a
patina that seemed centuries old. The odd thing about India
is that, although everything looked and felt old, the construction was rarely more than thirty to fifty years old at the most.
It was the ten-thousand-year-old Hindu culture that made the
place feel so ancient. Most of the buildings were as common as
lopsided New York tenement buildings and a vaguely yellowish
glaze hung over everything like a varnish.

Thea, a quiet Englishwoman I met in Switzerland with UG,
just happened to be standing across the street. Her white skin
and flowing white clothes stood out like a beacon in the mess
of the street. She showed me a restaurant for lunch near the

54

station where she knew the proprietor and half the people in the restaurant. Speaking in barely a whisper, she'd been traveling from one end of India to the other for years, like a quiet island in the teeming bustle of humanity, and knew the streets of Mumbai like the back of her hand. After eating a decent meal for pennies, we went back to the apartment building to find out when UG was due to arrive. An older man appeared behind the latticed wooden door of the flat wearing a white Gandhi cap and kurta, signifying loyalty to the standards of Indian Independence. Indifferent to our presence, he never looked directly at us, instead he held his head down and to the side in a way that reminded me of a priest in a confession booth.

Thea inquired about UG's whereabouts.

"He's not here," he said flatly, eyes averted as if avoiding our unholy Western presence.

"Do you know when he'll be arriving?"

"Not today," was the monosyllabic answer. "Come back later."

CHAPTER 11

But in spite of all that, in spite of the fact that the whole
atmosphere is religious (whatever that word means; to me the
religious thing you are talking about is nothing but superstition;
celebrating all these fasts, feasts and festivals, and going to
the temple is not religion, you see), those teachers have not
produced another teacher. There can't be another Buddha
within the framework of Buddhism. There can't be another
Ramanujacharya within the framework of that school of thought.

The sound of UG's voice echoing in the cement stairwells told
us all we needed to know. When we entered an Indian apartment two thousand miles from where I'd last seen him, his
greeting was exactly the same:

"Don't say the age for miracles is over!"

Then of course:

"Why have you come aaaall the way?"

Being the only Westerner (somehow Thea seemed like an
Indian to me even then), I felt self-conscious in the home of
orthodox Indians. UG was seated at the head of the room, his
white silk Indian pajamas glowing in silhouette from the light
of the porch windows behind him. I was taken aback when he
got up and came over to me, standing over me with those steely
grey, slightly vacant, but warm eyes. Smiling, his handshake
was like a cool drink of water from a natural spring.

"Ohhh, you look very spiritual, that does not mean you are
spiritual, just that you look spiritual!"

I laughed and made a comment that a shaved head was a

fashion compromise for my hair situation, not a spiritual statement; his joke and especially his greeting helped me relax
in what turned out to be the home of a Jain family. In such
moments his sweetness knew no bounds. It was like having
someone, a very important someone, personally clear a space
for you to sit among strangers.

We sat and he spoke for a few hours until mealtime arrived.
His presence was like that of a visiting relative with his hosts.
The table was set and I made an excuse and headed for the door.
Thea followed me outside where I stood feeling slightly confused.

"Why did we do that?" she asked me.

From then on, I took my cue from a quiet nod of her head
that it was ok to stay on for meals, since she already knew our
host, Mr. Pareek. Her presence became my reference point in
the back of the room during the entire visit.

UG went about his business in India in much the same way
as anywhere else: tearing apart everything human beings have
built up inside and out for centuries. It was a fantastic universal, verbal laying to waste of ideas and institutions Western or
Eastern. Anything related to human thought was worthless as
far as he was concerned and his way of leveling the whole thing,
lock stock and barrel, allowed me to feel at home among strangers in the heart of Mumbai.

It was as far from where I was born, bred and brought up
as I could have imagined, yet in his company I felt on common
ground with everyone else on the planet. We were all screwed.
It was indescribably liberating.

"You cannot be interested in what I am saying! You, as you
know yourself, you as you experience yourself, will come to an
end! You will drop dead, I'm telling you! You want me to talk of
love, bliss and beatitude like that filthy bastard J Krishnamurti?
Not a chance! I am not interested in selling you a shoddy bill of
goods. You can find plenty of gurus in the marketplace for that!
But I need not tell you, you are not going to get anything from

me, and you are not going to get anything from them! You will find that out for yourself, but what brought you here will take you somewhere else."

His host, Mr Pareek, a tall stern-looking man, never said a word to anybody, including UG, during the entire week. He and his wife were UG's hosts for over twenty years. She was nowhere to be seen, busy somewhere in the apartment with the cleaning or cooking, giving orders to the servants, always out of sight. His background as a Vipassana meditation teacher and a friend of Goenka, the founder of a school of Vipassana, was eroded and then terminated by his exposure to UG. Early in their association, when he heard UG condemning every religious and spiritual practice, Pareek asked UG point blank if he should drop his meditation practice. UG's answer was:

"Don't force it. It should drop by itself."

After another two or three visits from UG in the coming years his interest in meditation fell away almost unnoticed.

When we went out for a 'constitutional' drive, UG invited Thea and me to ride in his car. We drove the length of Mumbai from Juhu to the Queen's Necklace, a peninsula of upscale neighborhoods and the business district. The young Indian man whom UG called 'The Air India Pilot' wanted to take UG to the Mumbai Officers Club near the Queen's Necklace, but foreigners were not allowed, so he declined. He had a way of referring to people by their professions at times. No doubt he would have gone if we were not there.

Instead, we went to a beach at the Queen's Necklace coastline just as the blood red sun was descending into the ocean. The city lights were starting to twinkle along the curve of the necklace to the north. Taking in the sunset at the side of the road, we made jokes about UG's critique of the JK schools.

"That bastard used to drag all the children to watch the sunsets! It's all a pleasure movement, no different from watching the bouncing breasts of a woman I'm telling you!"

Driving back, the famous Mumbai slums along the side of the highway were a spectacle of human wreckage. Villages of makeshift hovels starting at the curb of the road ran for miles all the way up to Juhu in the north. It was a startling display of economic disparity. UG had no sympathetic remarks about any of this:

"The rich steal everything from the poor and then give them a few pennies to make themselves feel better, calling it charity. Those filthy bastards have stolen everything on this planet! I am not excluding myself. You and I live like this, the life of Riley. There is enough food on this planet to feed us all, so why are they starving, I want to know?"

His generosity as a young man revealed a side of the economics of charity few people knew. Once the poor school chums he helped with books and shoes achieved financial security, they ignored the poverty of others with a vengeance. They became, as he put it, 'greedy selfish bastards like anybody else.' Thus charity served no purpose as far as he was concerned. He condemned India as a land of beggars:

"India got her freedom handed to her on a gold platter, whereas all the other countries worked so hard and fought for their freedom, died for freedom—that's really the problem."

When we arrived in the mornings, he would be sitting in the living room, the light from the sunroom at his back illuminating a halo of white hair, the white silk pajamas shimmering as he moved constantly, talking with wild, graceful gestures. He was rarely quiet: the continuous movement of a shaft of white energy flickering before us like a flame. The sounds of the nearby school came from the windows behind him, filling the room with the rhythm of the day's activities. At a certain hour, the sounds of children playing and shouting grew and then again faded. Evening descended slowly, imperceptibly, and once again the darkened street was the backdrop for the theatre of nothing happening.

It's funny how listening to him was like listening to yourself. That made it easy to sit for hours, like watching fire in the dark.

A simple Formica dining table was always set for lunch before you knew it. Despite a strict diet of *idlis*, he sampled the food to keep company and show his appreciation to the hostess. A big black crow joined us on the windowsill during meals. From the dining room we could see down the hall into the flat. The stone floors and walls were like sparkling clean minimalist film sets. Down the hall a servant girl washed the tile floor on her hands and knees, or carried something from one room to another like an Indian version of a painting by the Dutch master Vermeer. The rooms were furnished with spare wooden tables, chairs and cabinets of a sixties modern style while polished tile floors bounced light into the space, isolating objects from the surroundings with mathematical precision. The rooms were painted in cool greens and turquoise, slightly faded but pleasing to the eye.

As evening approached and another day evaporated, a single bulb dangling from the ceiling by a wire came on in the darkening room. Shifting light blended colors from one to another on the walls of the interior, as the sun's angle swept slowly through it and the day glided slowly into night. The place glistened under the influence of slowed time. Something in the universe came undone as he sat with us; his inexplicable fragrance infused ordinary objects and rooms. The personality was lulled to sleep and, occasionally, waking from a stupor with a start on a low sofa full of pillows, his voice reminded me where I was as I stared into a corner of the room, trying to recognize my surroundings.

It would gradually occur to me that I'd been staring at that light bulb hanging from the ceiling for half an hour without a shred of interest in leaving.

"Spiritual coma!" he'd shout, if you fell asleep, but it happened anyway.

We floated along on the sweet, rough or meandering stream

of his voice, a force of nature that hypnotized us, like cloud flares on the horizon, as he ranted all day and into the night.

"Prostitutes are the only ones that deliver the goods, and every dog has its day; even prostitutes have a limited life!"

On and on he went, just like before.

"That's my line!" he would remind us, again, about J Krishnamurti, "He was like a navy man. He had a girl at every port. But I admire that bastard for one thing! He managed to keep the whole thing under the carpet. When more than one woman is involved that is something!"

The phrases I would eventually memorize by rote were trotted out and wormed into the non-existent mind, no matter what the setting, and in his company the setting seemed not to matter much. Meeting him was like opening a door into some timeless place where you found the same sweet nothing suspended within ordinary life, like a comfortable cosmic chair. I never sat so long in one place without feeling bored in the conventional sense. It was a vacuum of activity that seemed like boredom but with another effect. The more I heard him, the less I was bored. It astonished me that whole days could go by in this way as I sat in that room of strangers, all of us suspended in the air like dust motes, floating carelessly in a shaft of light called UG Krishnamurti.

I can never forget the quality of light in that room. At times I thought of trying to videotape these scenes, but a mechanical device could never capture the quality of the field around him, living, pulsing with light and energy. At the time I didn't know why it was so easy to be with him. Sitting with this unknowable man put the world in its place: oblivion. The subtle colors of the walls, the murmuring street sounds and the feel of cool floors in the heat of a Mumbai September were all that existed. He erased everything else with his voice, his smile, his blasts. Even when they were painfully jarring, his comments lanced the wound of conflicted human consciousness.

He was talking about spirituality again:

"You all fall for that nonsense. I refused to thrive on the gullibility and credulity of the people!"

I was thriving on a voice that repeated phrases with mechanical precision. He unleashed that ongoing stream of multifaceted vibrations which were his particular music. As soon as they rose from his breath, they fell away again in one continuous movement to nowhere. He was building and destroying thoughts in a rhythm like the waves of an ocean eroding a coastline.

CHAPTER 12

You don't like what I'm saying because it undermines the whole Indian culture and the psychological superstructure that has been built on the Freudian fraud.

Until he arrived in the room itself, UG was always asking:
"Where is he? Where is that bastard?"
Mahesh Bhatt, his close friend, voice in the media, foil and biographer, finally showed up one afternoon. The big-voiced Bollywood film director/producer stepped into the room as if stepping on to a stage, tugging at the expanse of his baggy black shirt, wielding cell phones like derringers. Staring wide-eyed at UG from across the room, he was a big round man with a noble face and large dramatic eyes. He was dressed in a uniform of black shirt and cuffed blue jeans. Halting theatrically just inside the door, he shouted across the room in a booming voice that made us all flinch,
"*I have come!*"
"OhmyGod!" UG muttered, recoiling and covering his ears, then he shouted at him,
"Hey! Where have you been?"
Ignoring the question, Mahesh advanced to center stage, stalking like the hunter of a wild animal poised opposite him, growling and howling toward his prey.
"Hey! Why aren't you dead yet?" UG said while he was only halfway across the room.
Suddenly he was the wild beast, subdued by the presence of the master magician.

"*UG, No*! Yahhhgh! You are killing me already! I am a young man! I can't go yet!"

Again, the hunter, he made a gun out of his fingers and pointed it at him.

"Help me!" he said to us, sparkling eyes darting around the room, "I have to kill him before he kills me!"

Crouching again, teasingly threatening to kill him, with sidelong glances at all of us, he came side by side with UG, flopped down on the floor unceremoniously, legs crossed, eyes darting. Then he grabbed at UG's leg, which recoiled as he shouted at Mahesh with feigned surprise,

"Hey! You bastard!"

So he grabbed and shook the chair leg instead, shouting.

"Aaaagh! UG!!"

Suddenly UG looked like a tiny bird, frail and fragile. Mahesh now suddenly transformed again, this time into a wild boar at the feet of a delicate crystal, yet completely safe. UG put his hands over his ears again, matting the white hair to his head, as Mahesh yowled out a Moslem prayer:

"La ilaha illAllah Allaah hu *Akbar*!"

What a blast of fresh air he was. So much energy! He laughed as UG shouted,

"*Hindi motboliay! chopra hou*!" right back at him. Explaining to him, "Hey I mean *you*! That means, *shut up*, just keep your *big-mouth-shut*, in Hindi."

Then Mahesh got up and went behind him:

"UG! How is your breast today?" reaching down to his chest as if to fondle the evidence of his glandular explosion, made famous in Mahesh's biography of him.

"Hey you! Get away from me!" UG shouted.

Recovering from the shock of this fearless familiarity, I realized it was all in fun for both of them, there was no real shock from UG. I'd hadn't seen anyone yet who could match Mahesh for sheer energy and balls-on fun and games with the tiny sage,

and UG seemed to love it. He was concealing a smile throughout the performance.

Mahesh finally settled down on the floor, but the movement
didn't stop, he grabbed a newspaper and started reading the
headlines, launching a series of questions at UG about the political state of affairs in India and the planet and what he should say
or do, or what the Indian people should say or do. UG responded
with a feverish blast against Indian policies, politicians, gurus
and pundits all. Quoting history, finally damning the entire
'spiritual shitland you call India!' he reminded Mahesh:

"You must say that! You are the only one who has the guts
to stand up to those bastards!"

Mahesh would say anything UG told him to in the Indian
media. It would be easy to underestimate the danger of this
kind of obedience, but Mahesh had built up a powerful public
persona over the years under UG's coaching. He pushed him
to exploit his talents in every area without compromising his
freedom of expression.

The 'rabid dogs' in the White House had just unleashed wars
in Afghanistan and Iraq, and UG was addressing the American
influence on India. The emergence of India as a workforce,
a new economy to be reckoned with, was the topic of some
discussion between them. Long before George Bush landed in
India, UG was cursing the Americans:

"India has invited America to come and fuck this country!"

It was one of his more vehement explosions and I cringed
at the hard cursing in front of what seemed to be some delicate
Indian souls, but they drank in every word. I found out only
much later how rare it was for anyone to speak the way UG did
about politics in India and get away with it.

The Indian friends who stuck with him over the years were
serious people who saw the jewel before them. They would put
up with anything from him. In proportion to the numbers of
followers of many Indian gurus, most of them fakes, he was

hardly known in the larger sphere of spiritual India and couldn't have cared less. His first public talk brought thousands of people and massive media coverage in Bangalore in the early seventies. Having done it once, he never spoke publicly in India again. Many people who heard him for the first time that day stayed with him for years. He was absolutely, instinctively efficient in his every move.

"India is a spiritual shitland and it should be wiped out for what it has done to this planet!" he shouted, hurling a sweeping gesture into the room, rich with expression.

"What about America, UG?" Mahesh asked; then, spotting me, he said:

"Look! We have a Westerner in our midst!"

With a local public figure pointing an accusing finger at me, I cringed a bit. UG ignored this and continued:

"America should be wiped out too, but do you mean to say they are going to go gracefully? Not a chance! Unfortunately they will take with them every form of life on this planet!"

Mahesh turned to me again, reading out a headline about Osama Bin Laden from a front page article of a major newspaper, asking me what I made out of the whole thing. I felt the flush of confrontation. As far as I am concerned, all political parties are lying, thieving crooks, Bin Laden, Bush, all of them. I had no opinion beyond that.

Later, when he said something like, "What are you doing here?" commenting to UG, "He's just a mixed-up kid," UG turned the description back on him. "You yourself are a mixed-up kid." And let it stand.

It was the first time I felt any hostility directed at me, but it was a relief when Mahesh expressed what I at least imagined the others may have been feeling. He could be counted on to bring things into the open.

This talk went on until one of Mahesh's cell phones rang. Cupping the phone to his ear, he retreated to the sunroom

porch behind UG, entering into a hushed conference, gesticu-
lating wildly. He paced back and forth for some time in front of
the windows like a caged lion, tugging at his shirt and talking
into one or both of the phones that rang continuously for the
duration of his stay.

Other friends came and went, people who looked familiar from some of the videotapes I'd seen. It was like walking
through a dream.

Then UG left and my reason for being in Mumbai evaporated. With a month to kill before flying back, it seemed like
as good a time as any to tour the country and get a feel for the
place. UG spoke of traveling to places to 'get it out of the way',
checking things off on a list of things to boast about. I did just
that and saw more of the country in three weeks than I would
see in the coming three years.

CHAPTER 13
December 2002

Attraction is the action.

It was only my first year of association with UG and already I'd gone to Switzerland and India. Now I was headed for California in the same year, for the third time in my life.

People were coming from near and far to visit during the Christmas holidays; the Guhas came with the New Yorker, Yogini was there, a German couple came; as usual UG was doing all the talking. Every morning it was essentially the same. We met in his little cottage, attached to the main house, which was occupied by some local friends.

The furniture was slightly worn IKEA, neat as a pin, with a calendar on one wall, a clock on the other. Efficient, ordinary functioning was the essence of his message, rather than lofty ideas about spirituality, truth or logic. All that was relegated to the trash heap. His talk was focused on the situation around him, with no patience for speculative discussions about anything else. The way he lived, his living quarters and his mode of expression were one continuous movement, a three-dimensional, living book of teaching. If you were observant, you could learn from him on contact with no need for explanation.

To each person entering he'd launch variations on the same greeting like a friendly bomb:

"Good morning! How good is the morning? I don't see any reason to say it is a good morning! You all talk, talk, talk, what is the game plan? I am not going to sit here eyeballing all day!"

His functioning was always directed at the interference of thought as it happened around him, no matter what time of day or night. This was his action and it was in constant operation.

One of his standard questions, launched into the surroundings, or at an individual, was, "Does it operate in your life?"

Indeed, in the case of someone like Jiddu Krishnamurti, his talk was no indicator of a way of living and way of life. UG used to love to joke about the gifts people offered Krishnaji, particularly his late model Mercedes Benz. JK was a real car junkie and when the sleek luxury vehicle was offered to him his line was: "Don't give it to me, sir! Give it to the foundation!"

Never mind that he was the only one allowed to touch the treasure, let alone drive it. So much for the man who talked of 'no teacher, no teaching, no taught', as if he was a naked *avadhut* wandering the streets in a loincloth.

First thing in the morning, when we entered, UG would threaten or praise each one in his way then start reading from a compilation of internet references which came to be known as 'The Links', or pressing someone to come up with a destination for a ride.

"Cabazon!" the Reverend, whom I'd first seen in Gstaad ,would suggest.

It was a mall about an hour's drive away.

"You are not helpful!"

That was the standard reply to most suggestions.

He was always threatening us one way or another, threats that seemed idle, absurd; the threats of a child or an emperor, you could never be sure. Then of course he would launch into the stories. There was Naren's prediction about the relationship between Mario and Lisa, an Italian living in Germany, and an American living in Palm Springs. UG called Mario a 'fungus cleaner', but he smoked so much that we called him 'Fumario'.

"Ahh, ha, ha, ha! Made for each other! That's what he told them! Can you believe it?"

UG was talking about an astrological reading the couple had been given before their break-up and mercilessly teased Naren, a German astrologer who had known UG for years. As he repeated them from details patched together, stories emerged about each one that gave him something to occupy his words with. Once he had a few details, he sculpted a version sufficient to get him rolling, the more sordid the better.

Another means of sparking a session of blasts were 'The Links', a collection of postings on the internet related to UG Krishnamurti in any and every way. Lisa had begun this collection when her relationship with Mario finally shattered under pressure from UG. While reading a passage about the seventeen-year-old-girl who liked punk music, ice cream and UG Krishnamurti, with great apparent pride, he would read the date of the posting with as much emphasis as the essence of it. It was strange and hilarious.

Many people, both old friends and new visitors, thought he was merely blowing his own trumpet, carrying on like an egomaniac. What was actually happening is that by reading this 'nonsense' he illustrated its irrelevance, indeed the irrelevance of language to what he was about. In this way he was able to communicate in a sense, and at the same time, never compromise himself by playing the role of 'teacher'. He adeptly sidestepped this. At the same time, for anyone who didn't 'get it', who didn't understand that what he was saying didn't really matter, who didn't understand that it was the way he was living that was important—well, that was just too bad for them.

If, on the other hand, someone genuinely had a question, he was as patient or impatient, forceful, or gentle as the questioner in replying to their question.

Health food was another favorite target. He condemned it as a sham and ate bits of junk food here and there with the rest of us. He ate potato chips, pretzels and drank coffee. I watched him eat packets of ketchup without the fries at a truck stop

GONER

more than once, but his basic diet was that of an ascetic. He ate no meat or eggs, no cakes or cookies, and drank no soft drinks.

Fact checking was pointless around him. Our daily reality is based in our memory banks, every time the question of identity was raised he gave the example:

"Red bag, table, chair, hard soft! That is you, nothing else. You are a collection of memories, definitions. You never once look without telling yourself what it is you are looking at!"

In this sense, he cut right to the core of so many obtuse and well-worn spiritual stories, giving instead practical worldly-wise examples of the way we were acting from second-hand information. The stories he told of his friends' lives were similarly tailored to exemplify the limits of our big ideas.

"But UG, I spent one third of my life with him! How can I walk away?" pleaded one woman when her relationship was coming apart.

"If you really love him, go there and clean toilets for a living! You are not going to make this kind of money over there," he replied, sidestepping the usual sort of consolations we give our friends under challenging circumstances.

The hard realities of relating were laid out in clear unmistakable terms:

"The only relationship I have with another is 'What do I get out of it?'" he would say, yet his actions spoke otherwise.

What he was really talking about was the dynamic we were living within, using all sorts of lovey-dovey talk to justify pleasing ourselves at the expense of others.

The fascinating thing was how these communications came forth from that vacant space of whatever he was to reveal the hazy nature of facts under close scrutiny. Who said what, to whom and why? Just scratch the surface and they crumble. Truth is your word against mine, and ultimately all law boils down to weaponry used to protect our goodies. When he said of JK for instance: "All empty words and empty phrases, sir!"

71

in one respect he was talking about all of us, and on the flip side, that was his essence: nothing. Every time he left the room, his absence created a vacuum that was quickly filled with the words that went on in us or between us, despite us.

The stories about his friends poked fun at our images of ourselves and kept everyone on point as he molded each narration to the moment. There were few of the usual tales used by spiritual teachers; instead his friends were the subjects of his metaphorical tales. By putting yourself in his presence the story of your life was used to attack ideas, the second-hand filler of most human life, the things that stood between us and living. His storytelling was potent, immediate and painful or humiliating, cutting out the secondary nature of most teaching and touching consciousness at the nerve endings. He trotted out dirty laundry, but the target was thought of any and all varieties. If he wanted to bring in anything traditional, he had a way of summarizing it that contained the essential wisdom of an entire text in one sentence:

"Inaction is action! That is your Gita!"

He did it so you couldn't miss the point. It was beyond brilliant. He was a source, not a reference.

Occasionally someone would try to correct him and he would counter with: "Don't be a German, always saying 'I am right! I am right!' You always want to feel good about yourself!"

Sometimes the way nothing else was allowed to happen in his presence made me feel crazy. Often. He had a way of cutting off the outside; keeping you focused without your knowing it because it seemed that nothing was happening. People say it sounds cruel, but I never saw a more compassionate man in my life. He was not afraid to state facts, something most people avoid like the plague since it upsets the balance sheet of social maneuvering. When you have nothing invested in other people's image of you it gives an enormous energy to your expression. Children are so refreshing for this very reason, they simply state what they see, until we adults teach them the rules of the game: lies, lies, lies and more lies.

"I am undermining the whole of human thought!" he asserted, with a tone of theatrical arrogance.

His assault had the effect of lightening the burden of ideas standing in the way of life, the thing we are constantly protecting ourselves from. If you resisted it was painful, and it was impossible not to resist, since the tedium of knowing is the fiber of personality. Around him the idea was constantly set on fire. He dumped gasoline and tossed a match on everything you cherished, as well as the stuff you didn't like.

"You cannot be interested in what I am saying! It will be the end of you as you know yourself and as you experience yourself!"

Then what were we interested in? I guess it was the entertainment of an extreme variety. To be honest, if honesty is really possible, there is no other explanation.

"You are all looking for happiness without one minute of unhappiness. That is the ultimate search, whether or not you seek it in a bar or in a temple makes no difference."

If you pointed out that he used to sit and listen to JK, or meditate, he wouldn't deny it:

"When I was young and stupid I did those things, but not one bit of it helped me!"

"Pain is the healer!" he would say in some other context. "But you are all the time trying to fix the problem and run away and that only makes it worse!"

One look at the manipulations of the pharmaceutical industry, and the accuracy of his assessment speaks for itself. Our ideas about healing are cooked up by drug peddling industries who use fear tactics to keep us 'healthy'.

Hearing him talk about the fascism of thought, it occurred to me that the machine that generates ideas is a liar. The only real use of logic is to impose it on what is seen as a threat to logic, another idea of illogic. If there is no logic and no illogical thinking, then what? This vacuum is unbearable.

Identity is a fiction pieced together from information designed to keep us all in line with a holding pattern of causality. This holding pattern is a form of conflict, the fascism of ideas as opposed to the unknown. His calamity killed off the effectiveness of the personality induced by Fifth Avenue shamans of culture. Any 'understanding' from my part, any ability to piece these conclusions together here with words, does nothing to stop this process from going on and on. In fact it's all I can do.

This is one of the painful realities I faced around UG, and the source of a common pitfall for people who assume that because they 'understand' what he was saying, they 'got it'. That there is nothing to get, is not as easy as it sounds. Popular Zen books and the cheap profundity they spawn is proof of this.

"Thought has controlled this body to such an extent that when it loosens, the whole metabolism is agog."

After the calamity UG's identity was a collection of ideas lingering in the organism known to the outside as 'UG Krishnamurti'. For him that story was over. The disease of personality had been surgically removed by an accidental event. There is a point where I realized it came to me in a package so complete that it was pretty much impossible to get rid of. This was apparent when I tried to meditate and the noise in my head only got louder. Then there are mantras, a deceptive little white noise machine...

Yet the idea of killing off thought was never presented by UG as an option. Indeed, in its proper place, it is a healthy normal activity that helps us to survive. Memory and the impulse to survive are so hard-wired into the body that he said the cellular shift of the calamity nearly killed him. We usually seek a new way of thinking, replacing one thought or idea with another. The idea of not replacing ideas is unbearable.

According to him we were better off getting away from him

and making 'loads and loads of money' so we could 'live in misery and die in misery' as he so gently put it.

Yet if you tried to leave the room, he effectively blocked you.

A white-haired gnome, he greeted us every morning in his cream-colored outfit, with the muted morning sunlight filtering through the curtains to the east, bare feet sitting side by side on a rickety glass and plastic coffee table,

"How good is the morning?"

I sat cramped on a chair to his side playing with the band of my watch while he went on and on. At some point I broke the band and that gave me something to shop for at the mall.

Occasionally he would look up at us as if waking out of a dream:

"What's wrong with you people? Why are you sitting here? I just say the same thing over and over."

Some of the time I couldn't have agreed more. Even after going to Switzerland and India, two pretty long journeys, to see this man, I wondered to myself, if what he was saying was true, didn't that make me a bit of an idiot?

What the hell is wrong with me? What am I doing here? I'd wonder, flipping my watch back and forth, staring at the carpet or counting the number of people in the room again and again while the others went into trances.

Now and then I just got stir crazy and went out for a smoke, having picked the habit up again in India where the air in Benares was so filthy it didn't matter whether I breathed or smoked. I would slip out and walk up the wide empty streets of Palm Springs where one style of house multiplied itself endlessly into the distance, like UG's talking. Smoking came in handy. I'd leave, wander around for a while, have a cigarette, then suddenly, thinking I might be missing something, having absolutely nothing else to do, I'd go back and find him still talking away.

"I am a tape recorder here, you are pushing the button making me speak."

It was no wonder there were only about ten people in the room with the most amazing man on the whole goddamned planet! He kept a low profile long before the calamity and seemed to know what was worth fighting for: nothing. Instead of building a following, he put all his energy into a handful of lucky people who could see what was up behind the blustery denials and fierce blasting. There was something so vulnerable about him, he was a man stripped naked inside. The way he put it was that he'd been stripped and didn't know where the clothes were anymore. By that point, he realized he didn't need them and was trying to convince us of the same. He also had the natural humility that came from facing the obvious fact that you can't strip yourself. You are stripped.

Once it has become pure, of and by itself, then nothing can touch it, nothing can contaminate that any more. All the past up to that point is there, but it cannot influence your actions any more.

We went for long rides to malls, or sat for hours in the living room of the main house during the day. The details of that living room were burned into my brain, the worn arm of a sofa or a photograph of some underwater creature hung too close to the ceiling behind him. He sat there twisting words with inexplicably brilliant and completely ridiculous finesse. The monologue was a continuous improvisation, using language and meaning to put a vibration into the air that can only be described as a perfume.

Sometimes I literally got a sour feeling in my stomach that there wasn't a hope of getting anything. That's about the time my projections would intensify, but the charm of his company overrode these reactions every time. All in all he was exhausting. After a day of listening to him, reacting to him, reacting to the others in the room, trying to follow along hour after hour, failing,

GONER

getting bored, getting hungry, getting angry, getting depressed, then starting it all over again, I went home in a state of collapse.

Yogini and I retired to the Arnold Palmer Suite, named for a famous golfer my father always admired, at the end of each day. Since the previous summer, our sexual alliance had already collapsed. I had already messed up whatever was starting between us by stepping back into the relationship with my girlfriend, a venture that was doomed to another final collapse soon enough. I had done this in an attempt to 'clarify' the situation and focus on the most important issue, UG.

In the meantime Yogini carried on as if nothing had happened. She baked potatoes for dinner while I watched early episodes of *The Sopranos* on the old cable TV. We shared our mutual confusion and happiness to be with him, then she retired to the back room to bury herself under a huge pile of blankets and I went out for a smoke on the terrace under the cold canopy of stars to discreetly call the girlfriend in New York. I was grateful for Yogini's company. In the room with him her smile was like a little ray of sunshine in a stormy sea.

As the New Year approached, the crowd inside grew and the place started getting cramped. UG said he wanted to go to northern California to visit a friend. He didn't want a crowd of people bothering his friend. That night everyone rushed back to their rooms to make frantic phone calls to find rental cars and hotel reservations for the next day.

The next morning the air in the little room was charged with emotion. He had changed his mind. I made a joke the night before about how all the shoes outside the door made the place look like an ashram. Now he was using my joke as an excuse to cut the crowd in half, like King Solomon. He used to boast that his grandmother called him a *kara katulka*, which means *heart of a Muslim butcher* when he was a boy. When she refused to move out of her dead husband's house, he brought a family of untouchables to the building and she left within the hour. He never suffered sentimentality. I was shriveling in my seat while he repeatedly thanked me for pointing out that the house was turning into an ashram.

The Guhas, the New Yorker, the German couple and a couple of others were ordered on no uncertain terms to go sightseeing in beautiful San Francisco. He would, under no circumstances, accompany them.

"If you stay, I will go, and you can take that bitch with you!" he spat, not even delivering a glance at the lady from New York.

I waited to be sent packing with the rest of them for my smart-ass comment the night before. Who knows, maybe that was the reason he didn't make me leave. Eventually, the others were expelled.

There were long rides almost every day. I remember one trip to a casino in a nearby town. UG snatched the cash winnings from whoever was playing.

"What is mine is mine, what is yours is also mine!" he would say, laughing.

We all laughed with him.

CHAPTER 14

It is not thought-reading; it is just an echo chamber: what is going on there is going on here. You can't do that; you want to decode every thought, to translate everything.

In May of 2003 I sublet my apartment in New York for three and a half months to spend the summer with him. The SIM card I bought at Zurich airport didn't work in my phone, I couldn't get a refund, so I dropped another 200 francs on a new phone and a week later I dropped it in the Launensee lake by accident. The logic board on my computer crashed a week later. Having landed in Gstaad for three and a half months, when it hit me what I'd done, fear snaked up my back for days. I literally had an anxiety fever. What the hell was I going to do for three and a half months in this overpriced cow town with these people I hardly knew?

Yogini was one of the lucky few in this world who didn't have to work. She had rented a nice little apartment in town for the year and invited me over now. Despite what had happened, however briefly, she didn't seem to be holding a grudge. I was careful not to think too much about what I was thinking about. I'd broken up with the girlfriend again—this time for the last time—with a determination to focus on UG alone. Fat chance.

I had a room at Ludi Haus Hotel where UG was meeting people. Someone told him I had slides of my artwork so he immediately demanded a show in Room L, also known as Hell. The projector failed and I breathed a sigh of relief, but we got another that worked the next day and the show went on.

By the third slide he said, "Boring!" and fell asleep in his chair. Flushed red with embarrassment in the dark, I continued to the end, at which point he woke up and summed up, "You are a horrible painter!"

Maybe he was right. The fact was I'd spent years in office jobs to support myself. I loved making it and hated trying to sell it. Later on, he constantly blasted me about my horrible paintings that no one would buy. I still haven't been able to give it up.

My room was on the top floor with a skylight in the sloped ceiling over the bed, a hotplate, a fridge and a sink. The shower and toilet were in the hall. Yogini described the wood paneling interiors as 'early Dracula'.

The first afternoon she came up and flopped down on my bed with a big sigh:

"It's nice you can escape so easily" (we were meeting in the building all that summer), "I have to go all the way across town to get away."

The way she threw herself across my bed made me nervous. She was certainly making herself comfortable. I don't know what she was thinking, but I was thinking, *not again!*

When the crowd grew, we started meeting one floor below in a bigger apartment. I was given the job of coffee maker for daily high tea. Yogini helped me a couple of times, but when the Guha kids showed up and offered to help, she quickly evaporated from the scene. Shilpa would check out her hair in the mirror over the sink while Sumedha pumped the creamer and watched TV, whipping the cream, slower and slower until I had to snap her out of a cartoon trance. Yogini arrived at the door, gave a confused look and disappeared. She was so gun-shy that the slightest competition for attention sent her packing.

The first night in the big room an awkward situation arose while I was joking around with UG. It was late, nearly time to go, and I was already in a habit of pretending to disagree to get a reaction, or just for the fun of it. I couldn't resist the urge to be a smart-ass for a laugh while the others sat around in profound silence. At times it was like two kids at the back of a class trading jokes.

Anyway, I said something to provoke him and he shoved a heavy wooden coffee table at me with his feet. He was smiling, daring me not to push it back, so of course I pushed it back at him, also with a smile. He shoved back, forcing my chair into the cabinet behind me. I was surprised by his strength. Staring him in the eye I shoved slowly back again as his chair eased back and connected with the door behind him. Click. Very quickly this time, he shoved back and the glass in the cabinet behind me rattled. Now I was effectively pinned against the glass front cabinet that was fixed to the wall.

There was silence for a second. *Hmm, what now?*

I stood up, grabbed the edge of the heavy wooden table, and pretended I was now going to flip it over on him.

He just smiled up at me like the cat that ate the canary, but the room was now dark around the edges. The others apparently thought I might actually flip the table on him. He had a history of attracting crazy people and never, ever backed away from the element of risk, on the contrary.

The fun had gone out of the situation, it was time to back off. I sat down and adjusted the table quietly.

"Just kidding."

Wasn't it obvious? I guess not. A couple of people were actually crying. I turned red with embarrassment once the moment sunk in. The fear was infectious even though I wasn't going to do anything to hurt him, what if I already had? He never stopped me.

What if I hurt the guy? Shit! He's so old I could have broken his legs! These thoughts came at me in a rush, as sweat broke out on my brow.

The room was extra quiet when he casually broke the silence and said it was time to go. By the time the room emptied out I was planning to get a train out of town in the morning.

One guy, who must have seen the look on my face, said: "Louis, what happened is already over, don't worry."

It wasn't over for me, it seemed like it was just getting started. I left the building in a panic and took a long walk to get as far away from the others as possible. *What the hell is wrong with me? I have three months to go here and already I'm in trouble!*

After eating breakfast in my room the next morning, I went down hesitantly, still considering leaving town on the next train. Sitting quietly in the back of the room, when UG looked up at me, it was with a guarded look. That really hit me.

"Good morning."

"Good morning."

Then I noticed that when I relaxed, he relaxed. It was over.

That summer he slapped me once. I can't remember what he was talking about but the move was totally unexpected. I was sitting next to him on the floor while he was talking and all of a sudden, pow! He cracked me across the face. I sat there stunned, but not hurt.

"A real teacher will push you into a corner, blocking all the escapes."

He was acting on a phrase he repeated in conversation over the years, finding a corner to push me into and my smart-ass attitude was giving him ideas.

CHAPTER 15

You think the more you listen, the more these things become clear to you; but the clarity of thought is making it more difficult for you to understand what I am talking about.

For three months I sat on the floor next to him every day. Taking a break was out of the question. I sat leaning against the television cabinet, until I was sore from sitting there. He forced me to do imitations almost every afternoon and never tired of this nonsense. When I was fed up with it, he wanted more. I worried about the effect this might be having on the others, but he didn't care. He would pick someone in the room and push me until I gave in.

"He is very observant!" he would say over and over, praising the act as the others became a little more guarded each time.

"Not me!" they said, with pleading looks, but I had no choice.

I would have hated to be on the other side of it. The whole thing got wilder and wilder. After a while I'd do anything for a laugh. Luckily the others were rolling by the time the non-sense was underway. Nothing was off limits. One afternoon I was humping the big round table illustrating 'tantric sex-mongering' techniques. His laughter was highly addictive, he claimed he never laughed like that before. I didn't believe it but I wanted to.

The only way to end the routine was to leave the room.

I don't know what he was up to with this. When Mahesh showed up that summer he kept telling me, "He's pushing you, man!"

To do what? I thought. Perhaps this was his way of career coaching me. I wasn't making money as an artist. Maybe there was some hope with being a comedian. Too bad I'm so lazy. The idea of starting down that road was not appealing. I had a friend in show business, but she was a good business person with real credentials. I had nothing.

Still he pushed and he pushed. Maybe also it was a way of going after the others' self-image. Clearly he was using me. Yogini explained that he was using me to 'move energy around the room'. I could never understand what this sort of new age rubbish meant.

His smile was so bright that his darker moods were all the more alarming when they blew through like a sudden thunderstorm. He blasted me once that summer and it wasn't like the slap at all. I can't remember the question that triggered it but suddenly out of the blue he turned to me with a fierce look:

"If you really want to know about life after death you go jump off the roof and kill yourself!"

He said it so violently that I flushed red and fell back slightly. Before I could catch my balance, he started telling me, in a voice like a carving knife, that I should stop wasting his time hanging around eating his friends' food, taking up space. I was skewered like a raw chicken on the spit tone of his voice.

Again I started reviewing my options. Where could I go? What about the rest of the summer? What now? I ran through the list of things I was doing or not doing to offend, to bring this on myself. Catholic guilt flowered inside me, but I couldn't afford to wallow in that response. It was as if I'd been physically shoved back into a mess of shame and guilt by the force of his words. It took me a few minutes to regain my composure, like trying to stand up in a slippery mud bath.

If anyone had a question for you it was he. He had one question you couldn't answer for the life of you, "What do you want?"

He would follow it with an undeniable, irritating clarification: "You want ten different things! If there is only one thing in this world that you want, you will surely get it, but you all want ten different things. I'm telling you! You want all this and heaven too, you ain't got a chance!"

Yogini and I were settling into a stalemate. I was sitting on lust; she was always there, lounging on the other side of the room, those delicious legs, those luscious curves and sad starry eyes collapsed on the couch for hours and days. Occasionally she took a shot at my pretense of spiritual discipline. Handing chocolates out one afternoon, I was sitting next to him with my eyes shut ignoring her.

She kicked me and asked with a sneer, "Hey! You want one?"

I wanted to kick her back but instead I thanked her and took a chocolate.

One night while a few of us were standing around the dinner table she asked if anyone noticed how nasty my imitations were. Nobody said a word. In the room I heard her laughing right along with the rest of them. I rarely imitated her and used extreme caution when I did. Her ballerina moves and extreme yogic flexibility got an easy laugh and she was as amused as the others. She seemed so reticent and fragile in some ways, yet resilient as steel in others. She was a constantly shifting cipher. There was a little dance in every move, a sureness and confidence in her body that made her downright intimidating. She had a distilled set of facial expressions that could make you feel like a million bucks or a piece of shit with the barest glint of her eye, or her full lips shifting into the pout position. All this made up for her limited vocabulary.

That summer her father visited and UG handled the situation like a pro. This guy was a businessman from a pretty conservative background and I had to admire her guts for bringing him over to meet a man like UG. Sometimes I don't know if it was guts or determination. As he came in, UG jumped up and crossed the room to greet him at the door, his hand extended in welcome. He immediately dropped a bomb:

"She is such a talented lady! How could you make her drop her career as a great ballet dancer? See how she ended up wasting her life with that filthy yoga!"

Taken aback, her dad smiled and said nothing but UG worked some kind of magic on the guy. He relaxed right away into the theatre of the absurd, going on with complete strangers as if he was enjoying a family reunion, even contributing a line for the Money Maxims which UG was dictating:

"Boring is the man who only knows how to make money," a self-effacing comment from a man who had spent his entire life making loads and loads of money by sheer hard work and determination.

UG flipped that suggestion around on its head immediately:

"Boring is the man who knows not how to make money."

Her dad was a decent enough guy, but I was a bit shy of meeting him. He reminded me of my father in the sense that he brought that whole all-American thing with him, something that made me feel out of place in that setting. Of course I ran right into them on the street and she jumped up from where they were having a coffee and introduced us. Making my usual annoying small talk out of nervousness, I outlined all the great places to hike, chattering on like an idiot. When I was finished she paused and asked me with a little smile:

"Have you been on any of those hikes? "No, of course not!"

We all had a laugh and he invited me to join them, but I was on my way back to the room and took a rain check, walking away feeling just a little bit stupid.

Yogini's father spent the weekend and flew back on a Monday. He was a real hard worker.

At the end of every day I took a long walk around the town by the Saanen River to stretch my legs. As I passed Yogini's apartment at the edge of town, she would wave from her balcony. She was always fiddling with the flower boxes. I used to see a fox standing under the street lamp right around the corner from her place that disappeared into the bushes with a light, graceful step when I approached.

There were others who couldn't stop thinking about her either, but I didn't know about them at the time. She wasn't some wilted lily who sat ignored at the edge of the dance floor.

CHAPTER 16

The moment you use this to get whatever you want to get,
or to arrive at some kind of a destination, you are tricking
yourself into the same old game—this you have to see.

UG dictated the Money Maxims that summer. He started dictating them to Cindy. According to UG, Cindy was the 'spiritual' daughter of the Reverend and she was the actual daughter of Sharon, his silent partner. He took suggestions from the floor, carefully editing them to a fine point, each one designed to spotlight money to the exclusion of anything else, all and only money.

"I dictated 108 of them on the spot in twenty minutes!" he would claim later, but in fact it took some three months for him to reach the target number of 108 maxims.

It was one of his twists on the 'Great Spiritual Heritage of India' to use that number. A mantra is repeated 108 times, you chant the 108 names of a particular god, goddess or godlet during a *puja*; it was one of those auspicious numbers of the Hindu tradition.

Whenever the hint of money came up he would call out, "Mademoiselle! Take it down!" and the 'Sorbonne produit' would reach into a wooden cabinet next to the couch where she stashed a notebook with the rough draft, and start all over again, from the top.

When the subject of the Money Maxims arose, people suddenly remembered errands they had to run. I once escaped to the balcony, climbing back through a hall window and out of the building. If he spotted someone leaving, he would shout,

"Hey! Where do you think you are going? I need your help!"

Sinking back into their chair with a sigh, they would be submerged into the philosophy of finance for the hundredth time.

He liked the way Yogini said the word 'money' so he had her repeat it over and over. She had a way of drawing out the word that appealed to him.

"Mademoiselle! Say it! Say the word money!"

It was a way to bring her out of that languid silence and keep her tethered to him. She loved it and repeated it for him as often as he liked, softly enunciating the word with a hammered-up sophisticated drawl, "Monnay."

Each time they laughed like children, until we were all laughing and saying it, "Monnay!"

It was nice to see her lighten up and have some fun.

He composed the Money Maxims with a precision designed to emphasize cash to the complete and total exclusion of anything else and the exercise was a complete negation of spiritual and religious platitudes. He had already composed his Ten Commandments with the same blatant reversal of anything familiar to the spiritual seeker:

1. *Just fuck—don't talk of love*
2. *Steal but don't get caught*
3. *Yield to temptations—all and every kind*
4. *Kill thy neighbor, save thyself*
5. *Better to be a dog than a holy mackerel*
6. *Hate your mother—beat that bitch*
7. *Shoot all the doctors on sight and at sight*
8. *Better masturbate than meditate*
9. *Eat like a pig, a hog and swine all rolled into one*
10. *Get lost and stay lost*

In UG's laminated copy of the Ten Commandments was a photograph of him, pointing to a road sign that reads *Route de*

Misery, with a line under the photograph reading *Not just a place—it is your birthright*, and then below that of course, *Have a nice day*. This 'special edition' highlighted the built-in warning that was often lost on people.

He was always the trickster; maybe he picked that up from his old pal JK, whom he always accused of 'throwing abstractions at the people'. He took the sport to new extremes.

Despite all the nonsense, if ever there was a source of religious ideals or behavior way back before it was all muddled up by the priests and pundits, it must have originated in a man like him. Living words were the key; his life was the subtext of all this apparent nonsense, and the Maxims were another exercise in erasing himself by creating something so tedious, bland and blank it negated him. I found them, and still find them, surprisingly empty and confusing like little brick walls. His life was the opposite of what he was insisting was important and the Money Maxims are an illustrated manual for the way human beings actually behave behind all the phony idealistic talk.

He also found a perfect opportunity to exploit his fondness for 'American underground' slang:

Moola is the Ruula of your life!
Make money by hook or by crook.
Take the dough and hit the road.

Later a German friend created a deck of playing cards out of them and UG delighted in using them to give readings to baffled visitors, who came to meet a spiritual master and were handed a card festooned with fortune cookie wisdom, as if it were a secret key to the universe. Asking the person to pick a card without looking at it and then hand it over to him, he would read it aloud with great ceremony:

"Marry not maddies, but money-making guys!"

The people in the room would say "Ohh, ahh!" and the visitor would scratch their head. Some of the language was archaic but it didn't matter as long as it communicated something about the essence of monetary relations. A Biblical tone was fine; anything that mocked religious pretense was welcome, rubbing our noses in that obsession that ruled all of our thoughts, overriding any other: *How much does it cost? Where am I going to get it? How much do I have? How long will my money last?*

Round and round this constant worry goes like the Maxims. The priest in the church, the bum on the park bench, even Bill Gates is thinking about money.

Money talks, wealth whispers.
No money, no honey.

He later used that last one on me to great effect without even throwing the usual sidelong glances at Yogini. Probably the one central reason I never even entertained the idea of marrying was money. I never had any. It's amazing how I dressed that up with all sorts of other excuses, but I wasted enough energy worrying about my own lack of money; why add more worry about another mouth or mouths to feed? No wonder I always felt guilty when I had sex with a girlfriend, at some level I felt I should be paying her back. I must have picked this up from the Catholic church, the idea that a woman should be rewarded for the sin she was forced to commit or something twisted like that. It wasn't love I was afraid of, it was money. Is there a difference? I'm not so sure. They both produce the most extreme sensations of pain and pleasure.

UG used to say money was the acid test. He never made money from what had happened to him. A friend in Bangalore once accused him of being a parasite. UG said:

"Of course! Why not? Who is not a parasite?"

The money game had driven away some dear old friends over the years. I heard a lot of stories about people who were sure he was going senile, or had been corrupted by this element or that, one group always blaming the other for the bad influence. It seemed to me that he was touching a nerve, the biggest nerve. If you really want to know if someone is genuine, look at how they deal with money. He squeezed people for money over the years I was around, sure, but he never once charged anyone money to sit with him. He often doled out large sums of money on the spot to help friends in need, and he never spent lavishly on himself.

I learned from watching UG deal with money that words are misleading and he used this deliberately in his Money Maxims. What amazed me was the brilliance and precision in his editing of a quasi document that was so clearly designed to give a wrong impression of him. Some people were actually convinced that all he wanted was for them to make 'loads and loads of money'. If they looked at what was going on behind those words of his, the story was entirely different, and obviously so. Not that he didn't want people to make money, no that wasn't it at all, but the indifference to it cannot be imitated. His ability to play with money, with the deftness of a great artist in his chosen medium, was really effortless.

He made the girls sing about money that summer. They'd always sung for him and I still remember the first time they sang the song from *South Park* about Kyle's mom,

"Girlies! Sing that song!"

They of course knew the one he meant, the smiles said it all.

"You mean the bitch song, UG?"

"Yes yes! That's the one!" he said with an expectant look,

"Weeeeeeell, Kyle'smomisabigfatbitchshe'sthebiggestbitchinthewholewideworld."

They sang so fast you could barely make out the lyrics, unmistakably rude, ending with a resounding, "Kyle's mom is-a-*bi-i-i-cha!*"

Again there was that childish laughter from him.

The song had the added appeal of addressing the theme of another one of his favorite lines, "Mothers are monsters."

"The trouble all starts there with the mother! My mother used to say 'I'm your mommy I'm your mommy!' and I kicked her it seems. And then she died. That is when the separation begins, mommy, chair, table, red table; all those words separate you from what is in front of you."

The girls had been singing together for the better part of their lives and sang in unison like angels. They sang *Money (That's What I Want)*, a Beatles song, and Lucia, an Italian friend, composed a round:

> *I want money lots of money,*
> *Give me money lots of money,*
> *I want money I want money*
> *That's all that I want.*

There was a waltz from Naren, conducted with great German zeal:

> *Make money by hook*
> *Or crook or crook*
> *Beg borrow or steaaaal!*
> *Or steal or steal*

That summer I gave UG more money than I'd ever given anybody in my life. I did it as an experiment.

As his birthday approached, he repeatedly told us how people sent him money from all around the world. Often he made more noise about a small offering than a big one. He wouldn't hesitate to call the Reverend a cheap petty bastard for giving him a thousand dollars, claiming that he was shortchanging him. The New Yorker was a constant target of verbal abuse while pressing cash into his hands at the slightest hint, yet if someone else gave him a fifty-franc note, he might talk about it for the rest of the day or the week.

In a twist of my own financial good fortune I was hired to work at the Basel Art Fair that summer. The morning I left, Mahesh was in the room while UG was praising me for the only time I recall as 'some kind of an artist.'

I started to thank him on my way out and he turned on me with a severe look, "Don't thank me!"

Mahesh was standing there. Assessing the situation, he said with his usual intensity: "He's telling you something, man! Listen to the master!"

All I could get from it was that he was telling me he hadn't done a thing for me.

When his birthday rolled around I spent the day before holed up in my room making a book of his statements about money, illustrated with a collage of magazine pictures and cash. I placed the joke book on his chair the next morning with butterflies in my stomach. It contained the entire earnings from the work at the fair, one thousand francs, one thousand dollars and one thousand euros. It made me giddy just putting the stuff together. When he discovered it, he opened it with a big show, quickly snatched the cash from the images, full of praise for what he called the 'paintings'. I was a nervous wreck as he went page by page, counting up the sum with a big "Woooow!"

He figured out it was from me immediately; there was an image of a bald-headed guy doubled over, literally coughing up some dough.

There were stark reminders of his mortality that summer. One morning I came in and noticed he was covering his mouth when he spoke. Soon it was apparent his dentures were missing. Without them he looked shockingly old. They had broken and the others were trying to convince him to have them repaired, but he complained that they hurt his gums. From then on he started claiming that his thirty-two teeth were coming back, proving the dentists were all wrong about aging and the body. It was an excuse to be rid of them.

"Why do children have to go to a dentist I want to know!"

He had his teeth pulled in the early eighties because they were vibrating when he talked during radio and television interviews in the brief period where he 'went public', immediately following the death of JK. Now he said the new teeth were cutting into the dentures and he didn't want to wear them anymore. Shilpa and Naren insisted he should keep wearing them:

"UG, you look like an old hillbilly!"

Finally, he relented, allowing the dentures to be repaired for the last time.

Another morning he said he felt a violent shaking under his bed during the night. At first he thought it was an animal, so he got down to look but there was nothing there. He thought the vibrations meant he was dying so he gathered his financial papers and walked over to Ludi Haus, rang the doorbell for the Reverend's apartment since Sharon was a medical doctor and could presumably take care of what ever had to be dealt with. He was prepared to die at any moment without a hint of fear. They didn't hear the doorbell or it didn't work so, since he didn't want to disturb anyone, he went back home.

He didn't want to disturb anyone!

People came from around the world to be with him, to be of help to him, to do anything for him, but his concern was not to disturb anyone. Aside from the humbling reality of his ways, it was beyond strange to imagine a guy like that waiting outside in the night for death to come; calmly waiting for an appointment with the accountant of time, all his papers in order under his arm ready to file and be done with it.

A couple of times after this I noticed him looking and feeling around under his chair, then he would ask if others could feel something shaking.

In the evening when he 'closed shop' he would walk home with a parade of goners in tow. The locals were no doubt aware of the elderly Indian living among them long after that other Indian gentleman stopped giving talks in that tent across the valley. He would talk to us as he strolled along, sometimes stopping to make a point as the group drifted around him along a back route of paved paths. It's impossible to describe the sweetness of the little man in his off-white outfit with his white hair sticking up slightly in the back like a hook, walking in a relaxed, unhurried way, chatting with friends about this and that or silent, never for a moment idle, never making an effort.

In the evenings after leaving I took a path by the firing range across a meadow, down a stairway, across the Saanen River to the other side in the dark. It was cool in the woods. The night air was a relief after spending the day in a room stuffy with warm bodies. Pretty soon I could walk the path in near total darkness. Sometimes I'd sit on one of the benches and savor the smells of fresh cut field grass, evergreen trees and the sounds of the river. Once or twice I fell asleep on a bench to the sound of the river, waking up with the moon peeking through the branches with stars twinkling around it. I was constantly checking to see if anything was different inside me. Had anything happened? Nothing ever happened. So it seemed.

Each time I passed Yogini's apartment I'd look up to see if she was on the balcony. Sometimes she was there, and would spot me and we'd wave to each other. I was always relieved when I saw she was alone.

CHAPTER 17

This structure is born of time and functions in time,
but does not come to an end through time.

The travel was intensifying. I made a trip to see UG in Amsterdam. From there I followed along to Italy, back to Switzerland, and back to New York in October. I left immediately after Christmas to see him in Switzerland again. While I was applying for an Indian visa, I ran into Yogini at the consulate on the same mission. It was odd that for years we'd been in the same places and never met, now we ran into each other everywhere.

She stayed on in the States a little longer than I did and when I got back, I met the new member of the caravan, an old friend of UG's from California, who would be with him, with some breaks, until the end. The Californian was a slim quiet guy who'd closed up his restaurant business and come to spend time with UG. There were some others I knew from before and UG was talking about a trip to India.

First we went back to Baveno to see the Italians on Lake Maggiore, where UG had experienced 'the saints marching out' in a hotel room near the lake in the early days after the calamity. He used to say that 'those filthy bastards, the religious criminals', were all flushed out of his consciousness at that point.

It was another inexplicable event that he talked about rather like you and I would discuss a trip to the grocery store:

"At last there were three rishis who appeared on a lake. I told them, 'You just getoutofhere!'"

Mohammed, Jesus and Socrates appeared to him and 'so many others that I didn't know...', as if he'd just passed them on the street.

"I would ask, 'Who are you?' 'I am Jesus'. 'Who are you?', 'I am so and so.' There were so many of them and they just disappeared. There was no way for them to stay there anymore. There was one fellow, a very handsome man with a long nose. I asked him, 'Who are you?' 'I am Mohammed,' and he disappeared!"

It seemed he knew of the place because of JK. There was that connection again. He pointed out the hotel when we passed by, remembering how much the room cost and how they left his meals outside the door while he was holed up inside for weeks.

Describing the aftermath of the experience in *The Mystique of Enlightenment*, he said:

> *You are back in that primeval, primordial state of consciousness—call it awareness, or whatever you like. In that state things are happening and there is nobody who is interested, nobody who is looking at them. They come and they go in their own way, like the Ganges water flowing: the sewage water comes in half-burnt corpses, both good things and bad things—everything—but that water is always pure.*

He said the saints came along after the sages and started the 'whole mess' of organizations and so on. The sages would otherwise have been forgotten completely.

There were lots of rides and then we headed back to Gstaad through the Alps. Fresh winter snow transformed the landscape into a sparkling wedding cake.

As the days wore on, he started insisting that I had to go to India; he needed my help to 'entertain the people'. He wanted to see my return ticket. I handed it over. He had a way of thoroughly examining documents. After looking it, turning it over a couple of times as if it were some important complex legal document, he declared it was a cheap ticket and suggested I throw it in the fire.

Into the flames it went.

"Look! Look!" he said to the others. "Are you there?" pointing at his head.

I just laughed.

"Good."

Then I spent an enormous amount of money on a round-trip ticket to Bangalore. This was 'UG economics'. What else is money for? He used to say money must move from one pocket to another, preferably from our pockets into his; nevertheless I'd seen how he treated money, and he seemed to be doing fine. I had the money, so why not? After all, this might be my last opportunity to see him in India.

When Yogini got back to Switzerland the hostility between us escalated. She was freaked about the Californian and me sharing a place with a German woman. I was freaked about her unclear 'friendship' with the Californian. Tense phone calls were going back and forth between him and her, and in the room during the day you could have cut the air with a knife. By the time we got to Frankfurt Airport the situation was degenerating rapidly. Unspoken alliances were crumbling and new ones being built by the minute.

CHAPTER 18

You want to continue, probably on a different
level, and to function in a different dimension,
but you want to continue somehow.

A handful of us staggered out into the humid breeze of the old Bangalore International Airport at about 2am in December 2003. After one night in a local hotel, arrangements were made for the foreigners to share a rental house close by. This made for some awkward dynamics, as Yogini, the Californian, and some others settled into separate rooms. I ended up sleeping in a dining area just outside the Californian's room. Each evening he would go up to visit Yogini for a couple of hours while I wrestled with demons below.

In the mornings UG sat talking while our hostess, Suguna, served coffee. She cried when she saw him. His dentures had broken again and he had finally thrown them away some months before. It was a severe blow to his looks.

"After all, there is such a thing as the aging process," he would say when people reacted to his appearance.

"UG, what is wrong? You have gone down too much!"

"Nothing is wrong with me! I threw away the dentures so my thirty-two teeth can grow back! Those filthy doctors are making you all into frightened chickens! Look, even my hair is turning black again," showing a few strands of dark hair remaining at the back of his head of white hair.

He made these absurd claims and foiled every attempt to feed him a little extra. In Telugu, Suguna would implore him to take one more *idli*.

"No! It is important to lose weight as you get older. It makes it easier to pack up!"

Even the mention of it brought her close to tears.

On the very first morning, the role of current court jester was thrust on me when he introduced me as an FBI agent. To this day people I met back then are still asking me about my non-existent job with the Bureau.

"Have you filed a report today?"

"I'm working on it."

"Did you say anything nice about me?"

"How could I? You are a threat to our national security!"

Given my constant preoccupation with what was happening over at the house, this distraction was a blessing in disguise. Instead of sitting on the floor stewing, I was forced to entertain almost constantly during that trip.

"Do something!" he would say, slapping me on the arm over and over.

I had to think up silly songs, imitate, the usual. There were no road trips, or very few by comparison to what he got up to in the West. I hadn't seen him there before so I had no idea what to compare it to, but the hours he spent on the couch talking increased tenfold. He simply never left it. Accidental naps were the only break he took from morning until we left at night. Then he sat up for some quiet time with the family until eleven at night. He was up promptly at five each morning, ready to start the whole thing over again.

"Don't quote the source, you are original!"

If there was a lull in the action, he brought out The Links, hefting one of the huge volumes into his lap, leafing through it, reading something out loud. After comparing himself to a computer or a parking lot (the signs in Swiss and German parking lots for lower levels are U.G. or *Untergeschoss*), or a saint or a pop star, he would slam the book shut, dump it on the table and say, "Enough!" asking for a glass of water.

People asked more questions in India. He usually responded on a completely unrelated topic.

"That is not your question!"

You couldn't help but ask and he wouldn't answer and set you up with answers that would lead nowhere.

"The word *how* should be eliminated from the language! In this area, the how is the problem!"

He introduced the Money Maxims with 108 phrases composed for the illumination of our wallets. Pretty soon he had everyone singing songs about money.

"My Money Maxims, how popular they are, better than all the books, everywhere, even in the universities. Presidential candidates are debating them! What is his name? Kerry, and Edward and his wife had half an hour discussion with my good friend there in California. But that bitch, the billionaire's wife, ran away when she heard them!"

The American presidential race was on and he didn't hesitate to bring that into the picture to 'promote' himself. He was quite sure about his own non-existent fame.

His hosts became increasingly agitated as UG started a full-scale circus of song and dance in the house. The crowds grew to overflowing, many probably showed up to be entertained, as he increasingly used my antics to distract people from their spiritual preoccupations.

His long-standing host, Chandrasekhar, sang some of his poems; one in particular that struck me as apt for what was going on:

You can stand upside down and do penance
You can have powers to crush rocks to powder
You can have all yogic powers and siddhis
You can have lots of wealth and money
You can be very cunning clever crafty

GONER

You can master all the Vedas and Sastras
You can be very devout, pour out your heart
You can beg for grace

Yet this state you cannot achieve by any of these things
Even one in a billion may not get into this state
Constantly hammering this fact, there is no way out for you
So says UG, the true seer, who is dear to Chandrasekhar

"How are we to understand you?" he pleaded in his songs.

UG's answer came in real time, with full-stop finality: "Just forget about it, you ain't got a chance!!"

Once he turned and asked me: "What will you say if someone asks you 'Do you know UG Krishnamurti? What does he say?'"

The question put me on the spot, sitting next to him in a room of expectant faces. The room was quiet and he was listening carefully as I explained, as simply as possible, why I was interested in him and the effects of his company:

UG was a force of nature appealing to the force of nature in all of us who chose to be with him. The so-called 'self' in each one of us was an imposition of ideas resisting the phenomenon of what we all called UG, a natural force the body was moving toward all the time. The only natural thing for the body to do was what UG was doing and my so-called 'mind' was resisting it all the time.

He didn't interrupt or correct me.

CHAPTER 19

*You are conditioning your mind through all this
lingo—that is all it is necessary for you to see.*

We drove to Madras to visit friends of his, an industrialist and
his wife. Yogini always rode with him; it was his way of keeping
her close while ignoring her at the same time. The Westerners
stayed in lavish homes of his host's daughters. Yogini slept near
the children, a new one for her. I was grateful to have a private
room to hide in. The situation with the Californian was becoming more and more awkward. They were regular chums.

The city was hot and claustrophobic. I felt trapped indoors
by heat, and poverty. The poverty in the streets was grinding,
probably the situation made it seem more severe. Just walking around made me feel uncomfortably like a voyeur in a bad
situation. In Madras, like Mumbai, polished houses sat side by
side with thatched huts. People were living in drainage pipes
on construction sites. Then there was the pounding sun, day in
and day out.

We would meet each morning at his host's house, in the
living room or an air-conditioned room one floor up, when it got
too hot downstairs. The house was enormous with stone floors
and fans and still I was sweating all the time.

They'd built a separate entrance for UG years back. When
they offered him any room he wanted in the house, he chose
the smallest room in the back of the house on the first floor
instead of the huge one they offered. He demanded stairs be
built to a separate entrance in the rear of the house, "So that I

don't have to look at you people when I come and go." He never used them.

As it turned out, they were a convenient passageway for the servants to move around the house. He often appeared to be making demands for himself while others benefited from the result.

The host's wife was so devoted to the god Krishna that she had visions of him working with her around the house. After meeting UG her visions stopped. Once or twice she sang for him in a voice like a flower blooming in moonlight. Serpentine melodies rose in the air like a trail of incense. It sent chills up my spine. Her husband strode the length of the house like a warden, sitting for a few minutes until his man called from his office at the front of the house. He was a big man, the picture of an industrialist, a man of power, who also looked to me like a comedian from the early years of television, with a husky laugh that drew his grin sideways and very expressive eyes.

A face reader came to the house one afternoon wearing glasses that exaggerated his stare as he scrutinized the face of his subject. The locals said he was a deeply spiritual man who was poor—until he met UG who pressed money on him like never before, encouraging him to charge more. UG had a handful of these characters around him wherever he went. He seemed to enjoy the performance. Of the many I saw the face reader in Madras seemed uniquely unpretentious.

The room was packed as UG pointed us Westerners out one by one, asking the face reader what he saw.

He'd read Yogini's face during the last trip and his story stayed the same: she would become a Holy Mother, starting a spiritual center in Kanya Kumari at the tip of South India, where UG would visit her every six months to check on her progress.

Since I was sitting next to UG, being showered with a lot of attention, he laid it on thick. By 2007, I'd be living on a beach wearing a *lunghi* like Ramana, eating rice and curds from the hand of some nice woman who would look after me while I built a temple to UG. I was useless to women and had mafia connections in New York. He got one thing right anyway.

A South Indian musician who had known UG for decades came with his family. UG forced me to sit next to him and sing. He laughed right along with the others as I made an ass of myself, correcting his *thalam*, a way of keeping time by tapping your hand.

Occasionally I had stage fright, a humiliating experience with a room full of people staring at me. I didn't have the luxury of a stage, the audience was at my feet. UG's elbow would dig into my ribs, making it worse.

"You are no good! Come on! Do something!"

There was nowhere to go, no curtain to pull and no back-stage to hide behind.

"Boooring!"

Bush, Ashcroft or Rumsfeld were easy fallbacks. All I had to do was double-talk nonsense from a Bush press conference; any two-year-old could do that.

All this time I was absorbing a tiny portion of the thousands of facets of Hindu culture. The layers of complex ritual attached to every act in daily life were everywhere. The more I saw of it, the more radical UG became in my eyes.

CHAPTER 20

Why do you bother about those fellows? They are dead. You should pitch them in the river. And yet you don't; you keep listening to someone (it makes no difference whom), and you keep hoping that somehow, tomorrow or the next day, by listening more and more, you will get off the merry-go-round.

The early morning winter light at Frankfurt Airport was blue, cool, mercifully neutral. I discovered I had no Euro cash and no return ticket. Shorty, UG's nickname for a diminutive Rajneeshi whom I'd met in wandering the streets of Gstaad during my first visit, loaned me enough euros for food. I couldn't wait to get away from the ragged gang wandering over to the train station on the way back to him. The Californian, some Germans and Yogini all waved goodbye as I sulked away with my tail between my legs.

At the last minute she turned to me, "Stay in touch," she said sweetly.

What was that? For a month I'd been avoiding her and California like the plague, then suddenly this shot of sugar.

I bought a return ticket and basked in the tranquility of the airport lounge for a while.

There was always work when I landed in New York. The guys joked about all the traveling around with the 'guru'; was I enlightened yet? Despite UG's blanket dismissal of hope I persisted in hanging around with the idea that if he could live like that why couldn't I? In any case, I was determined to stick around until I got the hang of it, or die trying.

LOUIS BRAWLEY

Word came that he was 'wobbling' in Germany. The worst period came in April, while he was in the Black Forest. He was in horrible shape after falling and hitting his head on a table in the dark. One morning a wall was smeared with blood around a light switch from a gash over his eye from a fall in the night. This was compounded by the 'plumbing problem' and his inability to pass urine.

He sat silently, while the others sat with him unable to help. He refused medical care. Was it the end? The Californian said each time he got up from his chair, he would pause and look out the window, something he rarely did, as if he was looking at the last thing he would ever see. The view was spectacular; meadows sloped gently down to the edge of a dense forest land ringed by rolling green mountains. Yogini said it was a horror. She was never particularly fond of Germany but from then on she hated that little German town in the Black Forest.

He gradually recovered, but his weight dropped severely.

When I called, he betrayed no emotion about what was happening: "Come right away, I need your help. I will give you 50 thousand dollars to pack me up! I have lived long enough and taken advantage of everything this world has to offer. Come here and get rid of this body, just dump it in the trash somewhere!"

I was taken aback and relieved at the same time. He managed to dissolve worries with his usual black humor. I called Guha who advised: "If I were you, I would go to the airport right away and get on a flight!"

I would have, if I hadn't been getting ready for a show in Los Angeles that turned out to be a waste of time and money anyway.

Around that time Yogini resurfaced in New York for a few weeks to see her father. We met for dinner and I pressed for clarification about what was happening with the Californian. She assured me there was absolutely nothing happening, then suggested I spend the night since it was already late. I accepted her offer and restarted the engines of misery. The

GONER

irony constantly hit me in the face that the idea I'd picked up
about living a celibate life was completely impossible for me.
The woman had such appeal I couldn't shake her loose no matter what happened. If it hadn't been her, it would have been
someone or something else.

Considering his condition, as soon as I had enough money,
I flew back to see UG in Italy in April. My return ticket from
Frankfurt had expired of course.

When I arrived he shook my hand. It was a light and sweet
touch, a cool blast of reinforcement for what was about to
unfold. It was Easter and the Guha family was there.

The girls greeted me at the gate screaming: "Saint Louis,
Saint Louis, we are not worthy, we are not worthy!"

The 'St Louis' thing had started when UG spotted a brand
of sugar somewhere with that name. From then on every time
we went for high tea he pressed packets of sugar into my hand,
pouring it into my palm from sugar containers. "You need it!"
he'd say. "Clean it up!" popping some in his mouth to show
me how it was done, giving a little shrug and gesturing to me
to follow.

UG was staying at the hotel in Baveno with the others, after
falling in an apartment on the hill. He'd been staying there
for years in his friend's condo but his days of living alone were
coming to an end. Shuffling over the smooth wooden floors
of the Azalea suite in his bare feet, he was like a tightrope
walker gracefully easing over the void. One friend had a terrible
moment when UG fell and he tried to help him up. The offer
was met with an unpleasant refusal that could take the paint off
your stomach walls, "Don't you dare touch me!"

The poor guy backed off as UG lifted himself from the floor
unassisted. It didn't help that the man was a healer; on the contrary, that may have been the reason for his refusal.

Yogini arrived the day after I did. The initial pleasures of
our New York liaison evaporated into sexual paranoia. Since

109

meeting her, I'd cheated, gone back to a former girlfriend, gone away and come back from UG's company countless times, while she engaged all the other males in the pack in a manner that had all the women on red alert and me on a razor's edge of jealousy. I was eager to enjoy our new bond, only to be told that as long as she was in the same building with UG that sort of thing would be out of the question. I was panicking with frustration while anger and jealousy sprang up between the boards of my 'saintly' sinking ship.

She was always in another car, his car, next to someone else. In the room it was torture. There was no question of talking to her while UG was there, and he was always there. We were living in a weird bubble, a glass house, trying to 'keep the whole thing under the carpet' as he liked to describe JK's 'sexcapades'. Otherwise he put on the BBC, CNN and broadcast whatever was going on to fill up the time. If we wanted to play it like that he didn't care, he knew exactly what was going on. They all did.

As he so charmingly put it: "I didn't come into the town on a turnip truck!"

His commentary on sexual relations set Yogini on edge daily. "Marriage is a legalized prostitution," he would say.

He referred to her career as a 'famous ballet dancer', smearing the word ballet so it sounded like belly. It was a sublime act of terrorism against 'sensual pleasure'. That charming phrase was like fingernails on chalk board to me when she trotted it out to evade or avoid a little roll in the hay. I was tormented by sexual frustration and I was the idiot who had this idea of a sexless life in the first place.

There is a statue of the goddess Kali in the famous Dakshineswara temple where Ramakrishna lived. The Divine Mother stands on the chest of Shiva in a state of rage, tongue out, armed to her sharp and deadly teeth. Her eyes are bugged with wildness as she marches, garlanded with skulls. The story goes that Shiva threw himself under her feet to restrain her anger that threatened to consume the universe. The representation of female fury is a powerful symbol of the potency of male fears about women. The tidal surge of uncontrollable animal emotions threw me this way and that like a rag doll when I was around the little old sage and the beautiful Yogini. The only way to deal with either of them was surrender, but it never happened. I couldn't surrender and I couldn't walk away. The battle was on and I was losing all the time. I spent days sunk in despair with the occasional suicidal depression. Is it suicidal if you only think about it?

"The fact that you are here means you have not given up hope."

It was another comment repeated so many times it was burned into the hard drive where it lingers to this day.

The drives went on as before, with chocolate shops as a favorite outing since we were in Italy. One day I made a spectacle of myself for his amusement by eating the remains of a chocolate orgy in a disgusting combination of sweet slop. Having done it once, he started ordering at every outing, "Hey! You buster, clean it up!" I never learned. Everything I did to show off, make fun, blow off steam, added fuel to the fire.

Yet I couldn't get enough of it.

Then I did the Indian thing: they say when you leave, "I'll go and come back." I went home and came back to Gstaad for a week in May. UG was stabilizing but I wanted to be sure. While I was there I found a cheap rental for the summer and set myself up for another three months of living hell in Heidi land.

Why? Because I knew it was good for me. Anyway, whatever was going on, he was right when he reminded me, with increasing frequency as time went on, "You had it coming."

CHAPTER 21

*To put it in the boxing ring phrase, you have to
'throw in the towel', be totally helpless. No one
can help you, and you cannot help yourself.*

By the third summer he was asking for me all the time to play
the fool, entertain, or just sit there with him, with Yogini sitting
to my left, right and center, and go insane. I was bursting out
of my skin.

If I left, when I came back someone would say, "He was
asking for you." Then spotting me he'd ask: "Where have you
been? What did you do? What have you seen?"

I told him I was filing a report (the FBI thing came in
handy sometimes).

The walks gave us some private time, long enough to get
some air, short enough to be frustrating.

He almost completely ignored Yogini.

The desire for escape had become as persistent as the
desire to be with him. I suffered from hours of immobility,
sitting in a daze listening to him, while thinking about going
outside. If I went outside, sooner or later I wanted to go back.
I didn't know if he was going to leave and I might be needed as
a driver. The uncertainty was infuriating at times, yet I could
sit all day mesmerized, walking home exhausted at the end of
the day.

Yogini was living next door to where we were meeting, so
we escaped to her room and went for walks. We spent hours
wandering over the fields of the Bernese Oberland which really

is a most beautiful place. On one walk she told me about her favorite movie, where the heroine married men and then murdered them for their money. Nice. I lived with similar fantasies.

Looking back, I don't know how I sat like a stone every day during the first and second summers, wondering how people could be so frivolous as to go out and waste precious time in filthy nature when the real action was inside with him.

UG was leaning on me more often, doing his imitation of an old man. One day I pretended there was someone on the phone for him. When he took the phone and no one was there, he smiled and without missing a beat, threw a bottle of orange soda in my face. It went all over me, the phone and the carpet. He didn't care, he was busy laughing.

"I am not a nice guy! I am not a holy man!"

I knew very well what he was.

Then he started punching and throwing things at me. A new monkey was out of the barrel. He had me sit in the chair next to him while he pinched my arm.

"Should I?" he would ask whoever was sitting in front of him.

Then he would pour the hot water from his drinking cup on my arm, telling the others I was in a very high spiritual state. I played along, ascending to higher planes of consciousness. While he was talking, I started interrupting him, correcting him until he punched me in the arm and eventually the face. By then I didn't care, I was so bored, and joking with him was the most entertaining thing I'd ever done. He was funny and never tired of this foolishness. He could turn any kind of nonsense into gold. I took pleasure in interrupting the sacrosanct atmosphere around him. Once you give up on the futility of logical arguments and idiotic dogma, what's left? You might as well enjoy yourself. It's a pity I never could convince Yogini of that, let alone myself.

One night he emptied a pitcher of water on me. I poured another one into my pockets. Soon he was 'throwing' me around like one of those world wrestling shows. When he pulled my arm, I flung myself across the room for effect. Sometimes people gasped while he was dripping hot water on me; it was a harmless theatre and some of them, seeing the fun, encouraged him. If it went on too long, I ran upstairs and jumped over the balcony, hanging from the rafters and dropping to the floor in front of him. Dodging a kick, a punch or taking a fall, I kept at it because now he was demanding it.

Now he wouldn't leave me alone. He was like a two-year old-child who loves it when you spin them around; your fatigue means nothing to them. On the other hand, being in emotional pain I'd rather stub my toe, burn my arm, or be in a car accident. The timing couldn't have been better.

The other fact of the matter was that he was growing weaker physically and this was a perfect way for him to distract from that issue, and make it more nerve-wracking at the same time.

"You mean to say I am a veekling?"

"Weeeell, you are a tiny little old man..."

Pow! With this comment he had his excuse to 'throw' me down and put his foot on my arm or leg and stand on it to demonstrate his power! He was so light I barely felt it. Then he'd check to see if Yogini was catching all this.

"Look, look! She is watching! I should be careful!" Asking for permission, he'd say to her, "Should I?"

She would give him a troubled look: "Why are you doing that, UG?"

"He deserves it! He had it coming!"

Looking at me, he'd start again:

"You mean to say I am a veekling?"

"Weeeell..."

Then he kicked me until I moved away: "See! He is only playing!"

Soon he forced the kids into the game,

"Come on, girly, hit him!"

There was the initial resistance.

"UG, I don't want to!" Shilpa complained.

This of course also made Lakshmi nervous. He pestered until I stuck my tongue out at her, then she got a glint in her eye and moved in with a pop on the head with the pillow. The dam was burst.

"Shilpa! Be careful!" Lakshmi scolded, then Shilpa got mad at her,

"Mom! He told me to!"

That was final. With lots of sidelong glances and a harmless thump on the head, she apologized, then ga8ve me another. If I blocked with my arm, he held it, urging her on:

"Come on, harder! Harder! You are no good!"

Then he went after Sumedha. Soon he had them beating me with the pillow regularly.

"Harder!" he screamed, if it wasn't done with sufficient feeling. "Harder! Harder! You are no good!!"

Sumedha never really gave in. She would give a tap and move away.

The song routine was expanded. His favorite song was the ballad about JK to the tune of *Jingle Bells*. I'd composed it in India the previous trip and he demanded it whenever a 'JK person' came to visit.

"Hey Buster, or should I call you a bastard? Sing that song!"

Jingle Bells, UG tells, JK was a fake.
Only thing that I admire were his sexcapades.
Jingle bells, UG tells, JK was a fake.
Looks like ol' Theosophy just put on a new face!

"He composed it on the spot!" he reminded his audience.

I knew so many details about the story, it popped out like automatic writing. Then there was the demand for the imitation of two oddballs, a Russian and a Greek, that was exhausting.

He liked that. Sometimes when he demanded it I just headed for the hills.

Ray rented a station wagon that summer and I was ordered into the back, like the family dog. Luckily I didn't get carsick like so many others and in the back I didn't have to think about elbows. The dreamless sleep took over like nerve gas if you were in his car. Even in the cars people were affected by it. Hours went by without a word from anyone.

UG was up front in the suicide seat, Sharon was behind Ray, feeding him sweets, coffee and chocolate with the occasional poke to keep him awake. Ray's seat was reclined like a Lay-Z-Boy chair, with her feet wedged under it. Occasionally his long tapering fingers twiddling in midair, she slipped him a Snickers bar, coffee or a sweet. He kept a Red Bull on the dashboard as a last resort; one shot of that stuff would have probably finished him off. Sharon was on the alert with a snack for UG at any moment and the interior of the car was a mess after about a week. UG was indifferent to this.

If someone wanted to clean their car, he would say: "Go and clean your head! That would be more useful!"

As his birthday approached he grumbled:

"I don't want to see anybody, I don't want to talk to anybody, and I mean it. I just want to getoutofthisplace!" running the phrase together in a growl.

"I am not like you people with all your sentimental twadel!" pronouncing the word with a little lilt.

"Anyway, what's so happy about your happy birthdays I want to know? I am 89 years old according to the Indian calendar! You are always forcing that filthy Western calendar on the whole world, you filthy bastards! You want to feel eeng [*young*]! There is such a thing as the aging process after all. And anyway, how do you experience your age, I want to know?"

He was always challenging someone to try and prove it to him, "You just for-get it!"

As July 7th approached, he reminded us he would be getting 'loads and loads of money' in his postbox from all over the world: "They send it from all over the world! So many countries, Poland, America, Turkey, Russia, South American countries! I don't even know who is sending it!"

Some of this was actually true.

We were all eating breakfast in room 609 while he pushed for an idea about where to go. He appeared to be in a foul mood.

"Get this and get this straight, I don't want to see anyone and I don't want to talk to anyone!"

We ate lunch at 10 am in order to get it out of the way so we could go for a ride.

"Where do we go?"

Ray was full of ideas,

"London!"

"Don't be ridiculous!"

There was some nervous laughter.

"Too far!"

"How about Saint Moritz!"

That was about 6 hours one way, but the exclusive company of the master for the longest duration was the best option as far as he was concerned.

"Hey...Shut up!"

The rest of us couldn't agree more.

"What about Paris! City of lights!"

There was a groan in the room.

Thankfully UG countered, "Too far."

Then there was a pause, "Isn't it?"

"Yes!" came the chorus. A dangerous amount of enthusiasm was expressed there. The seed was sown.

"Noooo!" countered the Reverend, spasming with ecstasy in his chair.

UG finally settled on coffee at a friend's place in Freiburg, Germany. Not too bad, only about 4 hours away. He would occasionally drop in for a coffee during the summer months when they were too busy to visit him. If someone couldn't get to him, he went to them.

We arrived in Freiburg for coffee and sweets, chatted for a while, then he decided we should go up to Cologne. That was 5 hours north and Ray was in ecstasy. In the end, it was Cologne for the night.

The happy travelers arrived at eight o'clock, with no luggage, not even a toothbrush. Arrangements were made for lodgings with friends and hotels and someone had the presence of mind to bring us some toothbrushes. After a lengthy discussion about what to do the next day, UG settled on Amsterdam so The Reverend could see the 'ladies in the windows' in the famous red light district. Maybe he was thinking of Mary Magdalene, Jesus' friend.

We arrived in Amsterdam the next morning, well before noon on a bright sunny day. After circling the streets several times, a cheery young Australian couple gave us directions. By the time we found a window with a lady in it, she could just as well have been a cleaning lady.

Ray made a joke about prostitutes that set him off: "Prostitutes are the only ones who deliver the goods! You all look down upon them. What about you? The only way to make a living in your filthy society is to steal from someone! Money must go from one pocket to another. Are you any the better?"

He didn't hesitate to point out that at least they give tangible satisfaction.

"Artists are prostitutes," he said, including my line of work. "Of course, you have to take advantage of someone, convincing them of the validity of your filthy paintings! I am not impressed."

The parking laws were impossible so lunch was hit and run.

"I will not set one foot in a restaurant! I have my own food! I don't need any of that crap you people eat."

Of course, everybody around him tripped over each other to

provide that coveted service; it was usually one of the women, who maintained his supply of rice sticks with the protectiveness of a mother tigress.

We raced through the streets to find something while the drivers kept the cars running, ready to roll on notice. Ray ran for a take-away coffee at a 'coffee shop'. "Sorry, no coffee!" Mushrooms and dope, but no coffee. We would have been better off with drugs instead of the grisly mess of fat and grease called 'Turkish pizza'. It tasted like cardboard and most of it ended up in the garbage.

It was still early so we got back on the road after the brothel tour.

"Where to, sir?" asked the Reverend, ever eager to please the one person for whom pleasure didn't exist.

"I don't care, you are the boss."

The passive tone was loaded as he munched on a pretzel in the front seat, waiting for the melee to start. France was suggested, then London, and of course Paris. Again with the Paris thing! Having gotten this far, he was setting the bar high. No doubt he was thinking of the whole exercise as a Zen koan for the rest of us to suffer through.

UG settled on Brussels where we could snap up his favorite food, Leonidas chocolates. They were also cheaper there so since the driver was 'after all a Jewish guy' it was an opportunity to save him a buck, even if he was actually Catholic and spent money like a drunken sailor.

"Fine, if you insist."

We hit Brussels at rush hour in the pouring rain without a clue where the Leonidas store was. Frustrations were running higher than usual after the long day of driving. My ass was killing me as we circled the city five times. UG kept on rattling Ray whenever he got close or finally decided to pick a direction on his own.

"Religious people always make right turns."

One tunnel we passed three times in a jam. I recognized a pipe gushing with rainwater I'd already seen twice.

Each time we landed in another dead end, he would mutter, "Of course!"

He deliberately confused Ray until he was incapable of taking directions at all. I could see the toll this was taking in the rear-view mirror. Ray was exhausted.

"It's up to you all to figure it out," UG would say, then put us back in a loop around the city.

When Ray asked if a left turn was ok, UG encouraged him, "Sure, I don't care."

As soon as the turn was executed I heard him muttering, "Wrong!"

If Ray dared point out he was just following orders, a fresh blast was sure to follow:

"You people always have to blame someone!"

It was unbearable. I don't like to be told what to do so I was impaled on my personality. Ray's inability to act on his own meant our dragging around in one of Dante's circles of hell. I knew I'd do a better job if I was driving, which made me even more miserable. The mumbling submission of the Reverend burped out at regular intervals, "Uhh huhh", "Yessir", "Yessir." Leaning in, giving him that bug-eyed stare instead of asking for directions, common sense had long since evaporated in the car.

The calm demeanor of the girls was amazing to me. Shilpa sat beside me reading a book or playing a game as if we were in a living room somewhere. Cindy and Sumedha were jammed into the back of the station wagon for the second day in a row, while Shilpa taught me sign-language to pass the hours, playing game after game of 'hangman'. Sharon betrayed nothing but good humor, but I noted a look of concern in the Rev's eyes as my murderous rage built up in the back seat like a hot poker.

Traffic was nearly at a standstill on our third rotation, when I finally got an idea: "I think the store is up there. I'll go look!"

I jumped out of the car and ran like hell. Dodging through the crowd with no idea where I was going, the fresh air and rain felt good. It was heaven. I considered my options. I had my passport and wallet on me. I could catch a train back to Gstaad and end this nonsense. I ran on, mulling it over. People in the streets were heading home after a long day's work, precisely what was waiting for me if I wanted to go back and 'take charge of my own life'. Who is in control after all? Were they? It didn't look like it. I was lucky in my particular torture, no doubt about it.

Just then I spotted the yellow awning of the Leonidas shop, with the New Yorker standing in front. I jogged up to greet the others and the questions with no answers started.

"Where are we going now?"

"Does anyone know where we are going?"

"Where is Shorty's car?"

Suddenly UG's car was at the curb. Shorty pulled up behind. The other cars miraculously emerged from traffic. We ate some chocolates, compared notes and joked. The New Yorker handed UG his favorite treat through the window, the box was passed around and soon he gave a wave of his hand indicating 'time to go'.

I got back in the car. Freedom means nothing left to lose. I'd seen that in the little man occupying the suicide seat already so I knew what it looked like. I still had way too much left to lose. That much told me I was not finished yet.

We headed back to Cologne with no further explanation and the whole routine started all over again, "Where do we go tomorrow?"

The morning of the third day he was teasing his host, who was feeding the whole lot of us, and paying for his rooms at the most expensive hotel in town. There was a free breakfast and complimentary extra one for a guest but no one ate there. There was a shelf in the bathroom lined with free shampoo, soap and toothbrushes from hotels where UG stayed, his gifts in return for the hospitality.

"After all, you paid a lot of money for those!"

Our host groaned theatrically, disappearing into his office to pull out some money he was 'hiding' in there.

"Tell me where he is hiding it?" UG would stage-whisper to his wife. "You have performed a miracle!"

"No UChee, it was you!" she would say.

"Noo!" Then a pause,

"Did I?" then again: "You tell me, where is he hiding all that money!" and she laughed.

Meanwhile, the guy had work to attend to twenty minutes after we left the house. Assuring he would have no time to prepare, UG preempted any preparation for work, reminding him:

"If by now you do not know what you are doing, you will never know!"

He said the work always went smoothly despite, or maybe precisely because of, these visits. Efficiency was a side-effect of UG's company. He would push people to the limit, and establish them more effectively in their professions, if that was what was needed. This man had been with a guru before. He told me that when he met UG, he was worried that he may, once again, have to give it all up for him. UG made sure he worked even harder, pressing him for cash as he made more and more money and established himself solidly in his business. The hotel bills and 'donations' were within his means, as dramatic as it looked from the outside. In fact he told me that he would fix the amount he was going to give UG before he arrived. With all the back and forth there would be some confusion, and UG always pressed for more along the way, but by the end, without saying a word to him, UG always left with the figure he had decided on beforehand. It was an impressive, invisible sleight of hand.

By day three, the girls were swapping clothes to break up the monotony of their wardrobes. Sharon was showing no signs of fatigue, but she had to be feeling it. Local friends were making Herculean efforts to get out of work in order to join the mad caravan. UG threatened one of them, the head of a local spiritual organization with an outbreak of 'fish poisoning' that would shut down the office for the day. Most of the senior members of his staff were hanging around UG. Rama would groan with a nervous laugh, "You are a real troublemaker, UG!" pulling at his lower lip.

UG held court at breakfast, wondering what was next on the agenda, collected 'birthday money'. It was a sizable amount. The people working at the institute never hesitated to show their devotion with money.

Rama gave a big sigh, a throaty laugh and confessed, "I don't know, UG!" as he handed over an envelope with several large euro bills. It was snatched away with lightning speed.

"Wow! Look! Look!"

UG hid his eyes, peeking through his fingers at the contents like a kid at Christmas. Sometimes he grabbed money and tossed the card or the envelope with some message in it after reading it as if it were in a language he didn't understand.

"I love you, UG?' What does it mean?"

I was keeping out of sight and out of range waiting for the question, "Where is that bastard?" Any minute he could pull me out of the crowd and I was in no mood.

"Where do we go?"

That question pierced the air like a knife.

"Gstaad!"

"You are no good."

Ray went for it, "Paris!"

"No, too far."

Then there was a pause...

"Should we?"

We were doomed to it.

The girls were excited. The rest of us groaned.

The drive was beautiful. Within a few hours we were in the French countryside. Miles of farmland rolled out to either side of us, no-one in sight. Clouds shifted spotlights over the industrial farming that brushed aside everything; small farms, charming towns, all pushed to the fringes. The flood of progress swept the landscape clean in a splendor of opulence. The few lucky rich fuckers robbed, stole or outmaneuvered the competition, clearing the way for an arsenal of food, the ultimate weapon. A two-lane highway cut through a green expanse with a dotted line. Trucks rushed past, sucking our car to the side with a sudden vacuum; the smell of danger jolted me away from the view time after time. We stopped at gas stations to refuel with diesel and junk food. It could have been the Midwest of America from the way it all looked: the same chain stores, the new highway hamlets, carrying all the same brand name goods, Pringles, Coke, Snickers and coffee. Gradually inching toward Paris, we cut through the countryside, monstrous combines and gargantuan barns, grain silos and hulking machines everywhere.

Towns sprang up on the side of the road like brush, suburbs leaked into view, industrial muck smelled up the windows like a grease stain on an old bathtub; all the signs of dense population. A grey sky began to rain as the tone of the ride slipped into a minor chord.

By the time we reached Paris it was pouring rain like Brussels the day before. Easing into rush-hour traffic, the sound of tires on wet pavement was hypnotizing. UG seemed fed up with the exercise, or with us. Our driver was hunched over the steering wheel under the lash of a verbal beating. Without a map he was at the mercy of his demon-navigator, taunting him with absurd directions. Despite all this, the little white-haired gnome riding shotgun was inexplicably funny.

"Use your eyes! Not your non-existent head!"

In the streets of Paris, the game started again; the closer we got to our destination, the more impossible the directions, insults and condemnations became.

He ordered Ray, "Go straight!" despite a sign forbidding entrance or a gendarme standing in front of it with a threatening look.

"UG, I can't turn there, he is saying no!"

"I don't care! What right do they have?"

Ray was sweating and spasming into another wrong turn as our destination retreated again. It was like a recurring nightmare where you keep trying to get up the stairs as the next landing retreats from view.

Soon it was dark and the hope of relief was repeatedly dashed in the delirium of confusion. We circled and circled until we were on the wrong side of the city, losing Shorty's car for the second day in a row. Pretty soon all turns were banned. At an hour when it was obvious that everyone was exhausted, UG turned the flame up to full. I sat behind him squirming, resisting the urge to grab the wheel from Ray. He clearly expected us to plow right through the heart of Paris regardless of traffic laws or laws of physics.

While he was pushing our noses into the oblivion of Paris the girls and I started singing to Ray:

Don't turn right!
Don't turn left!
Just go straight,
Just go straight!

Laughter from the darkness of the front seat indicated broken tension. UG was laughing. It was not too long after that that we arrive at his hotel at Rue Amsterdam in the dark, in the rain, with no place to stay for anyone but him.

At the hotel the others staggered in with blank stares. UG sat in the lobby, in a foul mood, while Ray and company cowered in terror around him. The idea of dinner at a local Indian restaurant was broached.

"I don't even want to look at you people. You are on your own. I don't want to see any of you here!"

Responsible parties rifled through an assortment of bags for bread, cheese and water for him. The rest stood or sat, vibrating like dazed fools. The New Yorker, who had lived in Paris years before, was instructed to take the girls out for a tour of the city, at around nine o'clock. Needless to say, this idea was carefully ignored.

The concierge took all this in from behind the counter with an expression of perfect French contempt. Later, the girls dragged cots into the elevator without help from the staff, but they seemed remarkably indifferent to all that; after all, they were in Paris. The enthusiasm of youth was on their side.

UG disappeared to his room. Shortly after that someone entered the lobby of the hotel looking for him. The concierge summed up the situation, "Your dictator is in his room."

We split up and wandered in the wet streets, looking for food and a room for the night. After a perfunctory meal we retired to cheap rooms in the neighborhood.

I showered, put aside my clothes to air out in the night and switched on the TV that wasn't worth watching. Switching off, I looked across the street into a bright apartment opposite and wondered what life was like in there. No doubt some snotty, self-assured Parisians eating *foie gras* somewhere inside. I was envious for a moment, then I lay back in the dark. You could hear every noise outside the door. Seedy linoleum floors, crackling with rot, bounced laugher and conversations off the walls late into the night, creating disturbing dreams.

In the morning we met at the hotel. Finally it was UG's birthday, the day we'd all been running from. His mood was no better, despite sunny skies. He was eager to hit the road, but first, it was time to give the girls a tour of the city.

"Come on! Let's getoutofhere!" he growled. "Take us for a tour, they must all see the city!"

It was a classic UG tour: three cars in a row flying past the Louvre, the Champs Elysees, the Eiffel tower, along the Seine to Notre Dame, back across the river to the Champs Elysees from another direction. "Look! Look! Look!"

As we circled the Arc de Triomphe, the New Yorker signaled from her car, veering dangerously close, holding out her cell phone,

"Tell UG Mahesh is on the phone!"

"UG, Mahesh is on the phone," I relayed.

"I don't want to talk to that bastard! I don't care who calls, I am not going to talk to anyone!"

I gave her the thumbs down and we sped off in the only direction The Reverend knew, toward the airport. It was day three of this nonsense, and UG was fresh as a daisy, yelling at him again with the usual pep, hit and dash.

The driver was losing steam, mumbling: "Strait is the gate and narrow is the way," to which UG replied, "...and look at what you have done to yourself!"

The Reverend's composure cracked and spilled. I heard a quiet pleading, "UG, please stop."

I looked into the rear-view mirror. He was in tears. There was a quiet pause.

"Fine," UG said softly. Then, "I don't care."

Raymond later gave me the full quote; "Strait is the gate and narrow is the way, which leadeth unto life, and few there be that find it." From Matthew 7:14 of the King James Version of the Bible.

We all had some feeling being around UG that we were so close to that gate, but the way was impossibly narrow with a huge chasm of the unknown to either side. Being around him was a challenge to him to 'give us what he had'. He showed us the degree to which we could not take it. Ray had given it his best, and UG pummeled him into a mash of pulp, it looked like to me, but he never regretted it later, that much was for sure.

We drove on as Ray regained his composure. Eventually UG went back to his harangue as we headed south toward Dijon. We got as far as Annecy before finally the signal came to head back in the direction of Gstaad. When we finally pulled into the drive of his chalet he tottered out of the car and people thanked him for the ride with glazed expressions. The group dissolved into the night like tattered bits of wet tissue paper.

CHAPTER 22

The absence of this movement probably is the beyond,
but the beyond can never be experienced by you; it
is when the 'you' is not there. Why are you trying to
experience a thing that cannot be experienced?

UG sat in his chair fiddling with a piece of paper or hollering about filthy religious bastards, coaxing money out of one, teasing another about looking like a terrorist, or scolding the New Yorker. He was constant motion, indifferent yet absorbing the flavor of each person. He knew me better than anyone, yet I knew him only vaguely. No conclusion stood for more than a few seconds.

He was a light that said, "I am not a light!", disclaiming itself just so you couldn't fit it into ideas cooked up by a dead mind. My thinking went on as usual but its irrelevance was constantly exposed.

Sometimes the heat of his light was maddening. You couldn't help it. If you let go, you succumbed to it. Often people came for a discourse and got bored and left without ever sensing it. He was a torrent that threatened to sweep you out to sea if you allowed it. The surface froth kept me focused on his words, while lives were uprooted and reshaped in the torrent. Closets were cleared, then the hallway went and the next thing you know your house was washed away. Whenever I went away for some time, there was a sensation of lightness. When I came back, the 'first person singular pronoun' tried desperately to maintain order.

"The desire for permanence is the cause of human misery!"

He never took sides in the personality skirmishes that went on around him. He seemed to deliberately fuel conflicts between people, making them burn more intensely, faster. He might drop a remark that would set something off between two parties, then smile slyly, making you hate his guts for a moment. Then you couldn't help laughing.

"Your question is not your own, it was put in there by those bastards! What is your question? What do you want?"

That one question was surprisingly difficult to answer.

"You are a pretentious bastard!" he reminded me.

I wanted what he had, sure, but I still wanted at least one other thing as well. She was sitting right across the room. The expression 'I didn't want to want what they wanted me to want' took on new meaning. He would look at me sometimes and say, "Take it easy!" at exactly the moment I thought I would explode.

"Hey! Don't be so serious!" he'd say to a woman sitting with a tight-knit brow, her eyes clamped shut. She'd look up and ask, "Am I serious, UG?"

Turning to another, a man who was staring at him intensely, he asked his girlfriend sitting across the room, "What's the matter with him?"

"Whaat? I didn't say anything!" said the man.

"The look on your face is more eloquent!"

Then again addressing the girlfriend: "What's the matter with him? Look at that face!"

The guy played along...

"Whaat, UG?"

"Where is bank-o-mat?"

UG was always squeezing this guy for cash.

"Ahh, unfortunately, they are closed today!"

"Ohh ho ho ho! Don't try to be clever! You think you are very clever. If I see some trace of cleverness in you I would be the first to point it out, but you are not clever, except in making money! And sharing it with a *poooor* Indian! Now come on! Where is ATM!"

For a while, he would look for Yogini, asking her to pronounce the magic word "Mon-ayyy!"

"Come on, Mam'selle, say it?"

"Mon-ayyy!"

Turning to another he'd say, "You call yourself a religious person?"

In his company the word sounded cheap.

"There is no such thing as spirituality! Spirit means breath! You are alive, you are breathing, that's all!"

I was counting the trees out the window.

"All this and heaven too! You just forget it! This is a thing you would not touch with a ten-foot pole!"

A truck went by outside. I looked over. It was ten o'clock. Still two hours to go before lunch. All we did was sit in the room, then eat. Or we sat in a car, and then stopped to eat.

Despite his apparent grabbing and hoarding of it, the minute you needed anything, he saw to it that it was provided. He gave a doctor friend $70,000 on the spot one summer when he was having financial as well as health problems. He whipped up $10,000 to buy a friend's son a piano when the grandfather offered a measly $50 toward one. He gave people financial advice, often saving them from bankruptcy and bad business. He oversaw the career-building of one woman who went from being a stripper to a successful independent businesswoman.

Once UG bumped into someone's foot in Bangalore. Later the man said: "The way he looked at me with genuine concern and apology was something I can never forget. I was in the way, yet he apologized with such sincerity for touching my foot."

UG practiced elementary manners and common decency to an extraordinary degree, yet never hesitated to tell a brutal truth about someone to their face if they could take it. He sensed who could and who could not take it. If someone insulted him he laughed like anything. You can't get a man's goat if he doesn't own one.

People said the scene around him at the end was like life in an ashram. I knew nothing of ashrams, but it made sense. You couldn't dress up your problems since you were under surveillance twenty-four seven. Try and dress it up and your little outfits were scorched off like a Barbie doll standing by a blast furnace.

One of the biggest battlegrounds was the kitchen. In years past UG cooked for his friends. He would make simple meals, which I'm told were delicious. Those days were over but he was still very much a part of the kitchen. It was a real drama to see how people took charge of the cooking, sometimes graciously, sometimes by sheer force. It was a position loaded with territoriality. The scramble for the job of feeding him heated up whenever new people showed up. Everyone had their idea of how it should be done and the arguments were usually kept under the carpet to avoid bringing him into it. He was well aware of every move and toyed with the situation deftly.

He knew kitchens "inside out upside down and if there is a fourth dimension, in that too!" as he used to say.

CHAPTER 23

Every time a thought is born, you are born. When the thought is gone, you are gone. But the 'you' does not want to let the thought go, and what gives continuity to this 'you' is the thinking.

A man who had been a friend for decades asked UG some questions on the topic of relationship one afternoon on a day off from rides. UG clarified, after a sidetracking explanation about his books and his lack of involvement in them. While talking about the image-making process in the non-existent mind, he brought out one of his stories about the physicist who 'hit his head so hard on the table' when he explained, in his unique way, the irrelevance of theories of a so-called space-time continuum. It was all related to what the man asked, you just had to sit with it and pay attention.

At first he set up the situation with some reference to Ray's poetry, an expression of pure unadulterated love for him:

"All these books published by people, you think I give a damn for that?"

"No!"

"I am not impressed, it's your problem. You are doing it for your sake and not for my sake."

"Yes."

"You wrote a thousand poems on me, for what?"

"Myself."

"What?"

"My sake!"

"Yeah, it gives you some good feeling. It's a self-centered

activity. Anything you do for anybody is a self-centered activity.
You can make a living on that shit. Start churches, temples. All
ashrams are… brothels!"

Here the other man interjected with his question, "UG?"

"Hah?"

"If there's no relationship, what is there?"

"Nothing. You are creating a relationship. Not me."

"But what word would you use, for your connection with us?"

"I don't have any links with anybody. When I look at you
I don't tell myself I am looking at X. If I turn this side (*away
from him*) you are completely and totally wiped out! If you are
looking at your wife and children and it's not that you are suffering from Alzheimer's disease, you will never know who you
are looking at unless there is a demand, and that demand always
comes from outside. If you ask me, 'Who is that lady?', 'My
wife.' What is that 'my wife'? You have an image, of what you
get out of that. But as far as the word is concerned, it is only the
dictionary meaning, nothing else. If you turn that side, you will
never be able to know how she looks like.

"Nobody has been able to explain this to me: 'What is
the mechanism that is there, operating in you, that creates an
image?' You know how your wife looks like and what is it that
creates that image inside of you? What is that that if somebody
asks me, 'Who is that?' I will say, 'That is my daughter.' But
there is no relationship, the word 'daughter' does not mean
anything, 'my' I have to use it to say that's not her daughter,
not your daughter, for purposes of communication. If you
don't know how they look like, not that you are suffering from
Alzheimer's disease, what is that other shit?"

Here he could count on someone to fill in:

"Senile dementia."

"Senile dementia; there is no way that you can tell yourself
that you are looking at your wife. What will be the relationship
with your wife?"

Then the story came in:

"Recently one nuclear physicist, top fellow, he's doing research to come out with new ideas, and he is interested in getting a Nobel Prize. He came to see me with his girlfriend. And then he went on talking to me about some idiotic nonsense: 'There is no such thing as space.' 'I know all that. As a student of physics I studied all that,' 'No such thing as time. No such thing as matter! No such thing as space, but what is known as four-dimensional continuum.'

"I listened to that crap for twenty minutes. I asked that bastard, if there is no such thing as space, can you fuck that bitch, or any bitch for that matter? He said, 'I have never heard of anybody talking about space the way you have.' And he hit his head on the table! 'What am I going to do? The whole project of mine will collapse.' 'Go and wash dishes in a restaurant to make a living.' I said, 'Getoutofhere!'"

Then he continued with another comment that drew a line which no-one can cross deliberately:

"You want to have all that and heaven too. In my case, the relationships are created, and destroyed in the next moment. Not that it is emotional. 'What do I get out of it?' That's the only basis I have for relationships. In my case, you understand? Even if you give me two hundred thousand dollars, I don't use it. I'll throw it in your face, 'Getoutofhere! I don't need your money!' Why you are doing it? Because it gives you a good feeling, that you are helping this poor, poor, poor Indian. You are helping me only because it gives you comfort, and a 'do-gooder's-high'. To put it in a psychological shit."

Then he launched an absurd disclaimer:

"Have you ever seen me helping anybody? Never, do I do it!"

Then the truth came out, sort of...

"In a particular situation, if it demands... then.... But even then, it is not an enlightened scoundrel! They don't exist at all. There's no such thing as enlightenment. How can there be

135

any enlightened bastard? All of them are criminals! Right from the beginning, all throughout history, they should all be put in prison, not the criminals we have created, grabbing everything that rightfully belongs to everybody on this planet, it is not communism, it is not socialism. It is not any of those things! We are only five and a half billion people on this planet, and the planet, or whatever you want to call it, can take care of the basic needs of fifteen billion people, at this moment. There is a statement made by somebody, that if we hit the fifteen billion population, if we survive that long (the chances are none), we will all be wiped out! We should have been wiped out a long time ago, for what we have done to all the forms of life on this planet. Grabbing everything, those scoundrels telling you, 'This is necessary, that is necessary for you to eat, twenty-five course meals"

He then referred to an outburst from a friend who was hurt when he made fun of the eating habits of JK: "He was angry. Fine, if I don't see him, who I have known for 25 years, it will affect me? Eh?"

"MMMno."

"Nothing. No power in the world can influence me, in any area of existence. Got it?"

"Mmm, hmm."

"Huh?"

"Yep."

In the course of the explanation, which I viewed later on videotape, there is a remarkable expressiveness in his every move, gesture, the ballet of those exquisite hands that formed movements as expressive as his words. His entire being was an expression of pure movement. The language moved deftly to clarify, and if it was hard to understand, that's only the manifestation of the blocking mechanism that helps people survive, 'living in misery, dying in misery'.

CHAPTER 24

This consciousness which is functioning in me, in you, in the garden slug and earthworm outside, is the same.

Every year, UG's friend, Salvatore the architect, would come to see him from Rome. There was a joke that he always said he was coming on one day, and showed up much later, the 'Italian way'. After thirty-some years coming to see UG, he was still bringing his questions, a way of interacting with him that he clearly loved, and he did it with so much grace and humor, you could see UG enjoyed it. This time, he was asking about culture and of course UG brought in their mutual friend, JK.

UG was explaining:

"Breath controls the music. Nothing to the music. You developed a taste, or a liking, that's why you like it."

Ray was seated next to UG while he was talking to Salvatore. This was the position of the ground for UG whenever he talked. He seemed to need one person who provided a bridge or grounding for the talk with no beginning and no end. Ray could be counted on to provide "Hmmyeah!" or "Yes!" or "Right!" whenever there was a pause, to get him going, or keep him going, as the case may be. It was an exhausting job.

"First time when I went to London, somebody dragged me to listen to one of the top fellows, playing in the Albert Hall."

Then, indicating Naren (the German loved music), with a slight wave of his napkin in his direction: "His favorite, Beethoven's ninth symphony... he started...I got up and walked out. Then I was in Moscow."

"Myeah."

"My guide, a bitch, insisted that I must go and listen to the concert, very famous concert in Bolshoi Theatre…"

"Ahh."

"Madame, I don't want to set my feet in that bullshit theatre!"

He said this with a pat in the air in front of him, continuing:

"You have not come out with any creative music, you are still playing Mozart." Here he warmed up to the insult on creative expression, with Naren in mind.

"Myeah."

Then exploding with his growling German, "Baaach!" with a big mocking grin.

Naren barked it back at him, "Bach! Bach!"

"What, Naren? *Baaach!*" taking a swipe at him and grinning as everyone laughed at his pronunciation.

The Reverend kicked in a pun: "His Bach is worse than his bite!"

Naren ran with this one, slapping the table, going a bit wild, "Bach! Bach! *Bach!*"

"Bach Bach!"

UG was not to be outdone, "And Wagner worst of all!"

Bringing down the pantheon of German cultural treasures with a final blast: "I know a lot more about music than…"

"Mhhhmmm."

"…even the top musicians!"

"Mhhn!"

"They could not stand it."

"Noo!"

"Eh? What?" He wanted to know what he knew from the Reverend again.

"You know a lot more about music!"

"Top musicians!" UG reminded him, laughing and pointing up to the sky as he leaned back into his critique with the glee of a boasting five-year-old.

Salvatore jumped in again,"UG, you are verry right, because..."

And here the room laughed at the agreed-upon silliness of the whole discussion, as Salvatore looked around to see what we were laughing at, laughing himself, but not before UG could counter, "Don't' say that I am right!"

"But-a wait, because I can a-with you..."

"Ahh?"

"... because-a this is also music," he said, tapping on the table with a pencil, "also de lift-a that you-a like in my house," referring to his elevator and the noise it made, "Brrrrr! You like, do you remember?"

"I know that."

"Moorty he told-a me, 'This is music!' Laaa laaa," he said, playing up and down with the pencil like a conductor.

"D'you remember? So also the sound, the music is the sound..."

He continued tapping, then adding a beat with his other hand. He had the beginnings of a nice tune going.

"But after, the man he do something else with the sound."

UG was not moved.

"Nothing."

"Ahh but-a UG, in de beginnin' is da sound, but after... the creativity..."

"Nothing."

Then Salvatore began humming, making the violin mime of strings, "Hhmmmmm, mmmmm, emmmmm."

UG laughed a little.

Smiling again, "Ah UG, you don't understand."

"I agree, I don't understand."

"Ahh, but natural-a, you are joking..."

"Nothing to anything."

Smiling, he took this opportunity to sidestep a little again, turning to Ray: "You see when I was addressing all the musicians

I used to tell that way. 'You see, harmony in the Western music. Melody, in the oriental music.' In India, they never used any instruments in those days."

"Mmmheah!'"

"I was surrounded by top musicians in those days in Adyar, the Theosophical Society. How many years I spent? 1932 to 1951?"

While he was talking to Salvatore, Maggie, our hostess in Palm Springs, was laughing hysterically with her brother, Naren, aka 'the holy man', yet another nickname. The whole thing was so joyously ridiculous. The two of them were a sublime comedy act.

I was in the back of the room on the couch with two people in the computer section playing the role of goon squad, commenting from the background. Others were scattered around the room in various states of declutched consciousness, and while UG spoke, there was an infectious giggling going on. I would interject some silliness in the midst of the conversation, cracking up half the room while UG explained things we'd all heard so often before it was like a rerun. He was like a child when he spoke, arms and legs moving around, giggling, smiling, leaning back in his chair.

He was rolling now and nothing could stop him.

"They don't know, I knew Krishnamurti very well, we were very good friends, he liked me very much."

The Reverend kept the ball rolling, "He liked you a lot!"

"Every day he was taking walks with me...in Madras, Adyar. My daughters were playing with him. And he did not know how to drink orange juice."

With this he smiled again, patting Rev's arm: "My wife invited him one day, 'Come on, eat with us.' 'No, If I accept your invitation, I have to accept the invitation of so many people.' And he invited me to have lunch there... Never!"

With a sweep of the arm, leaping ahead a few decades, he

launched into the oft-told tale of JK offering him a ride just down the road in Gstaad. There was no need to go into the details: if he missed any, the whole room filled them in for him. In the story, it was raining and JK pulled up alongside UG walking along. UG continued, "Bob was there. It's not a made-up story."

As if we were accusing him...but to be sure, the Reverend backed him up completely, "No!"

"I asked him, 'Do you have third-party insurance, Krishnaji?'"

With another wave of the hand he indicated that Krishnaji had no such thing, so we all knew that he told the old man:

"I would like to walk in the rain, singing in the rain!' 'Suit yourself, old chap!' He always talked like that, 'Old chap', it was the English way. That was the first time I met him, and last time."

Despite the inaccuracy, perhaps because of it, it was confirmed by Ray, "First and last!"

"...after 1961, never saw that guy!"

Salvatore tried to jump in again: "UG, a-say to me 'yes' or 'not'..."

But before he could launch the question, UG answered him resoundingly, "No!"

"But-a do you-a think..."

"No! No, no, no!"

"But-a the question..."

"No, listen to me!" as if he had an option. "I have only two words in my entire vocabulary. No for everything, yes for money!"

Regardless of the missing logic of this explanation, the case was closed as far as he was concerned, and yet.... and yet and yet...

"Yes...a..." Salvatore agreed, without stopping, so UG asked for clarification, "Got it?" Smiling.

Salvatore didn't give up so easily though, pressing on

through the jungle:

"Do you think he was in some special state, or not?"

"What?"

"Krishnaji. He was in a special state, or not?"

UG deftly slid aside the question with another question: "You want to hear what I said about him?"

Now the room was laughing again, we could all see it coming.

"No UG, yes or no!"

"Neither yes or no, but he was a stupendous hoax of the twentieth century!"

"Hoax, hoax, ok," Salvatore hung in there, "so he was not in that state?"

"No no, *no*!"

Then the inconclusive conclusion was broken in two by another question.

"What state?"

"Sometimes yes, sometimes not?"

"He was a very clever guy."

He was hanging in with the non-answers.

"Hey! Don't forget, we lived in the same atmosphere, his teachers were my teachers. Huh? You know all that."

Here again, he smiled widely and looked around the room, while everyone laughed, enjoying the crumbling dialogue.

"But I chose a different master! Kuthumi was my master. Morya was his master!"

Then, looking around to Naren for a music consultation again: "And Kuthumi was a great player, hey what was his ah..."

Naren was right there with the musical answer! "An organ zat vas resounding ssrough ze w-whole universe."

He had done some homework on that one. UG was pleased: "You heard it? Resounding through the whole universe!"

"... ant all beinks who vere rezeptif, vere shaking, viss egg-stazy ant bliss!"

Too much information! UG said "Shut up" in Telugu to that

filthy word, *bliss*!

"We don't want to talk about him." (Patting the air toward Salvatore.)

"But-a you are-a talking about him; I say nothing!"

Salvatore said this smiling, with a shrug.

UG reminded him again, "You knew him very well!"

"I... also can't disagree, but I loved him."

Salvatore was a diehard romantic Italian.

"Huh?"

UG was decidedly not.

"I-a love him... in-a some way."

"You loved him?" As if he didn't understand.

"Yes, I'm-a grateful to him for many things."

"For what? Name one!"

Here there was more laughter, in response to UG's tone of theatrical challenge as he explained to Salvatore, leading the court in another direction again:

"Because he was a close friend of Madame Scaravelli."

Laughing and pointing to Salvatore...then of course he went a little further, pushing and pushing:

"Because he pushed her husband to commit suicide."

"Ohh, I don't-a know."

"You were there when she invited the whole lot of Krishnamurti followers, in Rome, and I had to give a talk," he reminded Salvatore.

Then, sidetracking again: "Hey, her son is he died or still alive?"

"Oh, he died."

"You should have heard him talk about J Krishnamurti. What he said! He didn't like the mother to spend so much of money. In Rome! She collected so many people there! Come on!"

He said gesturing sweetly to Salvatore again, continuing:

"No, we don't talk about that nice fellow! He was a good friend of mine. Right? What?"

Now everyone was laughing again, the whole thing kept going round and round, he was laughing too, leaning, coming forward, smiling that toothless smile, teasing Salvatore with the obviousness of his answers, the refusal to be drawn in, "What?"

"Wellll you-a know-a UG, you-a know-a...I have-e a kind of gratitude to him."

"To him?"

"Yes."

Here UG reminded him of some of the ways in which J. Krishnamurti messed up the lives of his so-called friends, leading them away from practical careers: "You know he didn't want you to complete your architecture degree."

"Yes."

Telling the others: "He didn't allow him to finish...now he's very famous. I pushed him: 'Don't listen to J Krishnamurti! He ruined the lives of so many people!'"

"Yes."

Here UG pointed to him, a sort of 'see what I mean!'.

"Yes, I agree with you."

"He agrees with me."

"Because he take you for-a the beautiful, the beautiful trip..."

The Reverend tried to stay involved: "Right!"

UG was not going to let that one get away: "And when they met me, I pushed them away, (*from him*). All of them are on the top of the world now. He is also a great architect!"

Indeed, more than one career was saved by UG's intervention.

"But the ride was-a so nice," trying to salvage some bits.

"Heh?"

"The ride was-a a nice..."

"What ride? "

"Wiv the tinking, where it-a takes-a you, lettle by lettle," with this, he reminded UG about the Journey, the bogus-chartered thing:

"I told him, 'Yours is a bogus chartered flight!'"

GONER

"UG, I liked him."

"I also liked him."

"J'des amore," a phrase that sounded romantically jumbled between French and Italian.

"Why are we talking about him?" UG smiled.

"No I want to speak about many other tings."

"Heh?"

"I want to speak about many other intelligent questions."

"Do you have any intelligent questions?"

"Yes-a. I put a list, three-five pages."

UG didn't seem so interested and everyone was laughing at the famous list.

"How long have I known you? Thirty-five years?"

"Yes."

Still Salvatore pressed on:

"I also want-a to write down-a some of what you are-a saying, so I can-a change-a myself during de winter-a time."

He was laughing as he said this, fully inviting the joke, and we joined in of course.

"What, Naren!" UG sought out the astrologer in the back of the room, laughing heartily with his sister, enjoying UG's antics.

Salvatore saw it coming, "Don't laugh behind there!"

"What's going on, Naren? He is my very good friend! And he was the best friend of J Krishnamurti!"

"Yes!"

Seeing which way the tide was going he jumped in: "I want-a to ask Naren a question; if I will-a change, next winter?"

"Ahh, ha, ha, ha! You heard it, Naren?"

The Reverend rephrased the question for the astrologer: "He wants to know if he's going to change next winter?"

The German barely paused to consult the stars. The answer came immediately, "No chonze!"

"You heard it? No chance!"

UG backed him up for once. Then added, "You are doomed!"

"OK, I know!"

There was a pause, as UG abstractly pounded on the arm of the chair softly with a fist, clearly enjoying all this.

"Oh mamma mia!"

Salvatore brought another question, "OK. A simple question, UG."

"Hah?"

"A very simple question, intelligent, but simple!"

"You don't have any intelligence... Do you?"

"Do you think that ecology can change the world?"

"No. It'll worsen."

"Worsen."

Salvatore held his glasses and smiled with the answer; this gave UG an opening to tell his story about the woman receptionist at NBC who made the mistake of asking him if he had any comments on ecology, and he reminded her that she was using toilet paper to wipe her ass after shitting... but that's another story!

CHAPTER 25

The structure which is always thinking of every possible situation, envisaging every situation, how to be prepared, to deal with each and every kind of situation that might arise during the course of your life, is a thing that has no meaning, because every situation is quite different.

UG fell one morning, but pulled himself up and carried on. He was not about to allow a discussion of it. The summer was over and he wanted to get out of Gstaad, so we drove to Baveno, where the Italians came to visit from Milan. Then we drove to Vence within a day, to visit another friend on the French Riviera. The playing around had become a convenient way for him to grab hold of my arm for support. The stick figure sitting in the chair could go on for hours and hours, but when he got up to wander aimlessly, the legs were not so steady.

I was trying to figure out whether to fly back to the States or let things go to hell in New York. I was tempted to leave my belongings to the dogs since the landlord had finally given us the heave-ho. After ten years almost to the day without a lease, we were out. A healthy sense of self-preservation and some sage advice spared me from acting on this plan. I could sell the art and, anyway, leaving it to friends to dump my things in the street seemed inconsiderate. I wouldn't have wanted to be put in that position.

Nevertheless, I toyed with these ideas as we made our way south. UG was asking about my plans. I let him tear up my return ticket at lunch one day for entertainment, but it was an e-ticket so I knew it didn't matter. I talked all this over with the guys after a long day of driving in Vence, while we stood talking on a little stone plaza overlooking a picturesque valley. California and I discussed our intention to stick around until the end if possible. Everyone knew it was inevitable and, we agreed, there was nothing more interesting happening out there in the world. I told them my decision to return was hinging on what I thought was UG's need for my support.

"What would happen if I left and he fell?"

Thankfully, an old friend of his pointed out that UG died a long time ago and never really needed anyone's help.

I decided I better go back and clean up the remaining mess in New York. I gave myself a week to put my life into storage. The rest I left behind. It would be interesting to see what living without a base was like.

Then I headed back immediately, landing in Frankfurt. I met a friend and drove up to Amsterdam to meet the gang, spent a few days there, then back to Cologne to drop someone off, then to Gstaad in the 'chauffeur's' new car.

The caravan had evaporated. Now it was one car, with the driver and UG up front. California, Yogini and I shared bucket seats in the back; two buckets for three people, most uncomfortable, particularly in that combination. UG wanted to go to London so we took the Channel Tunnel. On the way there Yogini discovered at the first petrol stop that a bottle of cooking oil had leaked all over her new luggage. My backpack was drenched, so I tossed it.

As for London, well I saw it and sweated a lot in an overheated apartment. We toured the English countryside to where 'that fat bitch' the Queen lived, then to Cambridge and Oxford and then out. The three of us were smashed together to stew in our juices until I thought I would burst.

Mahesh came. He took one look at Yogini and said: "My dear, you look as though you are waiting for the final bullet!"

He was always taking me aside to tell me to get away from UG. I thought this was odd, given his history with him. But apparently his view was that we were hiding out, in danger of being 'destroyed' by UG, and becoming complete misfits in society, as UG would put it. I took it as one of Mahesh's typical typically dramatic statements.

We met Mario in Luxembourg, a fitting country, bordered by Germany, France and Belgium. When he pulled up in a van with decent seats I could have kissed him.

UG dragged us all to the Amalfi coast, where he was looking for a base. He kept saying how he was like an elephant looking for a place to die, but the feeling was more like he needed an excuse to keep moving. For years he said that when he stopped moving around he would die. Some friends knew a nice place just south of Genova, so we went to check it out and came back within a day to Gstaad, where UG suggested that we Americans rent our own car.

The Europeans were doing most of the driving, a considerable expense, even when we were contributing to petrol. UG often wouldn't allow 'helping out' as he put it, forcing the driver to pay for everything. I was always well aware that I was cruising around on someone else's dime, an awkward feeling at times.

We went to Lake Como, and while we were there, California, Princess Yogini and Mr Rage, rented a little red Fiat. She and I had a fight about my driving before we even got out of the garage. Meanwhile California sat stewing in the back seat.

We headed off in search of elephant burial grounds.

Sestri Levante is a coastal village along the Mediterranean in the region of Liguria south of Genova. The coastal roads along the cliffs are steep with even steeper curves, a challenge to my limited experience of driving with a gearstick. It was so beautiful it was staggering. As soon as we sat down in a little apartment, light glistening outside as the sun set over the sea, UG wanted to go for rides.

"What are we doing in this place? Come on! I want to go somewhere."

The place was abandoned in the off season. The lot of us filled about four condo apartments that overlooked the sea from various heights. California and I shared an apartment, while Yogini bunked with a German woman next door.

I was miserable. "Live in misery and die in misery," UG would reiterate, but I was determined to prove him wrong. There had to be something about his company that would resolve all this, I could never take him literally. Returning, finding a job, these were all options for later. At present here was a man, a major force, an event of nature, something not to be missed, particularly as circumstances had cleared a path, not only for me to have found him, but to spend time with him. Having found him, there was no way I was going to lose sight of him; the point was to hang on, no matter what. Whatever nonsense I was going through, this fact was so clear to me that I simply felt no choice in the matter, it wasn't even a matter to discuss.

There was an added dimension now that he was becoming increasingly frail and clearly using me as a physical support. The attention helped enormously. In retrospect, his attention was like gold to me, which offset the painful emotional turmoil. If he was right, and emotions were the same as ideas, then I was just getting my medicine.

One afternoon we were all waiting for a light to change by the side of the road at an ancient one-lane tunnel, on the way back to the house after driving all day. I was kicking dirt and stomping like a fool on an eroded cliff over the surf. The others looked on nervously until UG emerged from his car. The sky was full of the tossed remains of a storm. A wind blowing off the sea swept his hair back into white flames around his head, exposing his huge elephant ears. With a grin on his face he 'pushed' me through the wooden fence. That night he claimed to have 'thrown me into the sea', declaring at the same time that the 'beatings' were over. Did the upcoming trip to India have something to do with it? Soon we were heading back to Punya Bhoomi, what he fondly called 'That filthy spiritual shitland!'.

CHAPTER 27

India 2004—2005
November, December, January

*I don't like the articles written about me. You are trying
to present me as a religious man, which I am not.*

For the first time Yogini and I were on the same flight with him
to Bangalore. As I stepped off the plane the night air of India
swallowed me up again. On the way to Chandrasekhar's house
in the dead of night, huge trees hung over the empty streets like
phantoms. The former Garden City was wheezing in a fog of
chaotic urban development under the moonlight. Thousands of
years of spiritual yearning that has yet to be completely buried
seep up through rotting soil, permeating the sky of a country
where everything is named for a god. The effect is of a stick of
incense burning with human longing.

Yogini and I took separate rooms in a guesthouse on the
ring road, a place swarming with servants, who let themselves
into our rooms before we were out of bed to serve us coffee and
toast. After a fitful sleep we argued over breakfast. It was like
talking to air when she disappeared behind those blank brown
eyes, lips pouting with a quizzical expression. She blew across
me like a breeze but the connection never quite took.

We moved to a large house on a hill across the ring road
selected for Western visitors. The roof offered views of the city
in every direction. UG came to the house dressed in loose cot-
ton whites, something like a jogging suit, to have a look.

After touring each room from the bottom floor apartment to the roof, he said: "It's a nice house. Do you like it?"

His attention to our lodgings was that of a gracious host or a concerned parent, making sure everyone was settled and the rent was paid on time. Yogini and I took the top floor with adjoining bedrooms and a shared bath.

Noting the arrangement, he said to me, "You will have to learn to get along with others."

I carefully said nothing. He had a way of making a note of comments that flew out at such moments, reminding you later in a crowded room. The first floor was occupied by a shifting group of visitors.

As usual, he stayed with Suguna and Chandrasekhar and the house quickly turned into a local Grand Central Station for seekers and friends. A lot of Westerners were heading to India this time, descending on the little house as he unleashed a fury, orchestrated to upend the expectations of all those involved. On that trip he earned his reputation as the living embodiment of Shiva the Destroyer many times over.

Later I would see videos of his visit from previous years in a new light. It seemed as if he was more energetic, unrelenting and potent than ever before. As he aged, he became more furious and challenging to his audience, or so it seemed. The odd thing is that he was older, more frail, yet he seemed to be on fire, constantly talking, shouting, blasting the order of things with more gusto than before. Why now? Why at such a late period was this fury unleashed? I had no idea. Sitting next to him preempted any and all contemplation of these issues. He simply made it impossible to think straight around him, and most probably if there was a point to it, that was it.

"There is no such thing as silence! A silent mind? Hah! Some idea, empty words and empty phrases."

If you watch a waterfall, where is the silence? A hurricane? An earthquake? This is how I saw him later, a naturally occurring phenomenon, where is the room for ideas about silence and bliss around him? And yet and yet...

By the time he was failing, falling, or growing frail, it was clear that he would never seek medical advice about his condition, whatever it may have been. Clearly he was failing in some areas, yet his vigorous attacks distracted people from this.

Since his illness earlier that year, we were all on the alert for signs of the 'wobbling'. His Indian friends knew little or nothing about what had happened.

He wanted the situation kept under wraps: "I don't want all those worried phone calls!"

People who had known him for years were hurt to learn that he had been ill and no one told them. That didn't keep him from playing on the usual fears and phobias about illness and death, once he arrived and people saw his diminished physique. The dentures were now out for good, and his weight had dropped yet again.

Seeing all that, knowing he didn't hold back in India, some European friends warned him not to go at all, but once he got there, he showered energy with more fury than ever. From the beginning, watching the way he pushed himself I was sure it would be his last visit to India. It was like watching him empty a vessel before throwing it away. He had vast stores of energy, the kind of energy you get when you live with a complete disregard for the idea of saving for a rainy day. It gave the impression of a bone-thin body as a well-maintained puppet for something much bigger.

Shortly after the calamity, all those years ago, he was talking about dying. Assessing the effects of the calamity, some doctors apparently thought he had cancer. He later enjoyed talking about how many of the doctors he'd known over the years were themselves long dead. One of his favorite stories was to point out how all the great spiritual figures, Ramakrishna, Anandamai Ma, Ramana Maharshi, Nisargadatta, had died of cancer. At one point he had a doctor draw up his death certificate prematurely, stating that he died of cancer, just to be a member of the club. It was all part of his grand joking of course, joining the company of those he allegedly held in contempt. Then he ended with the comment that the doctor himself died shortly afterwards.

When Suguna saw how thin he was, once again his diet became the subject of immediate concern. He threw out so much of what he ate as a result of the cardiospasms it was hard to imagine what he lived on. She had been feeding him for over thirty years, looking after him like a mother or a daughter, and now suddenly people were advising her about how to prepare his food. His movie star looks and slender physique of even five years before were gone. Now he was an old man and without dentures he looked even older.

Straightaway he created some tension by insisting that we take meals with him in the house. Yogini was particularly upset since she tried to organize eating at the other house during the last trip and was completely ignored, then she was blamed for not making it happen. Despite attracting attention for her looks, she was so quiet no one listened to her. Used to all that, she retreated as usual into her shell.

A young Hungarian woman who met him the year before came again and shared the house with us. Taking charge of the cooking and organizing, there was immediate tension on that front. She and Yogini were like oil and water. Yogini was poised, quiet and well-mannered and the Hungarian was a kid with a gypsy life-style and a brash way of taking over uninvited. Eventually we worked out the arrangements for cooking at the house for the Westerners and, despite UG's invitations, the only way to handle things was to quietly leave and take our meals there.

He asked me to sit on the couch again, "Hey, buster! How good is the morning?"

"Fine UG, fine…"

LOUIS BRAWLEY

"Come, come, you must keep me company."

He used that swatting gesture the Indians have as a way of calling you over, patting the cushion to his side with a sly smile.

Since he'd declared the beatings officially over in Italy, I assumed it would lead to the usual small talk, word play, gossip and teasing during morning coffee. As soon as I was handed the first cup of coffee, he gave me a quick whack on the head. It was so unexpected it was as if he'd never done it before. I flushed, ignored it, and pretended I wasn't as surprised as I was. After all, he'd declared a truce. What was this then? My face turned red. Next I felt a hard pinch on my thigh that told me things were going to be different again. I ignored this so he gave me another pinch and a quick slap.

People were surprised and there was some laughter around the room. Suguna was shocked. A look of discomfort and concern crossed her face. Then there was the usual cross-examination from Mohan, who was a big round man with full features and a jolly energy who refused to go to work as long as UG was in town. He was in the habit of unleashing a stream of rapid-fire questioning that could go on for hours.

"Oh ho! UG! What is this?"

Suguna was more pointed in her worry, "UG garu! What are you doing?"

With a couple more slaps, he said casually, by way of explanation, "He had it coming!"

Then there was another slap to the head.

"Oh my!" Mohan exclaimed from the back of the room in his booming voice. Then he shouted with one of his wide-eyed expressions, "Energy transmission!" chuckling over his big belly.

Only in India are such things immediately incorporated into the spiritual discourse. I could have smacked him when he said it. Now UG would take it as an excuse. In any case, the floodgate was open and he was pinching me hard on the inside of my thigh where it really hurt as I blocked another slap on the head.

156

His fingers found a soft spot on my arm and soon I was duck-
ing and blocking while he carried on with his usual morning
sermon, talking and beating me as casually as ever. I lost focus
on the coffee and started sweating as the caffeine kicked it up
a notch. As if he could hear me sweating, he told Suguna to get
me another cup of coffee before I could finish the first one.

"Hey! I don't want another cup!"

"You think you have a choice in the matter?"

"Come *on!*"

"You think I am a sweet gentle Jesus?"

Slap!

"I am not a holy man!"

Punch! Punch!

"I am not a nice guy!"

"Ok! Ok! I get it!"

"I don't think you get it! You are after all a dunderhead, and
a bastard! Which is it?"

"You decide!"

I gave up and gave in for the time being. Once again, I could
put up or go and I hadn't even been sitting there for ten minutes.

With this routine he found a new way of making a point
with his listeners. Soon we were right back to hot water on the
arm or head, snacks that went into his mouth and the rest into
mine. If I refused a snack or his offer of more, always more, his
hot coffee was poised over my head. I knew he didn't care if he
stained the couch, but my hosts were not about to blame him if
he did; I was the one causing the disturbance.

From then on I was very rarely in the room without him calling me over to sit next to him to take a seat and some beatings.

"Hey! Where is that bastard?"

"He's out here, UG!" some helpful person would clue him
in if I went to the front of the house.

"If I have to come after you, you know what the consequences will be!" If I didn't come up willingly he'd threaten

to drag me up. I didn't want to risk his falling, or a scene; my refusal would only make things worse. Each time he unleashed fresh beatings on me with a vengeance.

"You think I am a veekling?"

Slap!

Again and again he'd look at me and say, "When I look at you the only thought that enters my head is to *hit* you!" It was his only explanation other than, "You had it coming!"

For the most part it was pretty funny, but painfully, with an edge of desperation on my part as I tried to balance my reactions with humor. When the Reverend arrived I was wedged between the two of them, his crossed leg extending into my lap, while he went into a 'spiritual coma'. I made myself as small as possible with UG beating me on one side and the Reverend's foot edging into my lap on the other, hyper-conscious of my own feet being in the faces of the people sitting on the floor. As ever, they were inching as close as they could get to him.

If I was wearing glasses, they were in danger of being mangled. If I tried to block his assault, he sat on my hand. If I struggled, I risked hurting him. If things slowed down, he would demand songs or imitations:

"Say something to make them laugh!"

The slapping, pinching and punching would get wild if I didn't come out with something quickly.

"See! You think I am a 'holy bastard', like meek gentle Jesus. Not a chance!"

Each time I thought I was really uncomfortable he made it worse.

On top of all this, I was overwhelmed by an energy pouring off him that left me feeling drugged. At times I could barely keep my eyes open with a sensation of floating in infinite space that had me reeling. It was like sitting in the night sky without a planet to hold you while someone pinched you to keep you focused on the fact that there was still a body there waiting.

When he sat on my hand, his body held no tension, barely any movement at all. He was completely relaxed unless I tried to pull my hand away, then he grabbed it lightning quick, twisting the skin in a pinch, warning me: "Don't try to be clever! You'll get clobbered!"

Struggling to keep my eyes open, I resigned myself to the fate of sitting in a waterfall of energy going in every direction while he hit me.

"Hey buster, or a bastard! What is the matter with you?"

"Nothing! Nothing at all!"

His expression 'eyeballing' was the perfect description of a room full of people staring at him. It was a pool of life looking back on itself in a daze, blinking in a rhythm like frogs croaking in a pond. Some came for the entertainment but most of them were submitting themselves to him in the hopes of getting something... anything.

The people who engaged him this way were subtly altered by his influence. Usually these people got what they came for, despite his denials, and many only realized it much later. Stories about the suffering that was endured around him, followed by huge changes in life, were constantly being told.

He said to me once, "First you must torture yourself, then..." He didn't have to finish the sentence, the wave of his hand said it all.

He could be the sweetest human being imaginable some-times. His politeness was impeccable. In the middle of a thunder storm he apologized profusely when his foot touched someone else's. He was doing everything in his power to help people around him, not out of a 'do-gooder's high', he had no choice; it was his nature.

"Do you mean to say that if I had a choice in the matter, I would be sitting here with you people? I could have twenty-five Rolls-Royces at my disposal if I wanted!"

Watching his face change all the time was mesmerizing even

while he was hitting me. There was a thrill like being in a cage with a wild animal that you know won't kill you, but you can't be sure what it will do.

I got into the habit of going back to the house for a break. Playing with a tiger can wear you out, but one day I decided to sit next to him as long as I could. When I arrived he started in, "Come here, buster!" He was shouting it almost as soon as I was in sight of the house. He did this so often the people outside would relay an early warning.

"Where is that bastard?"

"He is coming ,UG!" Then, looking at me with an envious or slightly pitying look, or one of anticipation, "He's been asking for you."

"Hey! I know you are out there!"

I knew he knew. Often I stood killing time, talking outside, to delay the inevitable. There was an ongoing feeling of good fortune mixed with dread accompanying his attention. As soon as I set foot in the room I was dragged into the ring.

"Hey! Where have you been?"

"Filing a report."

"Come here, buster, or should I call you bastard?"

"Bastard! Filthy bastard! I'm a dirty filthy stinking bastard!"

Even agreeing with him you never got the last word, "That's too mild a term!"

With a little wave of the hand.

"What's going on?" he would start, as I squeezed onto the torture rack between him and the Reverend.

"Nothing."

"Where have you been? What did you do?"

Slap! Slap! Slap!

It always seemed like coffee was being served with sweets when I arrived. Even if I'd just had lunch, a meal no doubt giving me some kind of heartburn, he would force the issue: "You have to eat! You look famished!"

Attempts to sidestep Indian sweets only invited more trouble. "Wait, wait! Give me that!"

The plate was handed to him and he grabbed a handful of sweets, shoving them in my mouth.

"*Prasad!*" people were shouting. It's considered a high honor to be fed by such a man.

Stuffing bananas forcibly into my mouth, with his JK justification: "Hey, you have no choice! You are living in a choiceless state." I resisted for the fun of it, clenching my teeth as the sweet yellow stuff was mashed against my face smearing down my shirt.

"You are a pig, a hog and a swine all rolled into one!" This was his latest description of Ramana Maharshi.

Then it was time for another show, "Say something!" Grabbing me by the back of the neck he shoved my head down to the coffee table.

"Do you want me to split your head into four pieces?" he would say, looking around for Yogini, who was usually buried in the crowd in an uncomfortable spot for hours, with that perplexed, slightly tortured look on her face.

"Should I?"... "Should I?"

With a pained look, "Why are you doing that, UG?"

She also couldn't figure out why I took it. Suguna stood in the kitchen door wearing the same look. Some of the crowd was delighted. Melbourne, a young Australian, seemed to relish it, "Beat him! Beat him, UG!"

Mohan shouted, "Spiritual transmission!"

When I offered to share some transmission, he declined! "Oh! No, no, no!"

Sometimes I think Yogini was taking it emotionally in about the same measure I was taking it physically.

Her question, "Why?" was met with the answer, "He deserves it! He had it coming!" Then, "See, she's on your side!"

Sometimes I thought she might enjoy his beating me. No

doubt at times she wanted to herself. In any event, he had found a way to get at her: "She is saying 'No.' But her expression says 'Yes!'"

Twisting the reply to suit himself, he covered his eyes with one hand and kept hold of me with the other. Then, like a five-year-old, he started again.

Pow! Pow! Pow!

"Three times! Twelve times! Twenty-four times!"

I usually got fed up and left after a while, if it went on for more than an hour or two, shrugging him off and bolting from the room. This time I was going to sit through it all, no matter what. He must have heard me thinking that when he pinned my head between my knees, and started elbowing me in the back.

Thud, thud, thud!

Actually that felt good, since I had a lot of tension in my back, but then he picked out the Russian I was imitating. He was sitting right in front of the table on the floor in a Russian mystic sweat, his boney features strained with a fervor, sweat running down deep creases in his face. Here was a guy who would be compelled to do anything.

UG asked, "Now, you do it! Hit him!"

"Ziz is ztranch, Euwchee! I kyen nyut!"

I sensed the inevitable and foolishly fought it, intensifying the determination of the force of nature sitting next to me, holding me down in a locked position.

"No!" I warned him. "Don't!"

"I ccchave tyo!" he said, words writhing as they spat from his near toothless mouth.

"Don't!"

Melbourne was going wild: "Hit him! Hit him! Hooo hooo hooo! Yeah Baby!"

I wanted to take him outside and show him how I felt about that.

Sensing the inevitable I wanted to get this over with.

"Alright, hurry up then!"

"Eim syorrie, I chaave thu!" he said, slapping my head lightly a couple of times.

But UG was just getting warmed up, "More, more!"

"Ei chyan't, Yu Chee!"

Turning to the Hungarian, "Now you! Hit him!"

"No UG I kon't do dat, he iz a nize guy!"

"No he's not, he's a filthy bastard! Anyway, you have to do it! I'm telling you!! Now hit him!"

"Alright."

She also gave a little tap. But it wasn't enough for him and meanwhile I was down there with my head between my legs. I was feeling more humiliated by the minute. My resolve was cracking. I had already reached the breaking point and it was only an hour or so into the afternoon. He made a few more people hit me and the Aussie started inching forward. If that fucker went for it I would have to retaliate. UG was showing me the limit.

Suddenly, in the middle of all this nonsense, some guy from Canada who was supposed to be making a documentary about UG shoved the camera in my face, "What are you feeling now, Louis?"

This guy had been coaching me to engage with UG out in the front of the house. Seeing what was going on, he wanted some footage, but I got the distinct impression he wanted to play director. That was a manipulation I decided to ignore. Suddenly he was throwing questions at me like a director from one of those stupid reality shows. I turned on him instead of Melbourne and lost it completely. Even I was surprised.

"Fuck you, motherfucker!" I growled at him. "Stick that camera up your ass!"

I yanked myself gingerly out of UG's grip and hopped off the couch.

"I'm getting the fuck out of here!"

Jumping over the packed crowd I rushed out the door and down the street with tears welling up in my eyes. I was never in danger of being physically injured; it was an attack on my ego.

"Look! He is running avay!"

It made me sick to think that was all it took.

My head was buzzing like a hornets' nest as I staggered back along the hot dusty ring road. Dark-skinned strangers stared at me indifferently. As I walked, I was planning my escape one more time. The only thing I was 'getting' was humiliated. As I got closer to the house, the hornets dispersed and my options became clear. I could go back to New York.

And then?

"He wants me to do it."

He was right. I wanted him to 'finish me off', rid me of the burden of my ego, but each time he showed me how hard I was hanging on. By the time I got back to the house, there was nothing to do but turn around and go back and face the music. When misery is all you know, right down to the marrow of your bones, it doesn't go away on request.

I returned in the evening.

CHAPTER 28

It also knows that this body is going to drop dead as others do—you experience the death of others—so that is a frightening situation because you are not sure whether that 'you' will continue if this (body) goes.

One day it became obvious that he was sick. He was coughing, his voice was hoarse but he didn't stop talking all day. He didn't take a break and he would never have taken as much as a cough drop. When someone mentioned that he sounded sick, the response was a sweeping condemnation of the very idea.

"I do not have a cold! I am not sick. You are all sick people, those filthy medical bastards are making a living on you and you fall for all that shit! Be a damned fool! I am not going to listen to all that crappp!"

So we just had to sit and wait for it to pass.

"I do not have a cold!" Cough, cough. "I kick all those doctors! They all dropped dead after advising me!" Cough, cough.

By now the number of dead doctors spoke for itself; of late it was thirty-three, a regular massacre.

Meanwhile the house had filled to bursting with Westerners, Indians and a lot of singing and dancing. He was reviewing the Money Maxims again. His family members were showing up, the girls had come from the States and he was pushing them to sing and shout, mostly a combination of the two, for hours at a stretch.

His voice was reduced to a hoarse whisper, which didn't stop him from continuing his diatribe right up to the usual hour.

It was painful to watch. There are no words for this apparent madness. The next day he was a little better and the next day a little better and soon he was fine again.

When I caught the sore throat a day or so later, I decided to test his theory by talking through it like he did. Maybe it was a choice if you admitted illness. By the end of the day my throat was on fire. I woke up the next morning sick as a dog and unable to get out of bed. I was bedridden for three days.

"Don't try to act like me! You'll be more miserable!"

His actions couldn't be reduced to any ideas, let alone what I'd read about enlightened people. Verbal denials weren't enough for him and anyway his actions were more powerful than words. Taking on the collective thought bubble, he was battling a monster with a thousand heads, and with each one he severed, two more sprung up in its place. The battle took no effort on his part, so it was hard to say who was winning and who was losing.

In his later years his expression became more graphic than ever: "Motherfuckers have a better chance of enlightenment than tantric fuckers!"

He would go on to say that if you were enlightened, you would see no difference between your mother and your wife or 'your next-door neighbor's prettiest girl'. As always with him, it was easy to miss the point that if that happened, at least in his case, he was unable to have sex at all. He was fond of confusing the issue; giving people a moral code of conduct was the last thing he wanted to do. That is usually where the trouble starts.

"If you are not thinking in terms of right and wrong, you will never do wrong. As long as you are thinking of right and wrong, you will always do wrong."

UG never used curses as expletives. That would have been sloppy language and his language, as harsh as it may have been, was never sloppy. He used the crudest language available to describe human functions and blamed Sri Ramakrishna, the famous saint of Bengal, as his 'model' in that as well as his discussion of money.

"The first thing he (*Ramakrishna*) asked people when they came to see him was:

'How much money do you have? How much can you give me?'"

Sri Ramakrishna was an uneducated villager who used the extremely vulgar expressions of his village Bengali. UG once told Guha, a Bengali, to read the gospel of Sri Ramakrishna cover to cover in the original language, so that he could see for himself how the man spoke. UG used to point out that the translators had cleaned up the text. When he confronted a monk at the Ramakrishna Mission in London about this, he was told: "It would destroy the image of that man we have built."

One could sense that UG actually held Ramakrishna in high regard. He always reserved his most ferocious tirades for the real McCoys.

It's interesting to note that a man told me when he started using the word *bitch* after spending a few days with UG, his son told him: "Dad, it's OK when UG talks like that, but it sounds nasty coming from you."

I was told he used to be full of praise for Ramana Maharshi and Sri Ramakrishna. Now he expressed nothing but contempt for them. In fact, he was doing everything in his power to destroy the images people were building in their heads about such people. The complaints about his use of language were more revealing about the person I talked to than about him. None of them really touched him.

There is so much momentum in what he called "This filthy country you call Punya Bhoomi! It's a spiritual shitland!" The spiritual industry of India is its most lucrative export and his four-letter blasts were launched against this business, the phony products being peddled in the spiritual marketplace, "thriving on the gullibility and credulity of the people".

Aside from a few short trips out of the house for constitutionals, he stopped going out at all, sitting on the couch, talking for fourteen to sixteen hours a day, with short breaks for food. It was an unimaginably grueling schedule for anyone, let alone an eighty-seven-year-old man. He had never spent so many hours at a stretch talking to crowds. Why this kind of schedule at a point in his life when he was so old? People showed up early in the morning and stayed late into the night. If someone called to say they were coming to see him he would not leave the room if they arrived at his lunch hour. We had to coax him to eat. He never took a minute for himself. At times he looked like a white- haired monkey perched on the couch.

He would occasionally go blank and stop speaking while his eyes darted around, his hands clasped in front of his chest, the eyes following some light against the wall or the movement of an object, a chime in the breeze or the passage of some shadow against the wall. At these moments there was an unmistakably pure presence in his face. The restless movements of the eyes resembled those of an animal or a baby. His face was something untamed, with a continuous fluid movement of the body. He was the embodiment of silence.

A local businessman took me out to have a chat about what was going on.

"Why all the abuse of JK? What is the point of his coming here and talking if no one can ask questions and all he does is twist everything into some kind of joke all the time? What is his teaching?"

All I could say was, "Watch and learn."

It always seemed to me that the only way to learn from UG was to watch how he lived. The attempt to understand was a bottomless pit of mental masturbation. This so-called dialogue was, according to him, a way of adding more and more information to the instrument that was causing all the trouble: thought. By using dialogue, thought is always adding more to its arsenal.

As I listened to him, his claim that there was nothing going on, just noise coming out, played out consistently; he really had no point of view, he was smashing the idea that one should exist. He never made those absurd claims that there was no reality, pointing out that if someone puts a gun to your head that's a reality. He reiterated that there is a parallel movement of thought that runs along side of the natural functioning of the senses, separating one thing from another in order to maintain itself.

"Maya means to measure", was a definition he gave, attributed to his grandmother. "In order to measure, you need to establish a point somewhere. If there is no point (ego), there is nothing from which to measure."

These examples were startlingly simple, too simple I guess.

It was Christmas, so I expanded a ballad I'd made up about Jiddu Krishnamurti to the tune of *Jingle Bells*, and another called *Jala Samadhi*, about the enlightened ones who died a *Jala Samadhi*, death by spiritual drowning. It was sung to the tune of *Yellow Submarine*. He also liked it when the girls sang the bitch song from *South Park*:

"Ooooh... Kyle'sMomisabigfatbitchshesthebiggestbitchinth ewholewideworld!"

Local Indians were horrified by this display of UG's scholarship awardees; the American-born daughters of Indian-born parents, singing such songs.

If they started any song at a polite volume he shouted, "Louder! Louder!" until they screamed out the songs for hours on end.

The crowd was a mix of rag-tag Western seekers and Indians that grew as the word got out that UG was not only in town, but causing a riot of sorts. People joined in for as long as they could stand it. The living room was turned into a madhouse for hours at a time before lunch, stressing his hosts to the breaking point.

At one point Chandrasekhar lost his cool, storming out

to the front of the house in desperation, "That's enough, this is ridiculous!"

But there was nothing he could do. It was hopeless, but as UG was fond of saying, "Not hopeless enough!" UG was not the least bit concerned when Suguna was reduced to tears as strangers, some of them quite shabby looking, went into a dancing frenzy in her living room.

When someone shouted, "UG, the neighbors will complain!" he replied without hesitation: "Let them move if they don't like it!"

At these times it was hard to see the sweeter side of UG. He was acting like a certifiable lunatic. Why at this stage of the game did it come to this? Was this his parting shot? Was he really just trying to erase any idea people had of his alleged spiritual status? He pushed everyone so hard in every direction it was disorienting.

"How long can they take it?" This question lingered in the room. I was asking myself the same question: *How long is this going to go on?* But as soon as he began to complain that he'd stayed too long: "Three weeks we have been in this place? It's too long!" (He was forever making a note of the time, the day and the place), people begged him to stay:

"UG, we love to have you here!" Suguna was adamant; despite what was happening in the house, she meant it with all her heart.

"I have stayed too long in this filthy shitland! I am upsetting your way of life."

Despite everything that was going on, Suguna would fall into a sad expression at the very idea of his leaving.

Mohan suggested: "UG, you must stay here. Settle in Bangalore, that is where you are most appreciated!"

"Not a chance! You want me to stay in this filthy country, with you around of all people? Not a chance! Not on your life!"

He said it with a little smile. Everyone laughed, but there

was no apparent sentimentality for his homeland or his friends—quite the opposite. And yet he established that family and their home as a landing spot decades before and never failed to visit for months at a time once a year. He kept his friends close no matter where they were, or how they felt about it.

"I used to feel at home everywhere in the world. It's the strangest thing, now I don't feel at home nowhere!"

An interesting choice of words.

That same night during one of the 'wrestling matches' he pushed my head under the coffee table and slipped his leg over the back of my neck to hold it there. It occurred to me that I could lift him on my shoulders and carry him around. As if he heard my thought, he sat on my upper back and ordered me to lift him. Soon I was parading him around the living room on my shoulders. I was concerned about his head hitting the ceiling fan. Checking a reflection in the glass cabinets, I could see there was no danger. The toothless old face emerging over my shoulders was split wide with a grin of childish joy.

Yogini and I were having a hell of a time. She felt abandoned. I would come back and go to my room to read, paint, do anything to avoid her, trying not to aggravate a nagging lust. She insisted on keeping company but only up to a point. It was irritating to say the least. Then she would make some comment about how I didn't understand how she and the American Friend suffered, living without a base for much longer than anyone else. I simmered.

"Why are you cross?"

The question only made it worse. As if she didn't know. She had a way of getting me pissed off then backing away like a puff of smoke. I was always left swinging at air.

Once after a brief physical 'lapse' she accused me of being a predator. I wanted to kill her. The emotion was as simple as that. We were reviewing the incident on the ring road in front of a crowd of Indians. I called her every imaginable name until finally she punched me in the face. I goaded her on for another one. It was important that someone release that tension. If it was me throwing the punches I would have left her in a pile of broken flesh by the side of the road.

Once I had a half-dream vision of UG. He was full face in the image. His eyes were shut and his mouth was dribbling shit while he chanted something. I asked Chandrasekhar what it meant. He said shit from a guru's mouth meant money was coming. What a religion! Nothing is without significance. It all meant something and nothing to me. It was a powerful image though. There was nothing revolting about it at the time, just something really intense.

CHAPTER 29

I am certain that you have no freedom of action. In that sense
I go a step further and say that you are genetically controlled.

My return flight was fixed and, for whatever reason, UG decided he was going to be on it. Yogini was unable to change her flight or get a seat, which sent her into a panic of sorts. The fear of abandonment was thick, yet she was eager for a break. Making a plan to stay with some friends in Bangalore for a few days, she oscillated between relief and chronic fear.

"He's angry that I'm staying here. I don't think he wants me around."

He always praised her for "staying in the background quietly", making sure she was in his car. He mirrored her silence with silence. She and I were continuing our raging battle about this and whatever else was available, which he kept an eye on.

One afternoon someone invited me to Cafe Coffee Day. I was eager for a break but they did it in front of UG and suddenly he wanted to go. At that moment it was a little like looking forward to going out and having your little brother tag along. I knew it would mean a crowd, transplanting the situation from one setting to another.

While he was sitting across from me at an outside table, I tried to cover my scratched-up black and blue hand, the result of a wall-punching episode during one of our fights. He looked at it quietly, then looked into my eyes and said in a gentle voice no one else could hear, "Crying." The look in his eyes made my eyes water, I had to choke back tears. Luckily just then some people showed up to distract his attention.

On the day we were to leave, he sat on the couch all day as usual. Counting off the days until he left was a practice that began as soon as he arrived anywhere.

On the very first day, whenever he landed somewhere, he started in with that question he would ask: "What am I doing here? Why have I come all the way? Three weeks here? It's too long. What am I doing in this place?"

He seemed wonder daily why he was anywhere at all. You got used to it until the day came for him to depart. In light of all that, it's interesting that clocks and calendars were one item he was always picking up as gifts for friends.

He was particularly ferocious that day. Four-letter words were flying with pounding force. Every word was like a knife jab or the crack of a gunshot piercing the air. At times it vibrated inside me like a physical jolt. I could hear him from half a block away as I approached the house that morning. As the day wore on he showed no sign of letting up. There was lunch. Coffee was served at three o'clock as usual, to a packed house, overflowing rooms of people, many arriving at the last minute, having waited to see him when he was safely on his way out of town.

At lunch I went home to pack, returning later with my bags, ready to go. He was still going at it. After dinner he went right back to the couch. It was nerve-wracking to think I'd be getting on the plane with him alone after this. *Can he survive this?* I wondered at one point. It was approaching 9 pm and he was still pummeling away as if he would exhaust his last breath if he had to in order to make himself heard. After months of this his body was thin and drained, but the energy driving it was unmistakable: flaming hot. He was raining holy terror on everything in sight while I paced back and forth outside the house, mumbling to myself with agitation. He showed absolutely no concern for the time. I never heard of one instance when he missed a flight, so my concern was the usual waste of energy. Finally, at about

9:30 pm, just a couple of hours before the flight, he went up to change.

When he came down dressed in Western wear he looked as fresh as if he'd just arrived. He said goodbye, waving and giving *Namaste* as he moved swiftly through the crowd swirling around him spilling out onto the street. With a final wave in the dark he climbed into the car and the car sped off to the airport. Major drove him, as he always did when UG was in India. He was a retired military man, a widower who led an austere and solitary life in the farmhouse outside the city, refusing UG's repeated attempts to get him to marry again.

That night in the airport lounge a young Indian friend asked him a couple of questions that had been pestering him all day. They were phrased in a way that hinted at his background in J Krishnamurti. He was more impatient than usual, you could see it in his face, his respectful manner straining to contain his urgency.

"UG *garu*, is it possible to be earnest?"

"I never answer questions."

"He is attacking the very foundation of the questioner," Major said from behind him, pacing back and forth like a panther.

"That's right," something I rarely heard UG say, adding: "A scientist will listen to me and leave in a very short time, sensing the threat to him in what I am saying. A holy man can hang around longer, because there are so many nets with which he thinks he can capture me."

At the very last moment, as UG was heading for the security check, the young man was still behind him and his final question came with the blunt impatience of a last chance; he was practically chasing UG down at that point:

"UG, a lot of people came to see you without knowing anything about you. There was this constant talk about money, because of which some of them went back without getting what they wanted. More than anything else, they went back with the wrong, mistaken impression. Why did you do that, UG?"

UG stopped and turned: looking him in the eye, he said in a low voice with spine-chilling force, "They are damn fools to go back." And then he turned and left.

As we passed the security check, waving goodbye to the others, he already looked half-gone, drifting like a ghost. I wandered behind, keeping an eye on him. With no audience, there was no interaction. He carefully examined the various advertisements and details of his surroundings with that stone-faced expression. It was a relief to be alone with that particular quiet spaciousness around him.

Toward the end of the flight I realized I'd fallen asleep. Worried that something may have happened to him after such a frenzied journey, I went forward to check on him. He was alone, the only passenger in the large first-class compartment. At first the seat looked empty from behind and I could feel my breath halting. Then I saw his white hair sticking up from behind. He was covered with a blanket in the huge luxury seat sleeping like a baby. He looked like a fragile bird. At first I couldn't see him breathing, then there were some signs of life. I made a rustling noise and he woke up.

"Oh you are here!" he said warmly.

"How is it going, UG?"

"Fine! Couldn't be better! She is taking very good care of me," he said, indicating the stewardess.

"Ah, good!"

In the silence it seemed as if there was wonder in his face as he looked at the panorama of clouds in the soft morning light out the window, but that is my interpretation. I don't know what it was. He had a pure, primeval look. At that moment, staring out the window, he was the picture of total innocence.

CHAPTER 30

*What you pick out of that 'thought sphere' is
your particular background, your culture, so it's
like an antenna. This antenna is broken.*

Winter days are short in Cologne, with a cold blue light that gives way to the sparkling glow of neon in the streets at night. The cityscape is dominated by the Dom, a huge gothic cathedral on the river that all roads seem to lead to. It was nearly the only building left standing after the Allied bombing at the end of the Second World War. In his pre-war lecturing years with the Theosophical Society, UG once took a boat trip up the Rhine where he stopped in Cologne and took a quick look inside. He claimed it was the only church he'd ever set foot in, impressed with the scale of the building.

The young people in the streets were full of youthful sexuality, even in winter. After so long in India, Germany had a quirky feel, a disorienting shift of reality that erased the experience. There was one large neon figure on the side of a building that caught my eye. It was huge, dominating the surrounding buildings, suspended in the darkness, blinking back and forth from male to female; as the arm raised up to drink, yellow bars, representing beer, rose, filling the figure with bright yellow light; then with the magic of a few lines, the man became a woman.

It made me think of the way UG always seemed to be going back and forth from male to female energies, recharging himself after a long ingestion of the yellow light of India. Somewhere I recall an interview where he even said the light in his head was yellow in India and bluish in Europe. No matter where he went, he immediately reflected the surroundings. The places I visited later never seemed quite as charged up as they were when he was around. Something about his use of the means at hand, as if he were a conduit for the essence of a place, brought out the significance in the most ordinary, overlooked situations. His use of language was similarly grounded in his surroundings, in what people brought to him in their minds. He would throw it back at them, spotlighting the situation around him with that curious light he generated with no-one at the center, a light that was just a light. You could practically take a meter reading on it.

While UG collected cash from his friends, a huge pile grew on the floor of the apartment where we were meeting. It looked as if a drug deal was taking place. The renovated apartment had a wooden floor that sounded like a stage as you walked across it, the deck reverberating as the performance in the round took place. I was wiped out, with no idea where we were headed. All I could think about was doing laundry. In India I could never quite get my clothes clean. Somehow when this came up, he used it as an excuse to dismiss me: "You go and wash your head! I don't need you around here."

Plans were being drawn up for his next destination, and he was repeating that he didn't want a parade of cars: "You people are restricting my freedom of movement!"

It looked like the journey was coming to an end for me. I could afford to stay in Frankfurt for a few days before catching the flight back to New York. If it came to that, I had decided it would have to be alright, I wasn't going to cling. By the time we left that night, I was ready to pack up and leave. It was a strange feeling that something had come to an end, almost a relief.

At the apartment, Mario encouraged me to go early the next morning to see UG before running off. Taking his advice I showed up at about 5:30 am. I knocked at the door which was answered by the smiling face of Misha, a tall, rail-thin

German who lived nearby and took obsessive care of UG's place in Switzerland.

UG greeted me warmly. "You are so early! What's happening?" as if nothing had happened the night before.

"I wanted to thank you for everything before I go, so thank you for everything."

"Why are you thanking me?" He always asked the obvious.

"Well, I know you are going today and I may not see you again. So..."

"Where are you going?"

"Well I know you don't want a caravan. I have to do my laundry and all..."

"Well I don't see any reason you should not come!"

I was stunned.

Then he asked, "What about you?"

A huge grin spread across Misha's face...

"Ah well I ah..."

"Go and get your things. Right avay! Hurry! What about that other fellow? Where is he going?"

Suddenly we were all back on board. Then his host showed up to say goodbye, but now we needed another car. He had less than an hour to get ready to drive UG to Baveno. It was time to move.

It was January 5th, 2005, the third year of this sort of thing. I was getting pretty good at changing plans at a moment's notice. The relief of still being on board was quickly washed away in the stream of activity that pulled us along. UG's warm greeting was a huge relief; the horizon was still open and there was no end in sight. I was happy because I had nowhere else to go. I knew better than to take him for granted.

We drove straight to Baveno where the hotel staff of Residence dei Fiore was getting used to a strange gang headed by the little old man. He took the top-floor apartment suite called *Azalea*. The couch was comfortable and he could recreate the

Sahara Desert with the heating system.

The scene at the desk was the usual dogfight for rooms at the end of a long day. Tempers flared and turf wars ensued about who got what room with what bath and what view. I hung back until it was over, to avoid the fight over who got a better toilet, and ended up in a room with about nine walls. The Italian family on the other side of the wall was having an argument or a conversation; I'm not sure there is a difference in Italy. The bed seemed to be vibrating after the nine-hour drive as the television blasted away into the sweet Italian night.

UG slept a lot after the six-week outburst in India. Again, I was instructed to sit next to him. When he woke up and I was drawing or writing he might snatch the book away from me, grab the pen and sit on it, or give it to someone to hide. He was always on the look out for something left behind by anyone. He'd snatch an idle cell phone or, God forbid, someone's wallet, and demand a ransom. I'd started to write and doodle in a book while sitting next to him in Bangalore. Sometimes he asked me to read what I'd written. Normally I would have been embarrassed to do this, but it was better than singing and imitating.

Watching me doodle, he commented that when he was a student of biology he made drawings of plants. I handed him the pen and paper and he began to draw with childlike concentration. Hunched over the paper, he completed one drawing with a flourish of the pen. Then another. He made drawings of me in my new striped shirt or drew flowers from memory.

One afternoon while he was asleep on the couch, breathing heavily, I was talking about real estate prices in New York with someone. We talked for a good fifteen minutes while he slept. That evening he made specific reference to the conversation.

"You are all the time talking about silly things like real estate. Who cares? Why do you waste your time?" Then he repeated bits of the conversation word for word.

"UG, we all saw you were asleep during the conversation.

How do you explain your memory of it?"

"Sir, this body is totally relaxed. The recording goes on all the time no matter what. There is no UG there to focus on anything so it all comes in and is recorded. Even in you the recording is going on all the time, but you are all the time practicing selectivity and censorship. Since there is no UG here, there is no editing and I have much more energy than you do. I have to bring that fellow back and then he can select things but he cannot stay there. Also this body can hear even while it is what you call sleeping."

As always, his explanations indicated a fine thread of difference between how we functioned and how he functioned; essentially the same, but there was always that thread of a difference, so close and yet untouchable.

When Yogini got back I drove up to collect her from the train station a few hours away in the middle of the night. Her face was tight when I loaded up her bags. As soon as we got underway she started grilling me about who was cooking, who was my friend now and not hers now that she'd been 'left behind'. Carefully reminding her that she had chosen to stay back, I could feel the anger building. Feeling acutely baited, I made every effort to be diplomatic until I finally got dragged into the mudslinging contest. Maybe she was upset UG hadn't come with me to pick her up the way he sometimes did, even in the middle of the night. In any case her insecurities were hanging out all over the place. She kept referring to 'your friends' in a nasty accusing sneer as if I was conspiring against her.

I ignored, I comforted, I reasoned, and then I exploded.

We finally got back to Gstaad where the Alps sparkled under a blanket of white powder. Barns and chalets wore the holiday uniform of inverted glowing V shapes, Christmas lights along the roof edges.

A bunch of us took over the 'Hunting Lodge', a huge spread of rooms with a fireplace and antler racks. I slept on the couch in the dining area, since Yogini was acting fragile about sharing a room. The fight in Baveno left scars and luckily a room opened up across the street, so I could step out of the fire and the frying pan to cool off.

UG was just plain weak on his feet. I was amazed how he kept going. At that point he was throwing out so much food it seemed like he was living on air. He still had fun tossing me around and throwing things at me, but it was like a vacation after the assault in India.

"There is such a thing as aging process!" he reminded us. Then he acted like a five-year-old when we stepped out the door, shoving snow down my jacket and me into the snow bank.

We went off to Gruyere for a high tea and the driver drove him straight to the door of the restaurant so he wouldn't have to walk. It was freezing cold and the icy cobblestones were potentially treacherous. He got out of the car and walked all the way back to the entrance of the little medieval town with the excuse of checking the exchange rates. We straggled behind him helplessly as he monitored the demise of the dollar. His jacket was flapping in the wind and if you tried to tell him it was cold, you were in for curses and threats.

"The body doesn't know hot or cold! There is no such thing! You are all frightened chickens!"

He was interested in highlighting and spotlighting a more pressing matter: "Look, sir! Your dollar is down again!! Oh I'm de-lighted!"

I heartily agreed just to keep him moving.

In the café he made a drawing of me with my bald head, and a funny-looking shirt. With the whole table staring with rapt attention, he started drawing a female figure. You could tell from the boobs. Her wide eyes were giving sidelong glances at the man who was looking away in the other direction. Everyone at the table watched as if he was performing a magic trick. Then with a naughty smile he drew unmistakable nipples on the

female, adding some lines to the man's head extending to the woman that could be interpreted in a variety of ways. It looked to me like the woman was hitting the man on the head with something like a penis, of all things. Yogini interpreted it later as the male figure taking the energy from the female. I asked him for some clarification and he told me she was hitting him, but I bet if she had asked, he would have told her the guy was taking the energy from her. *C'est la vie*: it was true both ways.

It was flattering that he took such a keen interest, enough to produce these little sketches that are still something like a talisman, a reminder for me. Whatever he did was so loaded with information that it kept on giving over the years. Like the sugar packets he was feeding me, literally giving me a sweet infusion in the midst of a bitter situation I could hardly bear.

His attention saved me from total despair over what was happening with Yogini; he propped me up, more than I could ever have propped him up. It was like being carried around in the patient, watchful arms of a mother. He allowed me to make all the mistakes I couldn't help making, stumbling along burning myself over and over, and not abandon me for being a total idiot. When he joked: "I'm not calling you an idiot; you *are* an idiot", it was kind of a blessing.

That winter we drove all over the place again. Yogini was back in the saddle, safe for the moment, feeding him in the car. The competition always spooked her. When there were fewer people around, she was always there to step in and do the job. She would do this for a while then a new person would show up and she felt shoved aside.

Being well aware of this competition to feed him, he created a lot of mischief with it. He would try to stop them from packing food for him, repeatedly telling everyone he didn't want to eat. Then he would eat. It created a little drama each day.

"He said not to pack the food!"

"Yeah but he always says that!"

"Oh."

"Do you think he's serious?"

It was a guilty pleasure to watch him litter the immaculate highways of the world with his cups, napkins and spit. Sometimes you could watch the silent outrage from behind the window of a passing car. His comebacks were priceless.

"You clean it up then!"

He never tired of reminding us of the story of his friend who was complaining about the traffic jam, only to be reminded that they were contributing and were equally to blame: "So you might as well enjoy the traffic jam!"

We had ample opportunity to do just that.

There were also small moments that stayed with me, little hints about things spiritual, that came in unlikely places. At

a truck stop in Germany, I was sitting opposite him while a conversation about the Rajneesh *sanyas* life went on beside us. There was an orange napkin on the table, the traditional color of a *sanyasi*. Thinking to myself with some satisfaction, *I'm not fooled by that sort of thing*, I crumpled the napkin into a ball and tossed it into my cup. Mind you, I was just thinking this, I'd said nothing.

He looked up at me and said, "It's not that simple."

Wrong again. And yet he never gave up, never lost patience, or so it seemed.

CHAPTER 31

Listening to other people is what you have been doing all your life. It is the cause of your unhappiness.

Yogini and I again flew back to Newark with UG. Family members came to see him and Yogini went to see her father. I spent a day in the room, then went to hide out in Ellen Chrystal's apartment. I needed to regroup, savoring my privacy for a few precious days and hours until that also became boring.

"Where is she?" he asked over and over.

When we told him Yogini had in fact left to see her father, he would say, "Is she really going to see her father?" It seemed as if he missed her, no matter how much he ignored her.

From the information I gathered over the years, it seemed there was always someone around to ground him in his base on wheels. Sometimes these people were with him for decades, as in the case of Valentine, who was his companion for 28 years, sometimes it was for only for a year or two.

UG liked the 99 Cent Store down the street from the hotel, so we went out in the freezing cold to have a look. Despite chilly winds he never wore a hat. He enjoyed reading the various tee shirts in the shops on 34th Street, especially getting a kick out of the foul ones: "New York City Motherfucker! Get used to it!"

He carefully read them out loud with great comic effect, articulating every painful insult to taste and decorum, "Look, sir! 'I'm with stupid!'"

After a week or so, once again Yogini and I flew with him to Los Angeles. When we arrived, the California contingent was there to meet him. Coming in behind him was always slightly awkward, I felt like the great unwashed as the group gathered around him eagerly. Once he got settled in the Reverend's limo, the rest of us were distributed into various cars and my driver was assigned to follow behind the Reverend in her new car.

"Keep up kid! We're not waiting!" he said, with the usual consideration as he bolted away with 'the package'. She did her best with a nervous smile as he drove at unusually high speeds on the freeway in the pouring rain. It was her first drive on the Los Angeles freeway and Ray was taking no prisoners.

The desert around Palm Springs was bursting with color after a record rainfall. The mountains were green, delicate pastel clouds of color floating above the dirt and debris in the vacant lots around town. The morning after we landed UG looked like he'd been soaking up this light and space. His skin appeared a shade or two darker against the cream-colored wardrobe and shock of white hair. Something in his face contained the vast energy of the desert. The emptiness and ancient vibration of the surrounding mountains flowed through him while he sat harassing the German astrologer, his favorite morning sport.

"UChee, vyy can't you chust take it eeesy? You have chust aggived!" He laughed as UG took his shots.

Ray was sporting a cream-colored Lincoln Town car this time, parked next to the door handle of the cottage. Teasing the local gang of friends, UG was in rare form. It was a remarkable comeback after India. Our hostess, Maggie, slipped out halfway through the 'morning sermon' to make *idlis*, calling over to the cottage at seven sharp (German timings), to tell them breakfast was served. Then we sat and made a plan, a mall rampage was always on the agenda. He used the breakfast hour to torture her with the intricacies of cooking *idlis*. Dan, his host and the brother-in-law, as UG repeatedly reminded him, of Naren, the astrologer, occasionally tried to join in, but there was a difference...

"They are after all not sooo bad." Turning to her husband, "What do you say boss?"

He always agreed. "No UG, they are not so bad, not so good. I don't know…"

"Hey! What does that mean?" She was listening from the kitchen so he wisely corrected himself: "I think they are more than adequate for me, UG!"

Once again we sat with him in rooms and cars, driving to malls and coffee shops, restaurants. His presence was the mist of the absolute, permeating the ordinary, making it glow and giving it its own significance. Dr Lynn once aptly described him as a portal to the infinite. Lynn originally rented the house where UG was meeting on Via Esquela, which has been passed on to a number of friends since then. Lynn met UG in 1972 and had a soothing presence in the chaos around UG. Since Lynn had a tendency to move all the time, we often stopped in on his family in various locations around Europe for a 'Hi and bye'.

Yogini and I shared a car and a condo. The drive across town to infinity took twenty minutes without stops. I told myself we shared the room for convenience's sake, but there was more to it. I was still hopeful that we would get along, whatever that meant, but in tiny ways we got on each other's nerves all the time. She was always up by five o'clock in the morning. I couldn't keep that kind of schedule and it drove me nuts to be constantly reminded of it. I spread drawing materials, books and cameras around the room. The sprawl upset her sense of order. The usual bridges of communication were burned daily.

"I told my wife, you have 99.9% total freedom to do what you like," UG used to repeat. That tiny percentile of non-freedom contained the impossible factor.

He would say: "It doesn't matter to me who I am around, or who I live with. But for someone to live with me would be a horrible thing."

He acknowledged this daily. He would tell the story of how,

when Valentine's memory was fading, he once told her, "Soon you won't know who I am!"

"You deserve that!" she said.

Valentine also said: "Of all the people I have met in my life, he is the kindest…" Typical of UG's stories, the second half of the comment balances the observation, "… you can imagine the rest."

So how do I justify saying that he was so sweet? It had to do with his lightness. His rages would go on for some time yet he could turn in the middle of a sentence and ask for a glass of water in the most humble tone imaginable.

We were there for weeks and I postponed my return flight so I could go to Las Vegas with them. He made a pilgrimage to that city, built by mobsters, whenever he was out there. For some reason he loved the place. He used to say that if he was going to hang the photograph of anyone in his house it would be Al Capone, not one of those gods or goddesses.

We headed across the Mojave Desert with two cars. The land was alive with flowers that hadn't been seen in fifty years. Temporary rainwater lakes reflected a huge sky ringed with mountains like mirrors on the massive floor. When we reached Las Vegas it looked like a mirage. Roped in cloverleaf ramps, high-rise buildings appeared in the distance. Suburban sprawl oozed out in every direction with golf courses everywhere.

No matter where I went with him, it hit me over and over the way we are spreading the mess of housing. How the hell do people not see what this is going to cost in terms of the environment? On the other hand, as he pointed out, there is no turning back now. Just try living for a few days without getting into a car. It's impossible unless you live in a city.

"I have no problem with things exactly the way they are," he would say. "You and I want to live this kind of a life. America is consuming 25% of the world's resources. Don't tell me all that rubbish about ecology, sir!"

LOUIS BRAWLEY

The casinos were pumped on the steroids of the credit economy. Tee shirts and posters of Capone, the Sopranos and the Rat Pack on mugs, toys and handkerchiefs were on sale everywhere. There was a toy kit for the kids to play Al Pacino as Scarface with a plastic machine gun, a knife, and a bag of fake cocaine. There were fake tits, eyes, chins and hair parading through interiors of faux everything that gave off a plastic stench.

The cheap meals catering to the gambling minions which amazed me on my first visit, ten years before, were gone. Casinos now feature galleries full of multi-million dollar paintings by Renoir, Monet and Picasso. The price tag was $20 admission at a fine art gallery in one casino. A casino owner had just put his elbow through a $40 million Picasso while boasting to his friends about how much he just sold it for.

"Look! Look! For you!" UG said, handing me a sugar packet while we had a coffee.

He took all this in with his toothless indifference and a smile. He encouraged everyone to gamble, so that he could collect the winnings and the losings. He said he never gambled in his life and, as far as he was concerned, playing the stock market was the same as gambling.

Gambling is a universal human preoccupation. The allure of getting something for nothing is exactly the same as the allure of enlightenment, where you will be happy forever. The odds of winning the lottery are probably better than those in favor of becoming enlightened, if that's what UG was. The draw to these goals is exactly the same, an escape from troubles—and our troubles are mostly immediately centered on cash flow, money, moolah, dough, the subject of his Money Maxims. I was in a constant state of calculating my bank account, while keeping my eye on the prize, UG. Well, and the other prize.

"If there is only one thing you want, just one, you will surely get it."

When UG talked about his own finances, he would put

190

people into total confusion. There is a clip of him in Las Vegas talking to friends in the midst of a casino.

"What's the secret?" someone asks UG,

"You don't have any money at all, no resources, no tools to make money, no tools for survival! No money! And then the thought that, 'I wish I had money. How am I going to survive without money?' also should not be there, then it will never be a problem. Then such a man will not come and gamble here."

Indeed, UG went and watched this dynamic of money in Las Vegas, but never participated. Just as he had with the stock market, he summed it up: "When you win they win and when you lose they also win."

Like the holy business, where the promise was never delivered, in Las Vegas, the base resource of the industry is 'the gullibility and credulity of the people'. Yet how to step into that zone he was talking about? "The very 'how' should be removed from the language," he would say.

I have yet to meet another person with UG's total ease with money. Everyone else is worried about it, whether they have ten bucks or ten billion. Despite his constant talk of money, I am convinced, by years of watching him, that he really didn't worry about it. His talk addressed the worry lingering inside everyone; it highlighted and spotlighted this final barrier. Spiritual people were put off by this constant talk, bothered no doubt because they were caught in the web of religious commerce and hated to admit it. It's an acid test, more transparent than that other acid test, sex. Pretending not to care about money around him didn't fool him for a minute. He was always pointing out that most of the seekers in India were "misfits in the society, looking for an easy way of living".

He looked a bit surprised when I lost ten bucks in a slot machine because I didn't know how to operate it. Coming up to me he said in a low voice that I shouldn't bother. He saw right through me into the thin wallet of my heart, but it warmed me, I felt off the hook, cared for, as if I didn't need to prove something by doing it, even though he encouraged the others.

The party moved on to the Paris Hotel to lose some more money. Retreating to a Montmartre-style café I sat over a coffee trying to figure out if the cobblestone floors were real or fake. The effect was so convincing it was disorienting. I felt like I was sitting in a set from a 1950's musical.

With UG I traveled from the elite cities of Europe to the fake ones in Nevada on a slender budget, from highway truck stops to the adult playgrounds of the American dream, the European dream, the Indian dream, the human dream, unable to wake up; it made me sick to my stomach sometimes. He was the unmoving hub at the center of the roulette wheel. Around him the whole thing revolved like a glass house, you couldn't help but see the hopelessness and at the same time the beauty of our situation. I was constantly catching a fever around him, mixing clarity and displacement, slightly nauseous at times. Once when he was leaving the house I asked where he was going:

"I want to go and watch them all react."

All I ever seemed to do was react.

He lived in a de-cultured zone, passing through things like a ghost, nothing stuck to him. In my memory he permeated everything, the supreme indifference of nature looking at itself through a human form with a glance from infinity. You could feel this in his coolness, a constant balance that was like a salve to the frenzied mind. So then what? I got into a fever of heated disorientation because I was around him and then he would come and cool it off with his touch,

"Take it easy, buster!"

I found no ground to stand on, but with him there was space to accommodate this. Walking through a neon nightmare of human desire his presence bathed my anxiety with milk and honey nectar. He made the apocalypse more apparent and more bearable at the same time. He was a boney stick of life, a

GONER

white-hot ember with a straw mat of white hair throwing light everywhere, unseen, untouched, unimaginable.

"I like this place," he commented with enthusiasm. "Come on, buster, or do I call you a bastard?" he encouraged me as I lagged behind the crowd.

"As you like, sir."

Yogini was quiet that morning. The night before I went off with Gary and Lisa to a restaurant. Gary and Lisa got together after she and Mario, the Italian living in Germany, split up. When she first brought Gary to meet UG, he greeted the big man at the door with a less than flattering comment: "I told you to find a fat cat, not a fatsy!" Somehow Gary overcame the insult and grew fond of UG. She was small and blond, he was big and blond, with an impatience with the driving ordeals I could well identify with. It was slightly vengeful of me to run off with them. I reasoned that with her early rising habits Yogini wouldn't want to come anyway. Of course she was annoyed.

With a little wave of his hand, we were on our way.

Gary shot past the lead car at about 100 miles an hour, like a wild horse hopping a fence, after behaving himself for most of the day. The road dipped every few yards, throwing us against the ceiling like a roller-coaster. Out the window the sky finished up a purple glow over the mountains. With the radio blasting classic rock, it was a completely different experience from the sedate European rides. It seemed like the dark edge of death was always winking from the horizon with UG around.

CHAPTER 32

Man cannot become man as long as he follows somebody.

The summer of 2005 started quietly; the routine was in place with all the attendant joy and misery. I was staying in an apartment at the far end of Saanen by the airport. The idea of leaving was growing inside me, but having an idea means there is no action. Then one morning I arrived and UG was absent from the room at Cabana, the condominium that had become his 'headquarters'. He was never late. He had called Dr Lynn over to his place for a 'conference'. Then we got a call. He had fallen again. His leg was injured but he wouldn't allow Dr Lynn to examine him: "There is such a thing as aging process."

I was called over to the cave, alone.

When I opened the door he was sitting in his chair with an almost sheepish grin. He gave me a look as if he'd tripped and was regaining his composure, covering the seriousness of the situation with humor. Dr Lynn was sitting on the couch close to him with his usual relaxed attitude, but something was amiss.

"Look who's here, UG!"

Lynn's easy smile was a relief but I could hear the seriousness under his joviality. Right away UG jokingly blamed me for his fall:

"Look what you have done to me! I fell down last night and had to crawl over to this chair! It's your fault!"

"Sorry, UG, but you were getting out of hand. I had to do something!"

Then he made it clear why I'd been called over. He was

always joking about the 'Robot Fund' he was building to buy a machine to take care of him when he got old, so he wouldn't have to depend on any do-gooders getting one of their highs at his expense.

"You see those Japanese have not developed the robots yet so I must ask you for your help."

"Whatever I can do, UG. I am not busy."

"That is very kind of you."

He described how he had fallen while getting out of bed in the night and had to crawl to the telephone.

"Now it seems I will need your help to move around for a while."

I was the most suitable human robot for the moment. My lack of medical training probably made me the most likely candidate. There was the added advantage that I wasn't going away any time soon and I lift things for a living anyway. Experienced medical help was rejected on sight and at sight. Maybe he didn't want his friends in the medical profession to drop dead as a result of treating him.

From what Dr Lynn could piece together, he had strained a groin muscle, an injury common in athletes and older people. Any attempt to move the leg caused severe pain but it didn't seem to be broken. If the leg had been broken he would be in constant agony whether he moved or not.

By this point the physical interaction between us suited me for the job. It was as if all that and his 'old man' act had been trotted out in preparation for just this task. Going to a hospital was out of the question; he would never allow medical technology to interfere with his body—ever.

Yogini was being so evasive that I was going through severe anxiety daily. We would go out and have a nice walk, chatting away, when suddenly she would say something so cruel, so mean-spirited or weirdly out of the blue that I felt like vomiting. Why was this so difficult? As time went on the situation became more oblique and emotionally complicated. I was calling friends back in the States trying to figure out what to do. Should I leave? Should I stay? I dreamt of running off to Nepal for a while. Oregon was another idea. I had never been to either of these places. Anywhere but the beautiful Saanen Valley was looking greener. The most torturous thing about our interaction was that when I moved away, she came closer. When I got closer, she moved away. It was something I knew well, having made a lifetime habit of it myself.

With this new development I was thrust right back in the thick of things. This time UG actually seemed to need me. Of course if I hadn't been available someone else would have been right there to step in.

Once the 'medical conference' was over, the others who had been calling all morning were told to come on over. Pretty soon the tiny apartment was filled with people, as well as the flies from the barnyard manure pile next door. The flies swarmed in and kept everyone busy smashing and swatting. UG never killed one. He had no trouble encouraging George Bush to finish the job of killing off the human race, but flies and cockroaches, bedbugs and mosquitoes were another matter. He would yell at the flies, calling them names.

He was cool as a cucumber.

I talked to Dr Lynn outside, once there was a chance for a break. He said the injury might take months to heal. Any movement of the leg made UG nearly pass out. My heart sank at the thought of being stuck in there with him for an indefinite period. I was incapable of doing anything but move him around to shit or dress, pulling him up in his chair all day long. I was in the awkward position of invading the only privacy he ever had. The only thing for me to do was play robot.

That morning he said, referring to the calamity: "I started thinking again the way I thought before whatever happened to me, happened to me." I was thinking again like you people. I was thinking about what to do with the money in my accounts. I don't want the bank to swallow it. I am going to have to write a will."

He used to say he would never write a will and start a 'death-watch'. He was always preparing for the inevitable, 'ready to go' at any time. He just didn't want to depend on bastards like me to take care of him! Ellen Chrystal was a New York State notary, so she could verify it. The whole thing would be done in accordance with Swiss laws. UG, an Indian citizen, was drawing up a will with an American lawyer in Switzerland. His lawyer friend visiting from California was in for a rough ride with this exercise.

"I always follow the rules even if they are ridiculous. The Swiss laws have changed and I have to change with the changing times."

There were new laws regarding Swiss bank accounts held by foreigners. He had by then nearly one million US dollars in his Credit Suisse account. He reminded us how Yogini 'forced' him to give the money to his great-granddaughter recently. Now he needed to find more girls so he could get rid of the rest of it.

The talk of the will and his money went on that first day and when it came to a close, I was left alone with him for the first night.

Once everyone left I closed the door and sat quietly on the couch. I was on high alert waiting for something to do. There was no talk, no acknowledgement of my presence. The show was over. He sat silently in the chair while the ticking of the clock got louder. It was dead quiet in the basement except for that clock and the hum of the dehumidifier. After a few minutes I got up.

"I'll clean up."

"Yes, yes, go ahead."

For the next half-hour I busied myself vacuuming the floor, straightening the rugs, emptying the water from the dehumidifier and changing the water in his cup.

That night it was clear to me that for the man who said, "No shop! No wares to sell!" there was a shop and when the people left it was closed. His eyes became hooded and vacant as an empty building. What he had been selling would be hard to say. Whatever he had, he gave away freely: his services in the way he tended to his friends. If you were lucky enough to be a friend of his, it was friendship that lasted forever and was absolute and all-embracing from his side. You became a project of his, your career, love life, finances were subject to his influence. In every way they would allow, he looked after people with great efficiency. Yet as long as you sat with him, he managed to veil all this with riddling behavior. Being his friend meant being at his mercy. Aside from the emotional grief (and what is narrative without it!), there was a benefit to every moment spent with him that far outweighed the suffering. The emotional pain was like thick layers of crusty old paint being stripped from a piece of natural wood, revealing its true grain.

The minute the others left, my role switched from clown to nurse, housecleaner and cook. The tone of our interactions was a cold mechanical exchange. I hadn't expected anything more. I was there to do a job, not bother him with idle chat, and preferred it that way. I knew my mind would race, so I kept busy when there was nothing left to do or just shut up and sat next to him, awaiting orders. I was on the alert, since I didn't exactly know what he wanted me to do or not do.

The flies kept getting at the cup he was drinking from. He waved then off, covering it with a neatly folded napkin. When he wanted water he would softly ask, "Can I have some water, sir?"

In the silence after cleaning up, I made some notes about the day, taking care not to stare at him or think about the awkward silence. He said nothing. In the entry from the first night I made notes about his physical condition.

Today I saw the effects of the calamity up close. He needed a massage on his leg and to be helped to the bathroom. For the first time in his life he cannot get up and squat on the toilet seat to shit Indian style. His penis is like a child's. He said it doesn't become erect anymore. He says in terms of attraction he is more like a woman than a man. His hips look almost feminine.

Later I wrote:

It is 8:10 pm and he is asleep. Flies are everywhere. It's completely silent with him now that the shop is closed. He contacted family members today, telling them to come right away since they may not see him alive again.

The first time I moved him to the toilet, he was light as a feather, smelling faintly sweet. He registered the pain only in the instant it happened. There was no tightness in his body in anticipation of it, and when it happened that his leg was paining he would just say, "There is pain. Ohh!" and almost pass out. I had to be extremely careful.

He felt as fragile as glass, making me aware of the heaviness of my hands against his tiny frame. Every time I picked him up under his arms as carefully as possible, he looked down at his feet as they left the ground and said quietly, "Wow!" I noticed the innocent wonder of his reaction.

I lifted him carefully to the couch on the first night. Going all the way to the bed was something he didn't want to risk. When I finally switched off the light, the flies quietened down.

In the morning, he woke by four o'clock and I got him from the couch back to the chair. Then he went from choirboy to drill sergeant:

"Bring water!"

"Not hot enough!"

"Take it away, sir!"

For a second this military tone reminded me of my father's arrogant attitude toward his subordinates (the rest of the world). I recoiled with anger, thinking, *Look here, buddy—I'm not your servant boy!* I felt the vibration of annoyance, but the important thing was to keep moving. I was on edge with the certain knowledge that he could hear my thoughts. At such moments the voices in my head were bouncing around like a barroom brawl.

Later he used to tease me about my name: "You are a Brawley! Brawling all the time!"

He got that right.

One nice thing was the peace and quiet, once the games stopped as soon as the door closed. I went from being constantly harassed to being ignored. When the curtain fell we were backstage in the dressing room of oblivion where he actually lived. I don't think he was different when he was alone. Simply put, activities were unnecessary for him. That was for others. Without them around, the echo chamber was empty.

Truth is, it was pretty fantastic to be sitting with a guy like that at night, all night, night after night.

The first few days the pain in his leg was so intense that when I moved him to the bathroom to urinate he almost passed out. He would just say, "There is pain! There is pain!" His head would begin to sway and his eyes would roll back. I had to be careful because he wouldn't say anything until it was too late. His way of talking about his body was an indicator of the relationship between whatever he was and his body. If I asked, "Does that hurt?", he would never fail to point out: "Don't say it hurts! There is pain there!" as if the pain were happening to something else.

I thought of the difference between this automatic expression and the way JK often slipped while carefully referring to himself first as "I" and then correcting himself, "Uh... the speaker." In his case it was an ideational position, you could hear it in the delay and correction of his grammar; it was theatre of another kind.

In UG there was a functional response to phenomena. He never pretended to be less than a human being, boasting about being a total egotist, proclaiming his greatness to disprove any lack of ego. All that boasting was a theatre with a hollow ring after observing how he functioned. It wasn't that there was no pain, but that the relationship of that pain to the witness was on remote, giving the impression of a real no-body.

During the day everybody had a hand in taking care of his needs. He would eat or drink then spit everything into a cup. Then the cups had to be changed. He had his favorite cups, which started a competition for who could steal the most cups from the Brot Bar. The New Yorker brought massive quantities, then napkins were added to the list. She brought him napkins from then on, no matter where he went. He never made public pronouncements about it, but napkins had long been a priority on his list of important things in life. Once he proudly showed us his kitchen cabinets filled with napkins stolen from truck stops and restaurants, arranged in neat piles like money in a safe. They were about the only possession he seemed to covet.

The first few nights he wanted to stay in his chair. He said he was most comfortable there. Moving him to the bed was still too painful. I slept on the floor in front of him with a small blue keychain light and checked on him occasionally in the dark.

I barely slept the first few nights, on the alert in case he forgot his injury and tried to get up. The sight of him in the blue light of the little flashlight, lying on the couch with his shadow blown up on the wall, was like a dream. It reminded me that, during my first visit to see him in Switzerland, I had the idea to propose photographing him for twenty-four hours to document the nuts and bolts of his way of living. At the time I dismissed the idea as too invasive. I never imagined spending night after night looking after every possible physical detail like this. Occasionally I wished I had a camera, but dismissed the idea as crass.

The first morning he made me a cup of coffee. He had me bring all the ingredients, instant coffee, lots of sugar of course, and some cream, and made it at his table, sitting like an alchemist while I watched. He made sure I drank it before he had his breakfast. It was strong and bittersweet. I made it myself after that. He always made sure I had my coffee before I served him his oatmeal. "Have you had your coffee, sir?" he would ask.

For my part, I could never make the oatmeal right, despite having made oatmeal just right for myself for years. For some reason with him it was always either too thick or too thin. He never said a word about it. In any case he ate it and threw it up soon after.

He was methodically neat, lining things up at right angles, rugs, sheets, and napkins. "Esoteric training, sir!" he said politely, as he asked me to straighten the edge of a carpet. In the night when he awoke to go to the toilet, turning on the light, he would straighten the napkins on the table by his bed as obsessively as a military man. When I made the bed the first few times I knew it wasn't perfect but did my best and moved on. I tried to make myself invisible.

Yogini was scheduled to go back for a couple of weeks to visit her father. I sensed her hesitancy about leaving UG this way, but there was nothing to do about it.

He would ask me: "Why is she wasting her life here?" pointing out, "She is rich and good-looking." Yet each time the subject came up he would ask her why she had to go. She was bringing me breakfast and sandwiches for lunch. I was locked in place by his constant threat that he needed me there for shitting. When I drove back to the apartment every day to shower he asked why, pointing out that showers were unnecessary: "You are killing thousands of microorganisms every time you bathe!"

Thank God the New Yorker made her car available so I could race back and forth to the place in Saanen. Just getting out and breathing some fresh air was like a sensual pleasure. Even at high speeds. I had a cell phone with me the whole time, just in case, and usually by the time I was half-way through the shower the phone would ring, "Where are you?" He needed me there for shitting and by the time I got there the moment had passed.

Once the summer was in full swing I counted thirty-five people squeezed into the tiny cave. It was like a sauna in there. When he was able to pull himself up in the chair I retreated to a spot on the other side of the apartment and busied myself with writing and painting while he held court.

"Only thieves have property!" he shouted, as they worked on his will. Then he shouted to the girls across the room: "Hey girlies! What are you doing with the money?"

"We are doing *puja* to it, UG!" Shilpa piped in.

"Hey! Don't do filthy *puja*!"

He didn't want anyone to do spiritual rituals even if it was for money.

As for his bodily needs, we had to pay attention to them, because he wouldn't. If there were people in the room he wouldn't tell me he had to pee. He would deny it. A couple of times when everyone finally left it was clear that he'd been needing to go for some time. His selflessness was so complete and yet he never admitted to it.

"You think I am a sweet, gentle Jesus? I am not a nice guy!"

It was one of his lines, but his behavior was the complete opposite of this claim, he was serving people who came to see him all day every day. That's all he did.

One day he was in a particularly good mood. It was as if the universe was shining through him as he sat in the chair in his copper colored silk pajamas, looking like a dancing Shiva from one of those Indian temples. It was strange how he kept repeating, "It's a very good day!"

Late in the afternoon the sun threw beams into the basement apartment at a sharp angle. For about an hour he was
sitting directly in the sunlight. It was hard to say where the light
was coming from: him or the sun. He was on fire with joyous
energy. The copper color of his silk outfit was shimmering, his
movements were a mesmerizing vision of gold and yellow, like
an angel from another dimension. Something about his appearance sent shivers up my spine. Immeasurable life was bursting
through him with sacredness attached to nothing but itself. He
was a bursting flaming male/female form, dancing in place as
if all the gods from all the corners of the collective spiritual
consciousness had condensed into one form. Once again there
was a waterfall of light and nectar pouring around him. You
could have traced these elements in the air, billowing around
him from endless space to endless space—a storm cloud bursting on the rolling landscape of eternity.

That afternoon everyone was knocked out by a powerful
gentleness that split the mind like a watermelon, washing away
time and space in a golden wake.

Since he would not go to the toilet unless the room was
empty, and he wouldn't say he had to go, we had to devise
signals to give him a break. People would suddenly go for a
coffee, giving him a break he wouldn't take for himself. When
they returned there were endless inquiries about the success
or failure of his attempts so, to sidestep the question, I made
a drawing of a pile of shit with a circle and an X through it
and taped it to the door. He would change the day-count of his
constipation to drive people crazy, claiming it had only been
two days when it was actually five. Then he would toy with
everyone's worst fear: "I don't care! I can sit here until I die!
It makes no difference to me. I have lived long enough! I have
enjoyed everything this world has to offer, and I'm ready to go!"

He took no medicine, repeating Dr Lynn's advice that he
should wait a little while after eating before throwing out the

food, otherwise the blood would rush from his brain into his stomach and he would wobble and fall and maybe he would never get up again, which was also fine with him.

After eight days of constipation he started taking suggestions. There was no way to say what he'd be willing to try. One day the Reverend brought in some kind of oil, and he drank it on the spot. He eventually drank an entire bottle of prune juice the New Yorker bought, but only after it had been sitting in his refrigerator for about a week. Finally I just put it in a cup and handed it to him without saying anything and he drank it.

When he finally cleared his system, there was a huge relief. Even this was subject to jokes when everyone came in again. "The noise I make while shitting is more melodious than your Beethoven's ninth symphony or fifth symphony!"

He was completely unashamed of his bodily functions. When he finally did shit he was so excited he called out from the toilet: "Louis! I think that is the rest of it!"

"Wow, UG, that's great!"

The others left each night at around eight o'clock. At ten o'clock he would break the silence, "I'll go there," indicating the bed with a wave of his hand.

I would lift him up and carry him to the bed. Every time I lifted him he would look down at his feet leaving the floor, saying quietly, "Wow!" Settling on the bed, he lay on his back first, then as the leg improved he would carefully roll to his side, drawing the blanket over his tiny frame like a child, pulling the pillow into position.

"Thank you, sir."

Lights out.

I got my bedding, laying it where the two carpets separated the sleeping area from the sitting area. Then I would lie on my back and look at the ceiling beam that ran along the middle of the apartment, absorbing the atmosphere.

One night, after I switched off the light, I lay down on the floor for a minute and suddenly I heard a woman's voice whispering near his bed. I locked the door just before I lay down and it was silent in that basement, so there was no way I imagined it. I didn't dare look up at the bed. This went on for a few minutes with a rapid whispering in some language I didn't recognize, then as suddenly as it started, it stopped. The dehumidifier hummed away against the wall. Nothing, no more whispering, it came and went like the saints that marched out all those years ago.

At first I slept so lightly that if he moved in the dark, the sound of his sheets woke me up. I would shine the blue flashlight at the clock to check the time. Sometimes he would sit up on the edge of his bed in the dark. There was something magical about those hours. At times, with the light on next to his bed dramatically illuminating his face from below, he resembled JK with his long deeply wrinkled Indian face, his shadow looming against the wall. When he slept I never heard him snore but there was a deeper breathing indicating sleep at times. Occasionally he would wake up and notice I was also there.

"Oh. You are awake. What time is it?"

"It's eleven o'clock."

"What? Only eleven o'clock?"

"Yes, sir, it's eleven."

"I must pee."

"OK."

I would help him to sit up on the bed. It was a delicate procedure as I tried not to move his leg at all. Then I would get the bucket and steady him when he stood up listing slightly to get his balance, leaning into me. Then I held on to him while he urinated. What a strange scene.

It may seem even stranger to make a note of it but his penis really was like that of a child, which he said was a side-effect of his calamity.

A few times he said to me: "Look, sir, it's useless! You mean to say I could have sex with that? I never, never would have expected this to happen, you can't imagine; it's the end of you as you know yourself!"

It was chilling to see the physical evidence of that. Not exactly the image of enlightenment bandied about in the marketplace. The purely physical process he described was a rare and painful mutation that finished him, not to mention these side-effects.

Another night I heard him rustling around so I got up and shone the light on him.

"Oh! You are awake!" He turned on the lamp by the bed.

"Yes," I answered from the floor.

"Sorry to disturb you," he said politely.

"No problem, UG."

"What time is it?"

I looked at the clock.

"It's twelve o'clock."

"Oh." He shut off the light, an hour passed, then I heard the rustling sheets again as the light beside his bed came on.

"What time is it now?" he asked.

"It's one o'clock now."

"Only?" He sounded impatient, like someone waiting for a movie to start.

"Yes, sorry," I reported.

"Strange," he said quietly.

The light went off and there was silence again for a while. Listening in the dark, his breath became deeper. I drifted off to sleep again until I heard the rustling in the dark and his light came on.

"What time is it now sir?" he asked again.

I looked once more at the plastic clock on the wall. "It's one thirty now," I said. Only a half-hour had lapsed and he sounded so impatient for the night to be over.

"Why?" he asked in an exasperated tone.

"Sorry, I don't know why but it's only one thirty!"

We laughed and the light went out again until four o'clock, the usual time for him to get up.

No wonder he always said: "When you look at the clock it goes so slow; and when you don't look at all it goes so fast!"

What was the impatience about? It made me wonder just how much he slept at night. In Baveno he'd explained about the 'recording' that went on whether he was asleep or awake. So what was it like for him to sleep? And where did time factor in? At times he seemed impatient, eager to get out and go for a ride. Then at other times he would say he could sit all day in the chair and not feel any need to do anything.

There is an interesting passage in *The Mystique of Enlightenment*, which may give some idea about the way he functioned:

> *Perhaps I can give you the 'feel' of this. I sleep four hours at night, no matter what time I go to bed. Then I lie in bed until morning fully awake. I don't know what is lying there in the bed; I don't know whether I'm lying on my left side or my right side—for hours and hours I lie like this. If there is any noise outside—a bird or something—it just echoes in me...*

He goes on to talk about the sensation:

> *If the question is asked, 'What is in there?' there is only an awareness of the points of contact, where the body is in contact with the bed and the sheets, and where it is in contact with itself, at the crossing of the legs for example. There is some kind of heaviness, probably the gravitational pull, something very vague. There is nothing inside which links up these things. Even if the eyes are open and looking at the whole body, there are still only the points of contact and they have no connection with what I am looking at. If I want to try and link up these points of contact into the*

shape of my own body, probably I will succeed, but by the time it is completed the body is back in the same situation of different points of contact. The linkage cannot stay. It is the same sort of thing when I am sitting or standing. There is no body.

The day began at four o'clock. He would get up and I would move him to the chair. He dressed there and every few days used a plastic razor and hot water to shave, rinsing then washing with Mysore Sandalwood soap.

One morning, helping him with his clothes as he sat on the edge of his bed, I dropped his shirt by accident and, before I could pick it up, he snatched it off the floor, using the toes of his right foot, with lightning speed. His body was completely relaxed at all times. I never noticed any tension in his body, no matter what the situation. The couple of times the leg caused real pain, he just passed out, he never shouted or tensed up, just moaned as the eyes rolled back and out he went.

Another morning he was sitting on edge of the bed getting dressed as I handed him his trousers. Suddenly he pointed his finger past me in a gesture of accusation saying angrily, "Scoundrels! Filthy scoundrels!"

I didn't see anyone there, and didn't say anything. He was talking to someone behind me to the left, pointing directly at them. I had no idea what that was. I don't know if he was seeing someone or talking to himself. That morning, when I asked him about it in front of the others, he said jokingly: "Just because you don't see them, doesn't mean they aren't there."

Before, when I heard the woman's voice, I made a joke of that as well the morning after. He said it must have been someone in the driveway. I know it wasn't. So when he made the comment about the things you can't see, it was as if to put some balance into the picture that would short-circuit any conclusions. He never confirmed or denied, leaving that up to us.

It was like JK's answer to UG's question,"What about the existence of the masters?"

The old man replied, "If I say anything about it, it will be used as an authority."

Clearly UG learned a few tricks from the old man.

CHAPTER 33

Questioning my actions before and after is over for me.

By five o'clock he would have dressed and eaten his breakfast, after which he told me to unlock the door and open the curtain so people would know to come in. The shop was open usually for an hour before anyone arrived.

Once the door was open, we sat without talking until someone showed up. I sat on the couch writing or dozing. He rarely spoke and I enjoyed the silence. Even though at times I could only hear my mind racing, I would remind myself that the racket in my trash heap of a mind was barely a squeak compared to the immensity he lived in. I never felt judged; it was like sitting in the Grand Canyon listening to the wind, even in such a place, thoughts carry on. Sometimes I had the feeling he was reassuring me that it was perfectly normal to be so burdened by thoughts I had no control over. People like that are not bothered by positive or negative thought. It's all the same noise to them.

Eventually he started to make a show of his improving condition by standing up on his own. One day when I was out of the room he did a little 'dance', which probably meant that he stood up and shuffled his feet. Eventually he walked to the bathroom without help, again while I was away. Soon he was eager to go back to meeting people at Cabana. When he recovered his ability to move around, his routine was re-established independent of my help. I was there in case anything went wrong, but after some time the question of how long to stay came to mind. I was waiting to hear from him but he said nothing.

Then, early one morning when there were only a couple of people in the room, he said, "I want to look at the stairs." We watched as he walked to the door, stepped out and looked up at the stairs for a minute.

"No. Not yet." And went back to his chair.

On July 17th, he got up and showered, dressed, and ate breakfast without my help.

People arrived and things were happening as usual, and suddenly he said, "I want to getoutofhere, right now!"

He walked to the door, stepped out and looked up at the stairs again. When I moved to help, he growled at me:

"No, sir. I don't need your help! You think I need your help?"

After a pause, he grasped the railing with both arms and made his way to the top step by step and made a little stomping motion with his feet as he hit the drive, smiling triumphantly. Everyone cheered and that was that.

Then he climbed into the luxury Peugeot 607 that had been sitting idle for weeks and Ray, who was trying so hard to be careful, closed the car door gently and the window automatically rolled up with two of his fingers in it.

"Ouch, the fingers!" he said in his strange dislocated way while we all looked on horrified.

God help these people from people like us! Poor Ray was desperately fumbling around with the fancy goddamn remote controls in the car to free UG's fingers from the mechanical grip of the automatic window. By the time the window was lowered his fingers were black and blue. Of course he didn't care; he immediately diffused all guilt feelings by collecting one thousand Swiss francs per finger for damages. Ray was horrified but for the rest of the summer UG happily held up his bruised fingers as a reminder and an example that they healed much faster than those 'idiotic doctors' said they would. He had a way of insisting on something that never happened over and over until everyone agreed with him.

GONER

Later someone told me a story about Anandamayi Ma, that one of her disciples once wondered what she would do if a coal fell on her foot, she seemed so unaware of her own body. When they looked away, she dropped a coal on her foot and just looked at it, as if wondering the same thing to herself. Only when the disciple turned back and saw it burning her foot and shrieked, did she kick it off, laughing to her-self. They had to bandage her up afterwards.

CHAPTER 34

*I tell you, you are more unique and extraordinary than
all those saints and saviors of mankind put together.*

One day, just before lunch, UG explained exactly how he
wasn't a religious bastard. In light of the recent fall, his energy
was impressive by any standard. Addressing the Reverend and
Mahesh he was particularly dark on the subject. He launched
the blast with the sun blazing over the Alps at his back, taking
on the whole of religious history. The fury was more intense
than the previous days.

"I am not a religious bastard! And filthy bastards they are,
fooling people, how they should behave, what they should do.
Inefficiency is the result of all that shit! Inexactness! Worthless
people you produce, all the scoundrels, all the spiritual teachers. You are an animal! You can't live like an animal. You think
that you are not. That's the cause of human misery. Be miserable, and eliminate this whole human species from this planet.
It will be wiped out! You and I will not be there to see it and
say, 'I told you so, buster!' It *has got* to happen! I don't have to
do a thing. You have set in motion such hideous things in the
name of God, that non-existing bastard, a filthy bastard. If you
guys trust in that God, you think He's on your side? Be honest
for once! He should be on their side, not on your side and on my
side, filthy scoundrels, who preach all that shit in the churches,
temples, and mosques. This is not atheism. It is not iconoclastic
nonsense. Your religious shit has no place on this planet. You
survived this long only because you had the most destructive

weapons. Thank God there are countries to wipe out America, but you are not going to go gracefully, without taking every form of life on this planet (*with you*). That is what we are facing in this situation today. All Americans must be wiped out, even before that, all India, and Indian shit must be wiped out! It's not my wish. That has *got* to happen."

Pointing to the Reverend he said: "Now I'm glad, your spiritual daughter found a cockroach dancing, in what? A microwave oven! And it came out, and continued to dance. Now I believe what that bastard said, 'Cockroaches are the only ones that will survive a nuclear holocaust.'"

His arms were flying with the most amazing gestures, symmetrical flourishes, pointing up, down, backwards and forwards; he spoke with his whole body as the words came fast and furious, with pauses and facial expressions to emphasize a particular shot of disgust, his words held up and smashed sound against sound, meaning against meaning, in an instant, spitting in the face of so-called human civilization. It was spectacular, and he could shout like this for hours while we sat around him in utter amazement.

According to friends who knew UG from before his calamity he was in the habit of carrying around a book of his achievements with him even then. Part of his practice when things got slow was to drag out some of these materials and read them like The Links. Astrology readings, palm readings were all a part of this entertainment for him.

One day he read from a *Nadi* reading given decades before that contained disconcertingly accurate things about his life, years before any of it happened. *Nadi* readings are an ancient astrological practice originating in India. The *Nadi* leaves are dried and cured palm leaves of long narrow shape like a ruler with tiny inscriptions on them. A trained reader can interpret the leaf for the subject and UG had several of these readings in his notebook. His grandfather had one done for him when he was a boy that was pretty accurate, but he would always point out that the man did a similar reading for his grandfather and none of what was predicted came true. He would read from the transcription of one of these readings on occasion. It was an apt way for him to hint at what we were witnessing. In print it may sound like an exaggeration, but in his presence it was anything but:

> The native's intelligence is well beyond the result of usual academic studies. He is at the home with all languages. Wherever he is, he understands the terms of the particular region.

Leafing through a bit, he skipped some items, then continued,

> One can't say he's rich or poor, god or human.

Here he indicated a similar line from a family member: "Like my great-granddaughter says."

> His thinking is the most enigmatic thing in this world, no one can say anything about him. He knows everything, and his vision of wisdom is an incarnation and there is no parallel to this event among the eight directions of the earth!

Here he stopped to congratulate himself, making a joke of it with shrugs and facial expression.

> He has his own resources, yet he deals with them as if they don't belong to him. In this birth he married for the sake of companionship.

Pausing, leafing through again, he said quietly to no one, "Got it?" and leafed through some more:

GONER

The native has no job whatsoever. In the path of wisdom he is a unique man in the whole world, he is absolutely selfless!

He skipped some more, then he found the part that described the head of a nation being assassinated 'on one Wednesday' and we were all disappointed that this hadn't come to pass yet. "Your Bush!" Then, "This is interesting, eh?"

He doesn't believe in palmistry and astrology, he doesn't believe in Nadi readings, he doesn't believe in miracles, he doesn't give a damn to the existence of God, yet there is a great emphasis on the compassion for humanity. You are endowed with the capacity to achieve anything in this world. You have all the supernatural powers, yet you could not save your own son, a blood relation, from the jaws of death.

He read on silently to himself for a minute, then, "So?" he said to no one, and then read a passage we knew all about from personal experience,

You are a true Brahmin, an enlightened person of the highest order, but most people cannot swallow the blunt and naked expressions of your attainment, they go away from you in total disdain. All those who hang around you, who choose to come to you, are helped beyond their expectations.

The evidence of this sat surrounding him in rooms all over the world.

As soon as he was well enough, we went right back to the rides.

I spent the night in his place until August 22nd, by which time I was plenty relieved to go; I was waiting for orders. By that time he was moving around fine without me. The final

morning when the others arrived he started blasting me and my
'do-gooder's high' until I was seething inside.

"Your job here is finished. You think I can't take care of
myself? I could get ten nurses better than you just by putting a
listing up at the Co-op!" He said coldly: "You want to feel good
about helping! I don't need your help or anybody's help!"

I knew it was a routine, a little theatre designed to cut my
attachment to the role of caretaker, designed to make me happy
to abandon him, but it was remarkably effective. By the time I
left I was cursing in his direction. Not so holy. As a thank you, he
gave me a cashmere sweater, a DVD player and a farewell blast.
I knew he was grateful, the blast freed me from worrying that
I'd abandoned ship. So I went back to full-time private misery.

The next day I listed various suicide options in my notes:

1. *Stabbing myself in the neck repeatedly with a
    Swiss Army knife.*
2. *Hanging myself from the door with a belt.*
3. *Hanging myself from a beam in the Chalet.*
4. *Diving head first off a high waterfall into the rocks.*
5. *Potassium cyanide.*
6. *Gun in mouth.*
7. *Decapitation with Rube Goldberg instant burial
    device.*
8. *Driving into a wall at a high speed.*
9. *Stepping in front of a truck. (Messy, involves
    innocent party.)*
10. *Starving to death. (Advantages: mystical visions.
    Disadvantages: it takes too long.)*

In the meantime I realized, while showering one afternoon,
that I'd injured myself while lifting him around. I hadn't been
careful. My testicle was swollen and the self-diagnosis was
immediately cancer. More wishful thinking no doubt. That

didn't keep me from weeping. Couldn't I get anything right? Lance Armstrong was about to win the Tour de France for the 7th time and his bout with the disease planted the seed (sorry). I imagined dying a slow, painful death in some shit-hole apartment in Oregon with no medical coverage. Why was I so fixated on Oregon? I guess the Northwest Territory was my last fantasy refuge, which was easy since I'd never been there. He really got me this time. This time it was the balls. What to do? I was distraught that this could happen here of all places. Sitting opposite him in the cave I felt lower than low.

The disturbing thing about this was the storm of angry thoughts directed at him, a mix of resentment, gratitude and envy of his ability to manage his own body. I told myself that he would never have put himself in a position to injure himself. When the long rides started again I experienced real pain from the vibration of the car after hours and hours of driving. Far be it from me to say anything. I was too embarrassed. I just seethed about one more piece of evidence from the universe that I was fucked and would remain so. It seemed that just when my humiliation was at a low, there was another layer under that one, lying in wait with an evil grin.

CHAPTER 35

If you could be in a state of awareness for one second by the
clock, once in your life, the continuity would be snapped,
the illusion of the experiencing structure, the 'you', would
collapse, and everything would fall into the natural rhythm.

This collapsing and the specifics of the 'one second by the clock'
took on relative meanings, as the tale of UG's former life was
revealed in anecdotes recalled as he sat around 'making noise'.
Most of the interesting, and probably more accurate, items
emerged when he was reminiscing while discussing a related
issued through some other medium.

That fall we started bouncing up and down Europe, as a plan
emerged to spend some time in Italy. While we crossed back
and forth between Southern France and Italy that September,
revelations about his past came to light in the cozy setting of an
apartment in Menton, a town on the Mediterranean sea where
he and Valentine stayed back in the 1960's. He kept telling us
it was the place where the painters used to come. Those days
were long over. He wanted to check on the progress of a 'cave'
being built for him in Italy. With that in mind we headed for the
Mediterranean town of Vallecrosia not far from the French border. Squeezing the cars into the driveway at Vallecrosia, Lucia
greeted us with a big smile and a brush in her hand, busy right
along with the workers. The painters were putting the finishing
touches on the 'UG cave'.

The setting for that final scene, which we had no idea was
coming, was a low greenhouse-style structure with a bedroom

on one end and a kitchen on the other. The windows along the
front had dark maroon curtains to block out the view. The light
was beautiful everywhere. UG came in and took his seat on the
couch next to me and said with a little grin: "This is not a cave,
it's a palace!"

Lucia sat at his feet hugging her knees like a girl in front of
a Christmas tree. He was most interested in how the heating
worked. With two floor-to-ceiling radiators on either side of
the room and a little stove, all together it worked fine. Charging
up the radiators, and with the glass roof absorbing the sun,
the place got toasty after about five minutes. Soon after that
it became apparent that there was only one problem: the paint
fumes were so intense they drove most of us onto the garden.

He ignored our complaints about the fumes, focusing on the
humidity: "I can't stay here, it's too humid!"

After a coffee he ordered us back to Menton, the 'Pearl of
France', where we landed the night before. Lucia was in tears
as we backed out from the narrow gate, but he made sure she
knew we would be back the next day to check in. For the rest of
the week we went back and forth from Menton, now a geriatric
beach resort, not unlike Miami Beach. He would stop in to
check on the 'humidity', we'd have a coffee, bake a little in the
cave while the heating blasted away, then split again.

A friend from Freiburg found him a newly renovated apartment in Menton. There were white marble floors and a balcony
facing the sea. The view was so spectacular that even UG made
a note of it: "Look, sir! Look at the view! Wow!"

The rest of us found apartments on other floors. The weather
was perfect. He was in his element. In the mornings he sat in a
little avocado chair with his back to the window while the light
poured in from the sea behind him. The German sat beside him
on a white leather couch, his eyes closed with a slightly knit-
ted brow, next to the American with his hand to his forehead,
a headache meditation he was good at. The New Yorker was

either asleep or running an errand, keeping us all in supplies. The Hungarian girl was draped in a beach chair like a zombie with Yogini nearby, lips pursed, looking slightly irritated. The doctor and his wife relaxed in beach chairs and zonked out with a casual bliss. I sat at a glass dining table writing furiously to stave off insanity.

Sitting in a comfortable chair in the living room of a rented apartment he spoke about his family life and the end of his sex life. Despite all his claims about the uselessness of his spiritual discipline—"It was all an obstacle, sir! Nothing to it"—I never met a more disciplined person. In the area of sex, a turning point in his life began when he entered into marriage and ended after a one-night stand. The more information I absorbed, the more was mercury on a glass surface constantly tilted.

"Hey, buster, listen. This is the most interesting thing."

He was reading from a new biography about his life. It was a highly imaginative document. In between passages that had him being seduced by a woman in Chicago, he reflected on his family life as if talking to himself.

I made notes while he talked about his visit to New York in the 1950's with his wife and son. They were shopping at Macy's on 34th Street, and she 'went wild', as he put it, and got lost in the department store. He left her there and went back to the hotel with his son.

"She thought I would wait for her. Not a chance."

The snapshots of his family life were always telling in some kind of indeterminate way.

His wife suffered his ways for sure. Yet once he was gone, her own family turned against her, she went crazy with grief and their family was shattered. He often used the word 'shattered' to describe the effect he had on people, but it was most applicable to his own life: what he'd gone through, what his wife and children went through, while he was pursuing that one question of his. The price was everything, and sex was just the start of it. After the one-night stand he returned and immediately told his wife what had happened. She was no doubt used to his bluntness, but she must have sensed that this was the end. As he read from the biography we were able to throw in the occasional question,

"UG was different, leading the strangest kind of life…"

Someone asked, "In what way strange, UG?"

"I never wanted to have sex with her anymore or have her there."

I tried to make sense of the bits and pieces floating up, piecing together a broken story. There were too many fragments. Nothing explained what he had become. He was reading about his life all the time, as if even he were trying to piece it back together, not caring how the pieces went or what meaning emerged. According to what he said that day, the woman he'd had the one-night stand with even came to meet his wife, to convince her to leave UG. His wife knew him well enough to know that if he said it was over, it was over. Indeed, some time later while UG was in Paris, the woman took him to lunch and offered to give him money. At this point he was down and out, but maybe he sensed the price of such a gift, because he said he 'threw it in her face'.

This was no controlled celibacy; he said the one-night stand experience drove home the fact that he could not have sex without using another human being for pleasure.

"Even if the other party is a willing victim, the fact nevertheless remains, you must use the other. I simply refused."

Seeing the way he refused to sell himself in any other area was the proof of his conviction. These details are so simple yet, when you look at them, they reveal characteristics of the man that stand out as significant despite his casual rendering of them.

He often repeated that the two basic functions of any organism were survival and reproduction, 'fucking', he would say for emphasis, so there was no mistaking the matter. So then what is the state of a person who is no longer reproducing, for whom that drive is gone forever? I had no idea, but compared to all the usual moralism around sex preached by religion, his story is chillingly different. For him, the end of sex was the beginning of the end of him. He had a way of slipping these implications into the noise as they entered our heads. Being around someone like that was very odd at such times, like glimpsing into a parallel universe.

On the horizon behind him the clouds hung over the sea, tiny and delicate. The atmosphere over the sea was condensed, tightening as it approached the vanishing point. He also had a way of condensing space until the entire contents of the universe seemed to be converging into a point. A seagull's cry filled the pause between the rhythm of waves and the swish of traffic outside. The room was charged with that action of his that penetrated everything. We sat slightly suspended in his warmth, despite the discomfort.

As the curtains were drawn at night, the bleached Mediterranean view disappeared, as if in a magic show where room was changed into a place without boundaries. Once the curtain was pulled, it could have been any place, anywhere, in any country. He sat in the little slipper chair while the others slept a cosmic sleep and wave after wave of something nearly visible, a diaphanous wash of the pale, violet energy of the sea flowed through him, enveloping the scene, softly pulsing around him like curtains of eternity flowing in a waterfall.

"Come on!" you might say. "Knock it off! What is it with these descriptions?" Well, that's just how it was. Do you think I was a total idiot, sitting there day after day just for the therapy? Nope. It was something else.

The weather held like the endless summer. After all the traveling around it was hard to say what time of year it was, except that there were so few people around. He noted the lack of young people in the streets.

"Where are they? Why is it only old people? You should enjoy while you are ee-nng! Let these old people pack up and make way for the young people!"

I was thinking about money all the time and he constantly told me no one would ever, ever buy my horrible paintings. In the next sentence he would call me a billionaire. Millionaire wasn't enough? I certainly seemed to be living like one, hanging around on the French Riviera with a guru of sorts, for Christ's sake. He kept cutting at me deftly with a very small but sharp knife.

"You are not an artist."

Sure, I thought. *Fine! What the hell else can I do now?* I wondered what would become of me once this bubble burst. His cruelty was unnerving but, at the same time, his attention was invigorating, painfully so. But it was, after all, the attention of a man who had seen into things so deeply that I knew I would benefit from the interaction. I sometimes felt hurt, but the look in his eyes was not the usual insulting look, it was something unattached to judgment, a hard reality poking at a soft wishful thinking that your friends won't dare mess with.

Maybe to offset the apparent good fortune of my having taken care of him, and the consequent attention, he was subjecting me to this abuse. It wasn't mockery for the sake of revenge—he had nothing against me—it was in a way payback in the form of harsh honesty; sensing that I could take it maybe, he let me have it full guns.

The surf outside was louder that day. There were old ladies swimming topless, probably the same ones who'd first outraged the public in the 1960's by revealing beautiful young bodies.

A Greek woman who met UG and JK on the same day, decades before, was now traveling with us. She had the body language and presence of a child and the lightness of a butterfly, flitting in and out of the apartment. "Eets okay, it doosent matter, I will only bee an haff an hour or so." UG was always threatening to leave her behind, but she always managed to show up in time. "She's very undependable," he would say if she was missing for any reason, yet when she sang, he beamed with warmth and childish joy. She sang a Greek song with a catchy refrain that became a stock request when he wanted me to imitate or sing to entertain.

Yogini and I left around seven o'clock each morning to walk the few blocks to his flat. We'd moved out of the one in the building after one night in a musty cockroach-infested flat that was unlivable once we saw it in the light of day. A fiery-colored bush on the sidewalk filled the block with its scent in the rosy morning light. We were buzzed into the huge marble and metal lobby with a statue of a naked woman in the classic Greek style halfway up the staircase. As the elevator neared UG's floor we could hear his voice reverberating in the building. We put our shoes by the door, noting who was already there from the other shoes. The marble floors reminded me of India. He was talking about a friend's windfall inheritance:

"How much money did he get from that bitch he killed?"

Neighbors in the hall scurried into their apartments and quickly locked the doors.

He was always busy when we arrived.

"One who has done serious *sadhana* cannot brush me aside! They sit at my feet!"

He narrated the story of a friend who, after years of traveling with him and Valentine, taking care of her when she fell ill, came to UG and said: "UG, I think it's time for me to leave."

Without hesitation he reached into his pocket, "Here is $2,000, there is the car, bye-bye. Out you go!"

His friend was shocked. Probably he expected a discussion about the matter. Backtracking he offered, "I can stay and help...," but it was too late.

"I don't need your help."

If I thought I was indispensable, I'd better think again.

"The desire for permanence in every area of your life is the cause of human misery!" he would say, including the desire to hang around him.

He found a quote in The Links from Osho: "If you are fragile in your growth, UG Krishnamurti can destroy you completely."

Again, he read it in a tone casually laced with menace. Then, looking up at me: "We are the same, you and I, except for one thing."

He sunk the blade a little deeper, "I am lucky, you are unlucky."

Like a razor-sharp samurai sword, it cut so clean I didn't even see it. My chopped guts fell with a thud, blood spurting from the stump. He was as vicious as I felt toward Yogini, spewing venom with more clarity than I could muster. With her I was spewing a similar venom, I couldn't help it, my desire for reproduction was being hampered.

"You think the hippy is so peaceful; try taking away his guitar," he said on an early tape. "He will beat you!"

If I had gone, no doubt it would have become another story in his arsenal, but someone else would have stepped in. The thing to remember was that it was never personal. He had huge fights with some of his closest admirers and friends over the years, some of whom never returned, but he was sweet as a lamb when he saw them next. I knew that the areas of my life under attack were not working for me, he was the only one who pointed out these blunt facts without hesitation.

That night a fawn-colored dusk faded as the flickering sea reflected a pattern through the curtains behind him. Light boosted the colors in the chair where he sat with his legs neatly side by side, hands clasped in his lap, eyes closed but not sleeping, creating a perfect image of silence. Everything I saw around him filled me with an urgency to capture it. I wrote and wrote but nothing could contain it. Fail, fail, fail. The marbled floor and white walls bounced soft light against an audience of five, two on the couch, two in chairs and me in the back of the room making notes. We were waiting for the Hungarian to return from Milan with a visa. The traffic washed by below, mixing with the sound of the surf and the whirring sound of the electric heater inside, blowing at his feet, causing the fringe of his chair to sway gently.

The next day it was over. Time to go.

"I like this place," he said as we got ready to leave.

Doors were slamming, bags zipped shut and the anxiety of leaving was in the air. In the past they said he got pretty nasty when the time came to pack up. Never before had he allowed so many people to travel along with him:

"You are all restricting my freedom of movement!"

When he decided to leave, he was ready in five minutes.

"I am ready now. Why are you standing there?"

I closed the shutters thinking he was on his way out, but he was just going to the kitchen sink to throw up some food. When I saw him come back into the room I started to re-open them.

"No, no, sir, it doesn't matter. I live in darkness."

He said it with a twinkle in his eye. I exchanged glances with the German in a moment of subtle disorientation. A mental image of him blew through me like a breath from inner space. He was always suspended in the darkness of the unknown, with nothing to hold him, no need for light, no need even for space, nothing.

"The light shineth in the darkness and the darkness comprehended it not." It was one of his favorite lines to quote from the Bible.

The usual nonsense went on as we packed the cars out front. Old people wandered by on the sidewalks, some of them staring.

"Let them go!" he said, almost under his breath, watching them hobble by on canes. "Useless old people like me. They should make room for the young people to enjoy!"

228

GONER

The young people were busy working miserably hard so they could enjoy their old age.

CHAPTER 36

After all 'death' is fear, the fear of something coming to an end.

We headed back to the cave in Vallecrosia, which was finally habitable, the 'humidity' having cleared somewhat. During the first night there was a power shortage in the cave so he started a fire with some of the New Yorker's napkins and cracked the glass on the door of the new stove. In the morning he blamed it on a few different parties.

The New Yorker was thrilled that he used her napkins to build a fire, joking, "Oh UG, that's so romantic!"

Ignoring this, he blamed her for breaking the glass. Then when the Hungarian, now dubbed 'Cheapie', showed up it was her fault. I think I got blamed as well. We were grateful for the power outage, it meant the room was a little less overheated for a while.

Sitting alone in the cave one afternoon, I listened to him throwing up in the bathroom. He never complained about his physical condition. Shuffling out of the bathroom, he looked at me with a mischievous glint in his eye and did a little shuffle dance step. Making his arms into a little choo-choo dance step, he slid his feet against the floor to a rhythm. I laughed. He sat on his chair with a sigh, and said nothing. His feet were always up on the ottoman. He would draw up figures with the big toe of his left foot as he sat drifting in space by the heat of the stove. Despite the heat he was never without the cashmere sweater, longjohns sticking out from his slacks around his ankles. The room was already an inferno. The only way to make it warmer would have been to set it on fire.

"Burn it to the ground, sir! See what comes up in the ashes."

I often wondered if women understood UG better than men since his acute physical sensitivity was more akin to a woman's than a man's. Mothers are aware of things at a more immediate physical, non-verbal level, possibly as a result of the ability to reproduce life in their bodies, while men are prone to the distraction of the mind. UG used to say he learned more from his newborn son in the first two years of his life than from any spiritual or secular teacher. His ability to douse high-flown intellectual abstractions with simple practical observations must have been refreshing for women who were a constant witness to self-important men talking a good game about life and truth and blah, blah, blah, while the women quietly sustained the men's bellies and their children.

Lucia rarely spoke, but one night after a long busy day of running errands, she asked UG about fear.

"There is only fear there. There is the fear of not getting what you want or the fear of losing what you have. In the end it is the fear of losing what you have. That fear is you as you know yourself and if that fear comes to an end you will drop dead on the spot."

Fear.

He took this opportunity to tell the story of JK's death again: "The old man almost killed me. He wanted to take me with him." It was one of those mysteries he repeated until it was rote.

Picking the American out from the corner of the room, he reminded us how he saved him that day in 1986 as the 'old man' in Ojai was dying, trying to take him with him. UG was staying with him and another friend at the time and asked them to come in and sit with him. This may have been what he meant, since at times it seemed that other people's presence pulled him back to himself.

In any case he said: "Hey! Thank you for saving me!"

"You're welcome, UG," the American replied, with a slight bow and a wry smile.

The American Friend was one of those people around UG who showed almost no interest in spirituality, yet his devotion to UG was deep. In all the years he knew UG, he never wavered in his single-pointed fascination with UG. There was simply no interest in other gurus, spiritual people, or ideas.

The story of the relationship between the two Krishnamurtis kept on mutating in my mind as more details were revealed or repeated. I overheard the American telling the story of the death scene in the kitchen.

UG wasn't so sure he would survive the energy pulsing through him. He showed them where the important documents were with instructions about what to do with the body in case he didn't make it. He said there were waves going up and down his skin from his head into the chest.

The American also talked about how UG seemed to be dying in different ways at different times. In the early days he'd get a far-off look in his eyes and drop his head onto his arm, fading out for some time. If you talked to him at such times he would come back. Sometimes there was an ashy substance on his forehead but he'd quickly wash it off. Early on he was more open about such things, explaining that it was the result of thought being burned inside him, what he called 'the ionization of thought' in an early tape recording. In Indian religious practice people commonly smear ash on their foreheads and he said this would have been the origin of that ritual. In one of the tapes from the seventies he discussed this and mentioned seeing a similar substance on JK's skin: "Oh he is a real trickster I tell you! He doesn't like to let on to these things."

In private Yogini was more talkative than you would have expected. She was so often confused about what he meant by this or that comment. "What did he mean when he said ...?"

I had no clue. Most of the time the effect of what he said evaporated into thin air while you were standing there. She was uncertain yet she sat there hour after hour with him. Of all of the people around him, she was the most persistent, the most faithful. She sat there with a grimace or a smile. When I asked her about it she said, "I want him to dissolve me."

CHAPTER 37

*There is a sensation in you, and you say that you are depressed
or unhappy or blissful, jealous, greedy, envious. This labeling
brings into existence the one who is translating this sensation.*

As soon as we got back to Gstaad, UG started asking that nerve-
wracking question, "What is the plan?"

We were still vibrating from the drive yet it seemed another
move was imminent. Mario was driving—he had relentless
energy for it. Now he was suggesting Cologne as our next destination and I could have plugged his yap.

"Why should I go to Cologne?" UG asked.

He was scheduled to fly from Paris to New York soon and a
lot of driving could be packed into those few days. I had a roof
over my head for the moment but the situation awaiting me in
New York was less certain. I wanted to enjoy some down time
but there was little hope of that. Meanwhile, there were storm
clouds in the living room.

"I don't want anything to do with you people! I am going to
my place and I don't want to see your faces!" He ordered Mario
to drive him home alone.

The day was clear and beautiful. Puffed white clouds were
strewn over the Alps, throwing occasional shadows across the
field next door. Workers were banging away somewhere in the
building. It was so nice out that I walked to town with the
intention of shopping. Yogini was off shopping already so I
went to the supermarket and wandered around. The feeling of
freedom at such moments was like a drug. I was so contentedly

blank -headed I bought nothing. I couldn't think of what I wanted. Then I wandered over to see what was happening with the little white-haired gnome. The closer I got the more my stomach felt like a raw nerve-ending but I couldn't resist the urge to have a look.

When I got to the bottom step and peeked in I saw the others in there with him already. Someone noticed me and he quickly ordered me in. Suddenly full of charm again, he said he'd been invited to share a meal prepared by me. I played along and everyone piled back into the cars and headed right back to the apartment. I walked just to savor another few minutes of the alternate buzz of being alone, thinking about what just happened. The absurdity of walking over there hit me hard. It was like being a junkie, you could never get enough of him. Why? Was I that lost? Was I so stupid? The fact was I was being pulled along on a current I couldn't control, dragged along banging against all obstacles in the way.

Back in the apartment he was full of beans again, again challenging us to a ride… again.

"What is the plan?"

Any suggestion about what to do was rejected or ignored. He yelled at Mario. He yelled at the New Yorker. Then he started talking about painting, no doubt for my sake. I'd been working on a small watercolor in the other room. There was a group show coming up in New York.

"Nothing original there! No art, no painting!"

Everything was a big "No," until he started reminiscing about the fall colors in Vermont, Vancouver, and the great Northwest landscape he saw on his train trip across North America on the Santa Fe Super Chief in the fifties.

Then to balance the picture about scenic beauty: "Now I wouldn't even shit on that!"

It was clear and cold out the window, a peach of a day really. The big white room was full of light. The New Yorker read emails from people interested in him. A young Greek man wrote to tell her UG had changed his life. "Tear it up, throw it away!" was his reply.

She read another with 'some idiotic question' about the chances for enlightenment: "The check-out girls in the supermarket have a better chance! Tear it up and throw it away!"

Mario told him the friend who looked after UG's apartment in town was coming to visit: "Good! I'll hand it over to him and walk away."

That morning he had gone through his little kitchen, throwing things away, with the Hungarian girl. He always pared down his belongings to the essential. Once in California he emptied some box of items with disgust: "What kind of person keeps all this crap?" and handing out extra razors and bars of soap collected along the way. Now he was in the kitchen of the apartment snacking on cheese. Women loved the sight of him rummaging around in the fridge, popping cheese or a Leonidas chocolate in his mouth, poking around to see what was on the counter. He stood at the counter munching a piece of croissant or dipping into the plastic container of rice sticks, popping a handful into his toothless mouth.

"So cute!" they giggled.

The New Yorker offered to buy him a new shirt: "UG, can I buy you another shirt like that one?"

"Why?" he asked briskly.

"It's wearing out, UG."

"I myself am wearing out."

He *was* wearing out. It was only a matter of time before he would be finished with us, finished with that body, finished with the imagined world. Every one of us felt lucky to be there and hoped for the best, but in the back of every one of our non-existent minds we knew it wouldn't be long.

The plan for my accommodations back in New York had evaporated. I still hadn't gotten used to asking people for a couch to surf on. What had been unthinkable behavior all my life was gradually becoming a mode of existence. The transition was not so smooth at these times. He must have sensed the despair. He was patting me on the arm, giving gentle reassurances in his way. Ah, that touch! So soft and reassuring as the world outside the bubble was waiting for me like wolves snarling at the door. I could have cried. Probably I did.

CHAPTER 38

*Day in and day out, for the rest of your life, that
is the only question for you—'How?'*

It was a muggy Halloween night in 2005. The rain misted
Newark Airport and the streets smelled of trash downtown.
Having failed to confirm my stay anywhere else, I let myself
into a friend's studio on Christie Street to spend the night on
his floor. I slept in my clothes on a musty old futon mattress
from one of his sculptures. Mice scurried over me in the night
and early in the morning the grinding roar and stench of trucks
unloading produce on the sidewalk greeted the day. There is a
black tee shirt in the windows of a souvenir shop in the East
Village with a picture of a gun pointed at you on the front, on
the back was written 'New York... It Ain't Kansas Dorothy!'

No shit.

I felt like a bum. After washing in the slop sink, I made my
way down to the street. The building was a concrete hive of art
hipsters. My friend was chopping his studio in half again to make
another space to rent out to supplement an absurd increase in
his own rent. The ways things were going it seemed like pretty
soon he'd be working out of a toolbox. Christie Street was
opened up like a transplant surgery. Construction was under
way for a new high-rise luxury condo on a corner that had been
a dirt parking lot for decades. Workers were crawling around
inside the street wound; human cockroaches scurrying across
steel beams, welding and banging around. We were gradually
being flooded out by new money. Every few months there was a

high rise where there had been a tailor shop or a pizzeria. The stomping ground of Puerto Ricans, junkies and Jewish garment workers was being ploughed under to accommodate the new world orderlies.

I took the F train up to midtown to see what was happening at the hotel. What else to do? UG greeted me and went right on talking to the others. The gang was sitting around like collapsed coffee cups after a brief night at the Motel 6 in New Jersey. They were roused by 5am for the ride into town.

UG stayed for two weeks while the plan was taking shape for California. Yogini visited her dad, I visited my mom and then we booked our flights out to California. I had some work to attend to before I got there. The upcoming art fair would get me through to spring, so by early December I could rejoin them in Palm Springs. Yogini was staying with an ex in the city; staying in a hotel room he was paying for. UG's money maxim rang in my ears, "No money, no honey." How had she ended up with a joker like me in the first place? Clearly it was a matter of proximity. The tank was always close to empty and I was always floating around on fumes. Of course, having taken my cue from the old man, I kept telling myself, *I have enough in my pocket, what is the sense in saving for a rainy day?* It's dangerous to copy these people, but it was a test I couldn't resist.

I was going. I knew I was going, but that didn't keep me from entertaining escape fantasies daily. He heard me from two thousand miles away.

When I called he greeted me immediately with the echoes of my thoughts: "I'm glad to hear you are staying away. The happier you are, the happier I will be that you are staying away from this place."

I sat in my mother's basement, watching crime shows to kill time without going insane in suburban fairyland. Yogini was visiting her father and dropped by my mother's place. Her visit was a welcome cover of normalcy. We went for a coffee in town. It was like spending time in limbo for the two of us. When she got out to California I called her. She said it seemed crazy to be there again. What was she doing in that living room again? She went inside and handed UG the phone. We had a funny conversation:

"I am glad to hear you are not coming to California."

"I'm not. I don't like California. I'm going to Palm Springs instead."

"What are you so attracted to in Palm Springs?"

"There is a whirling vortex there."

"What?"

"I said, there is a whirling vortex there."

"I don't understand your American English."

"I don't either."

On the first night of the job in Miami, all my belongings were stolen from my hotel room. On the last day, the hotel management called to tell me they'd recovered every item from another room in the hotel. Life was getting stranger.

From the window of the plane out to California the human presence on the land below looked flimsy. Human occupation was like toys on a carpet. From the sky you could feel the universe poised to swallow the carpet in a blink. I savored the hours alone in airport limbo before diving into the rapids again and over the falls.

The street names sound like high school cheerleaders. Sandy, Nicole, Debrah. As I stepped into the house, familiar faces greeted me like an ongoing summit meeting in a madhouse. The head of the organization, the capo, the boss, was sitting by the front door, skinny as a stray dog and full of pep, hit and dash.

"Look who is here. Nice to see you."

"It's nice to see you too, sir. You are looking well."

"She is taking very good care of me," he said, indicating the hostess.

GONER

The crowd had been stewing for a few weeks already. Saying hello was a hurried affair. "Cut, cut, cut!" he hollered when people hugged. I took a seat on the wall-to-wall carpeting in the back of the room. I was back in the bubble; he was rolling as usual.

"If you want to know about what happens after you die, go and kill yourself."

"Don't use that filthy word 'compassion'! It's a shit!"

"And if you do you will drop dead?" someone asked, finishing his usual line.

"What will happen then you never know, it will be the end of you."

He was reading about his life again, a detailed re-enactment of a conversation from an episode in his life, from the same text he'd been reading in Menton.

"He knows more about my life than I do!" he joked.

The details of his biography before the calamity read like accident reports. Nothing I could find predicted what happened, the only thing that came across loud and clear was what he'd sacrificed along the way to get his answer, and along the way, that question disappeared.

"What happened to UG after the calamity?"

"He never existed!"

On the second day I asked: "UG, how is it that you are not more famous?"

"You have to sell something to become famous. I refused."

We had high tea at a condo in a gated community rented by two couples, on generic furniture with frills, under a tall slanted ceiling. Out the picture window a trippy ultra-green lawn lit up the view. UG sat with his back to the window each time and Choochi Baba, Sid and Kara's border collie, brought money to him in his collar. Sid was a Vietnam war veteran. His wife, Kara, joined him in a fervent devotion to UG, having hosted nearly every single spiritual teacher who passed through Southern

California after their association with Osho. Sid described his first meeting with UG in Palm Springs as resembling the sensation of being in a jungle in the dark with death breathing down your neck.

We had coffee, cake, cookies and potato chips. UG reminded everyone of all the additives in the food: "Your cheese has morphine in it!" Lisa had recently found an internet link to that effect. "Even oatmeal is addictive, that is why I have stopped eating it," he said, with a note of disgust.

He picked up the phrase 'ocular projection' from a link related to the one question he said he wanted to put to the scientists and medical people: "Where is the image-making taking place inside of me?" Since the calamity that capacity had been destroyed. Was that the area of consciousness where the image-making takes place and the 'continuity' of personality was maintained? He was unable to form images of people once they were out of sight. What was left, he said, were words he could use to describe things, but no image.

"I can sit here in this chair forever. I am never bored. You people are bored because you think there is something more interesting happening somewhere else."

It sounded like he lived on the precipice of the indifferent black hole of total dissolution.

"I am dying all the time. You don't seem to understand, life and death are one continuous movement here. Every time a thought is born it is burned out here. You don't seem to understand. Those bastards put all those thoughts and ideas into you. Nothing you see, nothing you experience is your own. I am not any the different. I have no idea, no thought I can call my own. I am like Humpty Dumpty here. That UG can never be put back together again. He tried so many times, but there was no way he could stay any more, any longer."

He took yoga lessons in the early years to help him deal with the pain of the transition but in the end he said it didn't help;

the energy was reversed, going from top to bottom instead of escaping out the top, he said—whatever that meant.

"You are not ready to commit suicide," he said to friends in a conversation in 1970.

UG was not suicidal but in the momentum of his search, the fervor of his question, his willingness to risk everything, finally pushed him over the cliff; and when he found himself still alive it was in a new and unfamiliar place.

"The old man hinted that there was nothing there," he said of his conversations with Jiddu Krishnamurti. "In my imagination I thought there was a peak to climb. He said: 'Boy, there is the valley, you have to jump.' But I couldn't."

He described a death experience triggered in a JK discussion group in 1953 that revealed the intensity of his relationship with JK at the time. He spoke to the old man about it and the response seems to have been a bit gruff: "Why are you telling me about it? If there is anything to it, it will operate!"

Then UG asked if this meant he should no longer attend the talks and the old man was adamant, "Not at all!"

This was a UG I never saw, the young ardent seeker, following every word of his teacher, letter and sound.

"Looking back I could see that this (*the death experience*) had its own momentum."

Eventually the momentum tossed UG into oblivion like a bolt of lightning, an accident of circumstances, an unpredictable event. Acausal.

"I was going potty! I was lucky I didn't flip."

The toughness of his physical body and the rigor of his intellect may have saved him from death or insanity. Otherwise why would he repeat over and over that it took the lives or sanity of 'all those saints and sages that meditated seriously'?

Again, a feeling of being lost in a ridiculous exercise started to overcome me. Why was I wasting my time listening to him go on and on in there? Escaping to the back yard I sat under the tree, savoring the dry desert air while thoughts pestered me about what the hell I was going to do if this went on much longer. I felt like I was hanging on to nothingness. He wasn't kicking me out, he wasn't telling me to stay. I was there of my own volition, if there was such a thing.

"A real teacher will block all escapes."

"What is the personality and why are we defending it?" I asked him.

"There is no such thing, sir, all nonsense put in there by those scoundrels!"

He warned us all the time not to hang around: "You will lose your drive!"

Then: "There is a fine line separating me from the maddies!"

"What is the difference, UG?"

"There is no such thing as madness!"

If he was not a religious man, how was it that the only people who came to see him were engaged in the spiritual pursuit? What else was the function of this man if not to serve the spiritual community?

"Anyone who has done serious *sadhana* cannot brush me aside!"

"If you walk out of here and never come back I will be the happiest guy!"

His friends were people who had already been to the 'criminals, the holy men and saints' and because of that they had some inkling of what he was about.

"They should stay away from me, they are not going to get a thing from me. Let them go and find someone who will promise them the goodies!"

Few stuck around; the ones who did, did it with a frenzy.

"You are afraid that if you listen to what I say and take it seriously you will lose me."

His company was its own *sadhana*. He was a concentrated dose of what all those practices were striving to attain. He said

244

they could never deliver the goods. His advice was almost without exception to drop spiritual practice. He was the very thing he warned against.

The Links were getting wilder:

"Hey! You bastard, listen to this! This is the most interesting thing. 'Think of Jesus while you masturbate!' What's going on?"

Where the hell did Lisa find these things?

"'Are brains really necessary?' What took those bastards so long?" He was always irate about that: "I said this forty years ago as a student of psychology!"

Then: "Pope has AIDS! Probably when he was shot and they had to give blood transfusion the virus entered his body! Whom are they kidding?" Filling in some of his own details: "You know that new pope was his boyfriend?"

His favorite lines were out of celebrity magazines from the supermarket or serious medical journals and The Links. Links from a teenage girl somewhere in cyberspace who was obsessed with heavy metal music, tarot card readings and the 'philosophy of UG Krishnamurti' were celebrated along with the punk rock band somewhere called The Peabody who like the 'philosophy of UG Krishnamurti'.

In between the reading and the talking he sat absently picking at his fingernails, his eyelids became heavy, and he stared into space. At such times there was a silence and you could hear everything buzzing in the world, but there was no movement in anything. The phone number at the cottage was a state secret, and the message was clear, no one was invited unless they already knew him.

A woman came all the way from Sedona and asked about enlightenment. "Madame, what are you going to do with that?"

The way he put it made me ask myself the very same thing: *What the hell do I think I'm getting? What am I going to do with it anyway?*

He presented the frightening possibility of being lost forever from what you know. I couldn't listen to it without twisting it into a pretzel of what I wanted to hear.

"If I could give you just a glimpse of this, I'm telling you, you wouldn't want to touch it with a ten-foot pole!"

He had no personal life and his entire existence seemed to be out of his hands, even while he was in total charge of all of us. Or was he? Was all this my projection? What the fuck? All this misery; really I was just looking for an escape and pinning all my hopes on him.

"If there was free will, do you mean to say I would be sitting here with all of you?" he would joke. "I could have had a thousand Rolls-Royce limousines if I wanted!"

Whenever the phone rang he'd say out loud: "Shut up! Who are you? What do you want?"

He condensed his teaching into two words: "Your job in life is to *shut up*!"

I wished I could.

CHAPTER 39

There was the same hypocrisy there too, in the sense that
there was nothing in their lives; they were shallow—the
scholars, master-minds and remarkable people.

UG was fond of reading an exchange of letters between JK and
a French person named Dominique from the internet. Whether
real or imagined, a young professor of French language translated
the exchange where Dominique asked JK about UG's approach.
He read and reread the letter allegedly written by Jiddu, where
he said that the conflict Dominique perceived between UG and
JK was in Dominique's head.

UG's favorite passage was where JK said, "He (UG) caused
us to reset our clocks about spiritual matters."

He had the Reverend repeat this phrase time and again.

Perhaps to him there was no conflict between the two after
all. If you have no position there is no conflict with anyone. He
liked another line where JK said: "UG's approach, if there is
such a thing, would be very dangerous for you."

The words paid homage to his methods. Whatever was left
in his head when the calamity hit bounced around in the emptiness for the rest of his life. I don't think it meant a goddamned
thing to him by that point.

We took a drive to Brawley, California, near the Mexican
border, between the Salten Sea and the Chocolate Mountains;
a landscape of salt and sweet, like our high tea diet. Along the
way a desolate-looking resort called Bombay Beach sat on the
parched earth banks of the lake. The land was split with huge

cracks and a silvery light bounced off the lake, creating an eerie twinkling midday atmosphere. We drove until we were 86 feet below sea level. As we passed through one broken-down town, a putrid stench permeated the car from an intensive cattle farm by the side of the road, a horror show of industrial efficiency.

By the time we reached the town, tension was winging in the air. Yogini was having an emotional meltdown. Temperatures inside the lead car soared into the high nineties. When she asked for the heat to be turned down the driver suggested if she didn't like it she could get out. We stood behind a building on Main Street and she cried. I lost the brand new cell phone Sid loaned me. It had been a gift from Kara that he just started using that day. Desperate hunger landed us in at the doorstep of a Subway sandwich shop restaurant around the corner from a gas station. For the rest of the day afternoon lunch sat threateningly in our stomachs.

It was not the high point of our travels.

Back in the house UG was getting irritable: "Let's watch the Bullshit. It's better than the bullshit going on around here."

The previous summer someone brought a tape recording of a cable TV show called *Bullshit*, that exposed the darker side of a variety of popular religious, political and entertainment icons. The episode in question showed the darker sides of Mother Teresa, Mahatma Gandhi and the Dalai Lama. Gandhi slept with young virgins and discussed his enemas with them; the Dalai Lama had been running terrorist training camps for Tibetan monks in Colorado with funds from the CIA.

Mother Teresa was taking funds from all kinds of dictators and corrupt wealthy donors to run her nunneries. According to the hosts of the show the funds were meant for the running of the leprosy clinics in Kolkata, but Mother Teresa diverted them to build her army of nuns. A former nun from her order, who left in disgust, said that family members were not allowed to visit patients who were forced to live in humiliating and insanitary dormitory conditions. It wasn't for lack of funds, the bulk of which were being sent to her nunneries; Mother Teresa explained that they were meant to bring them closer to God. She took the idea that 'Christianity shows us the strength of suffering' to sadistic extremes.

UG constantly blasted these three already, so the new information gave him ammunition. Michael Jackson's sex trial was in the news at the time and he was quick to point out that they should leave Michael Jackson severely alone. Catholic priests should be punished for molesting all the boys first, then let them sort out all the other stuff.

After that we watched a Bill Maher special. Maher was the only public figure to speak out against the administration after 9/11 during the fascist lock-down on the American media. On the show Maher quoted the famous Kris Kristofferson song, "Freedom's just another word for nothing left to lose".

I heard UG quietly say, "That's it."

Before leaving California UG took us back to Brawley. This time the ride was easy. Someone photographed the two of us in front of the Town Theatre under the family name. He was getting a big kick out of it and so was I. He took my arm and pulled me along the street, stopping an old guy to point me out: "This is the bastard they named your town after."

Charlie was an old geezer with a friendly face. "Well, nice to meet you," he said, smiling at the startling introduction coming from the elderly foreigner. I asked if he knew a good place to get sandwiches and he pointed to a place called The Rock across the street—a Christian joint.

The whole gang actually enjoyed eating together for the first time in a long time. It was a rare moment of harmony. I was relieved to have the family name redeemed.

A new passport was waiting for me when I arrived back in New York. With nowhere else to go, I booked a ticket to India while I was sitting opposite him in the hotel room. He warned me: "If you go to India, I will not set my feet on the filthy Indian soil."

The comment ignited some latent paranoia. They were going to Europe for a few weeks but I couldn't afford that leg of the trip so I headed to Bangalore to wait and see if he meant what he said.

CHAPTER 40

Why do you bother about those fellows? They are
dead. You should pitch them into the river.

It was nice to be in charge of my own movements for a couple of weeks, hanging around in Bangalore, going here and there with my new friends. People kept asking when UG was coming, as if I knew! I was actually afraid to tell them what he'd said about my being there, but he finally did land in the early morning hours of February 15th, 2006. The Major, Chandrasekhar and Suguna were there to meet him, with a few others waiting outside. He came out to the receiving area and waited to make sure the others arrived safely with their luggage. When we asked if he'd like to sit down or go to the car he said, "What for? What's the hurry!"

Standing with us he played 'old man', joking and clowning with me, talking with the others in a light hearted banter. I was struck by the graciousness and concern for the others. Common decency and elementary manners were his code.

A massive celebration was underway in Bangalore to honor the fiftieth birthday of a world-famous guru that month. Thousands were flocking in from around the world and tables were set up in the airport with volunteers to greet out-of-town guests. The famous guru was nowhere to be seen of course. Here in the midst of the ordinary crowd was the real McCoy, a man who was the essence of what all the great spiritual poets of India spoke of. I was choked with emotion at the sight of him.

The little house was full when he arrived. Chandrasekhar wandered around the edges of the room, answering the phone and disappearing into his office. I rarely saw him on the couch with UG. The visit had a softer tone this time. The smaller crowd was offset by the ferocity of his voice, no matter what was going on. His latest weapon was a book from an internet publishing site called *Stripping the Gurus*. Spiritual legends of the nineteenth and twentieth century were exposed and accused of various plausible and not so plausible sexual perversions, aberrations and scandals. It was manna from heaven for him. Right away he was reading off the lists of their misconducts: "Not that I am against it! Don't get me wrong!" The Major was sitting cross-legged at his feet, resting his head on the coffee table with a combined look of acceptance and resignation.

"What, sir? What is going on?" he asked him, reading a devilishly enhanced story about Ramakrishna fondling Vivekananda, with the idea of offending the Major, who was way past arguing with him anyway.

"What, sir? It's says here that he was playing with the penis, (*pronounced, 'pen-iss'*), of Vivekananda!"

Vivekananda is possibly the greatest spiritual and political hero of India, so UG read with great enthusiasm about how: "He visited all the brothels in India, that bastard!" The Major just shook his head, "Yes sir." Not exactly humoring him, but with a resigned laughter at the absurdity of the claims. After the previous trip, people were only occasionally disturbed by these crazy new accusations.

He left the house more often than last trip with the excuse of seeing a young woman who had given birth to a premature child. He refused to allow her to bring the child or leave it behind. Instead he went to her. She cried tears of joy every time he showed up. He predicted the baby would one day be a great musician.

On the way down the stairs from their apartment I flushed with sweat as he stumbled slightly. His visit was late this year; it was already March and Bangalore was heating up. As my

scheduled departure approached, I woke up crying one morning. I was thinking what would happen if he fell and I wasn't
there. I decided there and then to cancel my return flight.

Yogini and I took a room in a new hotel by the ring road. We
managed to get one at the end of a hallway, furthest from the
road. She was constantly making endless comically frustrating
trips to the tailor for new outfits. The Indians have a joke about
the man who orders a shirt and is thrown in jail the next day.
After two years he is released and goes straight to the tailor.
The guy tells him, "Sorry sir, ready tomorrow." It was like that.
Still she couldn't help it any more than I could help my chronic
habit of scribbling or painting my 'horrible' pictures. Yogini and
I took a shortcut to 'work' every morning through a minefield
of shit and garbage, to avoid the ring road. It was a routine we
never quite got the hang of.

UG wanted to go to Madras to leave the house clear for a
ceremony connected to the baby. We arrived at noon under a
blistering sun. The cool marble floors were a welcome sight, as
UG took a seat in the hanging chair in an enclosed garden. On
that verandah, with a hint of a breeze, he swung in the chair,
looking like a frail schoolboy.

He was losing his voice again: "Don't tell me I have a cold,
you are all frightened chickens!"

He toppled around coughing as new people showed up from
Tiruvannamalai in the afternoon. An older French man said he
felt his *kundalini* rising in UG's presence. UG denied the whole
thing of course: "I don't see any *kundalini*! Where is the question of it rising?"

He talked until he had nothing but a shredded voice. Mahesh
showed up, inciting him to riot. He was writing an article for
the Indian press and brought politics into the conversation.
George Bush was on his way to India and UG's assessment of
his motives was unmistakably clear: "He is coming here to fuck
the Indians!"

He cut to the essence of the situation in answer to Mahesh's questions, while swinging around in the wicker chair like a bored kid. As always, Mahesh brought out a fiery tirade from him and the two of them were shouting back and forth despite UG's hoarseness. Mahesh was using the expression 'storybuster' to describe him of late. A storybuster was the unmarketable man living outside the narrative thread, a thread that keeps the entertainment industry alive.

Out of concern for his failing voice, I forgot both myself, and the seriousness of the situation and stepped out of line. Worried about his talking so much and loudly, when Mahesh asked him what India could do to achieve the world power that China now enjoyed, I said to Mahesh in a sarcastic tone: "How can you ask him of all people?"

UG got out of the swinging chair, stepped over and slapped me across the face three times, hard. He was quick as lightening. "Shut up, you filthy bastard! Keep your big mouth shut!"

I wanted to disappear. I was red before he even sat down. He went right on with the conversation but I was sweating. I'd been slapped so often by then you would think another slap was nothing, but this one was delivered with an unmistakable message. You never, ever interfered with what he was up to with someone else. For him it was already over. On the other hand, I was vibrating for some time.

A woman came late one night after he had retired for the night. Our hosts informed him in the morning and we went all the way to Auroville to have lunch with her. He walked all the way to a pleasant little house where the Korean woman had fixed a lunch for us all. He had fun talking with various people and commented on someone behind a door who didn't want to see him. The hostess was surprised he even knew she was there.

Back in Bangalore, UG threatened to leave if things got wild like the last time. Never mind that he'd orchestrated it: "If you keep telling the people I am here, I will leave! I am not going to have that same mess!"

It was too late. The word was out and more and more people called the house day and night, wanting to see him. Eventually the room began to fill up.

He went for more rides, insisting on riding in the Major's car despite the fact that it had no air conditioning and the air was horrendous. As often as another friend offered the use of a new air-conditioned car, UG refused. He was proving his point that the need for air conditioning was psychological nonsense. We invariably got stuck in traffic and he kept the windows closed against the pollution. The interior became like a stove and he nearly passed out twice after a ride. Finally he relented and took the new car, but the Major drove. He was very loyal.

Even though he had kept himself relatively obscure in India by refusing to promote himself or get up on a platform, UG was frequently quoted in the press. This rarely happened in the West, where he was invisible, off the grid, obscure.

I'd come to the conclusion that JK was a liar who held a phony public image up to the world, making him far more famous, saleable, all the rest, but the fact remains that UG followed that man for over twenty years. I had become far more attached to UG, more than I could possibly have been to JK, yet my ideas about the twenty-year tie the younger man felt and followed right up to the calamity were shifting as time went on. A black and white dismissal of JK as a total sham was smeared with grey smudges. The fact that not a day went by that he didn't remember his former teacher was a testament to something; what that was I didn't quite get yet.

He continued to feed me sugar to 'sweeten me up' while the bitterness of my life felt like an enormous steel trap of repetition. At first I thought he was telling me to 'taste the sugar' as in that sugar of enlightenment. He used to say of the old man that he thought he must have seen the sugar, but not tasted it. Was he just telling me to sweeten my view of the world and the people in it? "A phony will make you feel good at least for a while, reassuring you, giving you some treats, but a real guy will make you miserable." The long-range effects of his company came in brief glimpses of a contentment and happiness like nothing I'd ever felt before. The intensity of our interactions overshadowed most of this in the moment.

While he'd definitely toned down the song and dance routine of the last visit, he went to great lengths to create an atmosphere of total absurdity in another way. There was more talk, talk, talk, this time, and less physical chaos. No one could get a foothold on anything as usual. He suspended the usual rules of normal communication, stabbing at the collective mind with his fire and brimstone ridicule. The exaggerations lifted from the *Stripping the Gurus* text were deliberately laughable. He smiled as he dispensed them. I sometimes wondered if he was so disgusted by the ways of the mind that he gave up and made fun of it all. His methods evolved as a result of the way he functioned. He took in information, processed it and dispensed it through the clarity he lived in. The rest of us were lost, but while he was in a state of 'not knowing', he was not lost. Or maybe he was the most lost of all, and happy about it. Anything you can find has a limit. He saw what was in front of him and his electric eye shot down the falsehood automatically.

He was visiting old friends, chatting away up there on the couch. Giving career advice to a young man from Mumbai, he encouraged the aspiring film writer to give up his film scripts: "You are not going to make any money at that. Don't hang around here. Go and make money!"

In the middle of a good hearty shouting denunciation of Rajneesh he said, "Oh, I have to take care of my burning throat." Then immediately corrected himself, "No, no." And went right on talking, smiling, yelling over to Bob Carr who was recording the proceedings. (Bob had first met UG before the calamity, when they were both 'with' JK.)

Compared to what I have since seen of his visits to India and his general tone in talks with others, at times his behavior seemed crazier in the last couple of years. The endless repetition of ridiculous claims, the insane amount of energy, these are signs of a crazy person.

A young man came and inquired politely, "UG, I have a question…"

UG leaned forward on the couch and pointed at him: "No! You don't have any question of your own. Go to the scholars and discuss that shit with them!"

He said the only relevant questions were practical ones. Only these could be answered, the rest were schoolboy's logic. In this vein, he stated with great emphasis that all the psychiatrists were now killing themselves because they found out that psychoanalysis is dead. That became a new refrain.

Day after day I sat in the bedroom opposite him with my attention split between his talk and my writing. Ellen Chrystal was usually in the bedroom helping the New Yorker organize The Links. The bed was turned into a desk with index lists of his favorite links all over the place to make it easier to get what he wanted. The system only created more chaos when he ordered something from the New Yorker and started yelling at her all over again anyway. In a rare silence, several clocks could be heard ticking in different places in the room, all gifts from him. The ticking of a clock was a sound I came to associate with him. In the bedroom the ticking clocks sounded like quiet echoes of each other, bouncing time around in the space, filling the air with a musical tick-tock of minutes, hours and days.

A journalist interviewed UG for a local paper, boldly quoting the bulk of UG's extreme statements about everything from feminism and vibrators to the hopelessness of India's future. The day after the article appeared, a crazy young man from a nationalist group called the RSS showed up at the door. He was angry about UG's views about India, threatening to bring a gun so UG could kill all the Indians. A group of men shouted back at him from the floor.

Finally UG got up off the couch, marched over to within inches of his face, screaming at him to go to hell, lobbing his most ferocious lines into his shocked face: "If the Buddha were here that filthy bastard would fall at my feet!" The vitriol poured out of the tiny old man without a trace of fear. I was sitting on the floor just under them, shooting video of the exchange.

As UG turned away with what looked like rage, his face registered a relaxed and amused smile for a fraction of a second after the explosion. There was no one there to be afraid. He went back to the couch and said with a satisfied look, "I like that guy." Then, as if to explain: "You can translate what I am talking as anger; no, it is tremendous force. To silence his noise!" He said, "A worthless noise! It's finished."

In the mornings UG greeted us and gave me the remains of his coffee. He would alternate between us, one morning giving it to Yogini, the next to me. One morning he started complimenting her, then teasing her about wasting her life hanging around him. She was never comfortable with his teasing. Her tendency was to take him literally while he contradicted himself from one sentence to the next. At the end of the day, when she asked me what he meant when he said this or that, I could never make sense of it with her. I could only hear that I was giving my distorted take on it. The questions kept coming until she summed it up, dismissively I thought, as my being an intellectual, which was why I could 'understand' him and she couldn't. After a little chat like that I would simmer. It was maddening. In any case, his praise remained the same: "She is always there quietly in the background." He would then spike the punch by calling her a famous ballet dancer, making sure it sounded like belly dancer.

Most mornings when I woke up and saw the ceiling fan the first thought in my groggy head was, *Shit. I'm still in India.*

GONER

UG went to the farmhouse more often, hanging around for an hour or so. He talked, gave tours of his bedroom and set Chandrasekhar's grandson loose on me to beat me, bite me, punch me and scream at me. I have a picture of him taking a bite out of my arm. "Hey!" he said, as soon as the kid was in view. "Beat that gundu (*bald*) bastard!"

CHAPTER 41

I have no regrets, no apologies; whatever I am doing is automatic.

The Hungarian, now known as 'Bitchie', had booked a flight to go back to work, despite his warnings to her not to leave. Why was it that he would encourage some people to stick around, and others would be sent off? I had no idea. Now that she was leaving, he was demanding she pay him back two thousand dollars she borrowed from him in California. Usually he could insult her all day without affront but this time he was pushing her hard and blocking every escape.

"UG, I dunt haave des kend off monay."

"I don't care! I want the money, now!"

All afternoon she had been trying to confirm her reservation with the airline.

"The most practical thing for me to do is I get out of here on the 26th, I go to south of France, I work, and I come to Vallecrosia, and I give you the money and bas!"

"Nope. You have a checkbook?"

"I have bonk card, but is almost empty."

He explained slowly, with long comically timed pauses: "I wanted you to enjo-oy … your first visi-it …to America. I felt so bad when you were struggling…. so I gave you two thousand euro, and you promised to pay it immediately!"

"No UG! I did not! How could I?"

"You did! Otherwise, you mean to say you think I would give that kind of mone-ey…"

Pausing for emphasis, "…to a bitch like you?"

Everyone was laughing but her. He was smiling like a cat with a canary in its sharp little teeth. He looked over and saw her boyfriend recording the transaction: "Look! He's recording!"

"Yeah, he likes that," she said with a slightly peevish tone in her voice. Then he looked into the camera and asked: "Should I continue to call her a bitch?"

She was nervously tapping her fingers on the coffee table. He suggested, "Comon'—let's go and get…"

"Hey! I have to get to France!"

"No! I want it. I won't let you go."

"Hey! UG!"

"No. Not a chance!"

Putting his cup down with a deft "Nope", he gestured in refusal, that slight wiping of the board with a movement of the hand, leaning back in the couch.

She launched another excuse: "I ask you when I should book my ticket, and you say: 'Don't book your ticket because I don't know when I'm going.' so I ask you again: 'UG, which day is a good day?' 'Ahh I don't know', and den, 'Ahhh twenty-six is a good one'… So I did it."

Now she was rolling her eyes at him, exasperated.

"And you cancel it! Today is twenty-six!"

Then making fun of her quoting his 'aah and ooh', "Not a chance!"

"And then you tell me, 'Tell to these Air India guys they can help, and I tell them and he all the day long he help me and he called Mumbai, the big boss and everything."

"Who? You are making up stories, bitch!"

"I'm not. I'm not!"

"Cash on the barrel!" he demanded, slamming flathanded on the table. "Two thousand, plus interest, three thousand euro you have to give!"

As it went on the laughter became slightly more uncomfortable, we were wondering how all this would end. She was playing with the napkin he used, slapping it around on the table. Getting more and more irritated…

"Come on! I will write off one thousand, and you will give me two thousand, which you took from me, in America-a! Otherwise…"

"UG I will give it to you."

Now he was deliberately ignoring her, making a list of her options on his hand:

"Beg…"

"I am!"

"…borrow, forge, steal! Do anything that is needed to raise money!"

The New Yorker started writing a check.

"What is she doing?"

"She's writing a check"

"Where is the cash?"

"It's a check!" explained the New Yorker.

"Your check will bounce!"

Finally he went to his room and brought down the money he was demanding, $2,500. He gave it to her Israeli boyfriend who was always broke, to lend it to her to give to him as her payment. Then he handed it to the New Yorker, as a part of a 'loan', a bit of a joke given the amount of money she had 'forced' on him over the years. In the end, 'Bitchie' owed her broke boyfriend money he would never demand, and UG handed the sum to her original source of borrowing.

People were scratching their heads for hours after that one; but her flights were all delayed, and she ended up not getting the job in the end. It was strange; he couldn't have known any of that. Like so many things that happened around him, it was just like he said:

"It's out of your hands, it's out of my hands. Just leave it alone."

CHAPTER 42

The culture has made it impossible for the personality to express itself in its own way, because the culture has different ideas.

He was emphasizing that he was a functional rather than an ideational being; his preferences and taste were still there, he pointed out, an obsession for matching colors, or a favorite brand of yogurt. I mentioned one morning that he cited tradition when it backed his commentary.

"UG, for a non-religious guy, you seem to like quoting traditions."

"I like tradition when it suits me."

He asked me to read his palm for the hundredth time, so I pushed that game to see what he would do. I should say I knew nothing about palm-reading other than what I'd been hearing around him, but his palms would make a believer out of anyone. They had the most amazing lines, even from a design point of view. The right palm had a huge break in the life line, indicating the calamity. It was full of other lines extending from the base up to and running right up through the fingers with very few obstructions. There were stars all over it, in significant points with boxes of support around all the major lines. There was plenty of material to improvise on. I said he didn't travel at all, since he obliterated all space, he was everywhere at the same time. JK was in his left palm and Ramana Maharshi was in the right palm.

"What about Ramakrishna?" a local asked.

I said he was integrated into both palms.

UG said nothing, smiling all the while.

Then I held the wrists together; he extended his hands at perfect right-angles. The agility was impressive. After the calamity his wrists had become more flexible, he said.

Chandrasekhar said that, shortly after the calamity, when UG was talking to a small group in Switzerland, someone asked if anyone else had achieved that state. UG stood and folded his hands in *pranam* and in Telugu he gave thanks to all those who had been in this state before and left the room. Later he said he was bidding them good riddance since they were now thrown out of his system. I heard him say on an early tape that after the calamity his hands would spontaneously go into the *pranam* gesture like two magnets forced together and could not be pulled apart. His explanation of these phenomena was always cut-and-dried physical science: "After all, all bodies are magnetic fields."

It was a perfect day, hot inside with a pleasant breeze outside, as we sat listening to him attack JK after lunch. There was a JK devotee in the room whom he had known for some time, so this went on for as long as she was in the room. UG read links from the internet, as filthy as he could find, delighting in the most outrageous passages. He was smiling and laughing all the while.

That afternoon we watched videos of him in Yercaud and Bangalore from 1996. It didn't seem so long ago. I thought about my life in New York back then: struggling with some stupid job, trying to get my career on track. I couldn't help wondering where I would be now if I'd met him then. Some of the people in the video had since died. An old friend named Brahmachari was dancing and making jokes with UG.

"Where is that bastard now?" UG asked out loud, then answered himself, "He's dead" in a monotone voice.

That night when dinner was over, the late evening session started. The Major told us that UG used to tell him what a fantastic cook Mario was. Overhearing this, UG covered his ears saying "Oh my!" In between yelling at the New Yorker about The Links and punching me, he was talking about *upma*, a South Indian dish she was fond of.

Then he brought the focus back to his favorite topic, JK, with a vengeance, since the lady who was a devotee of his was still sitting there. It seemed he was satisfied only when she was in tears.

"Stop, UG! Krishnaji was a god to us!" she said.

"I am not impressed."

I'd seen some early footage of this stunningly beautiful young Indian woman before. She was a little older now but still beautiful. Sitting at his feet like an exotic flower in a lavish pastel sari made of silk and crinoline, she spoke in a breathy English Indian accent. Her gracefully stylized movements reminded me of a geisha girl. Tears were welling up in her eyes as he blasted JK with more than the usual vehemence, particularly about his sex life. He repeated several times in front of her that, while JK was a success story, he was a total failure since he hadn't convinced any of us to walk out on him and never come back. This came in reply to the question:

"Has anyone come close to getting the hang of what you are saying?"

"Not one."

It was just like the old man.

It was a fact that, in that sense, UG had 'gotten it' from JK. He walked out and never set foot in the tent again. Had anyone walked out on him? "No," he said.

A local drunk showed up every night begging for money. UG always gave the man a few hundred rupees after a brief demonstration of yogic postures and a *bhajan* or two. UG borrowed from the New Yorker, slapped the rupees into his palm, giving him a *namaste* and telling him to go and get drunk.

"That is better than sitting around here listening to all this crap!"

New people had come, and from the looks on their faces, it must have seemed like the Mad Hatter's tea party from *Alice's Adventures in Wonderland*. There was no sense to be found anywhere. Anyone who took up a line of argument or spiritual question was demolished. He started making people dance again. Anyone who wondered what they had come for left soon enough. It was fitting that a deaf Australian musician from Perth joined in with great enthusiasm, playing his guitar and leading the room in songs like Abba's *Money, Money, Money*. Soon the chaos was going full swing.

The Major was convinced this would be UG's last trip to India but I thought the previous trip was going to be the last and he'd proven me wrong. It was almost the hottest time of the year and he was as energetic as ever.

A DVD was being played of a visit from UG's family while he was in New York (mercifully without sound). I thought of 2003 when they visited, and I felt like such a fool among the successful young professionals. The rift between life around UG and the average social life was stark on those occasions. The family members were successfully participating in the world and he talked about them as a proud father. Without sound the video took on the quality of an old-fashioned home movie. It was one of the last videos with him wearing dentures, and it seemed like decades since that visit. Time was flying and he was gradually withering physically.

He continued the reading with pornographic links full of the words 'bullshit' and 'motherfucker', some of his favorite words of late for shocking the audience. There were some passages about Osho, "The Greatest Pimp the World has ever seen!", and then he turned to obscure items about JK's failed gambling attempts in volume three of his magnum opus, *More And More Links*.

His repeated claim that The Links would end up in the archives of the government of India seemed like an almost

Dadaist gesture, guaranteeing him future obscurity. I cannot imagine anyone else making sense of the collection of comments about him or the letters U and G as they related to anything and everything.

The videos had the feel of something that once he was gone would be half dead, like staring into a grave. In the videos transferred to DVD format, the soundtrack drifted behind the image about halfway into the recording, "Sound follows behind light in perception". We watched one tape from a video camera someone left running on the floor under a table pointed at the bottom of a cheap metal chair. You could see the feet of two Indian women walking back and forth with some idle chat going on in the background. They were strangely hypnotic fragments. He used to say that, for him, the movement of an arm was as profound as any sacred verse. These were the things we looked at during the course of the day in real time while sitting with him. After sufficient exposure to him, such footage became as relevant as anything else. Watching the images, I wondered whose legs those were, and whatever happened to them. It could even be that they were also dead by now.

CHAPTER 43

Here the cumulative process has come to an end: the
only action is physical action—only on that level.

The week before he was scheduled to leave, UG was talking
himself hoarse again, grinding himself—or us—into a pulp
with a piercing, hostile tone. Many times I had the feeling that
if we were not there to listen to him, he'd disappear into thin
air, so maybe talking kept him in his body; if he didn't talk
he'd dissolve. From what I felt just sitting next to him, this
seemed like a possibility. Things became confusing and where
one began and the other ended was not so clear any more.

After almost two months in India I was exhausted. As the
finish line approached and one person after another asked questions he refused to answer, I felt the hopelessness of 'getting'
what he was about. I was fed up and the world outside the circus was worse. If he couldn't solve the problems with my head,
nothing could.

UG told Chandrasekhar to read the *Nadi* reading his grandfather had commissioned for him in 1926 that predicted significant events of his future.

In a quiet, nearly invisible, moment in the dining room UG
told me that JK had said to him:

"You have to carry on my work."

This comment was so surprising that it nearly disappeared.
I even thought I imagined it. He just managed to slide certain
things into you with such a subtle touch that they dropped very
far inside and the clatter of contact took some time to register.

Once you heard them, they never left.

Through the *Nadi* reading Chandrasekhar listed the major changes in UG's life in 1986, immediately following the death of JK. He went to India after receiving some money from English friends for a place in Bangalore. It was the year he went public, giving radio and television interviews for the first time since the calamity. The first book, *The Mystique of Enlightenment*, came out that year and Valentine stopped traveling with him. In the face of all this evidence it was obvious that the year JK died was a year of huge changes. In another moment of homage that morning he said JK had given him the push to stand on his own. That was the 'walking out' that no one around him had yet managed.

Not that we knew of anyway.

The next morning after breakfast a young Indian man named Nagesh, who had taken UG's Money Maxims to heart and was beginning to make a lot of money, teased Mohan about a passage he found in his notebook that made the declaration: "Mohan is the only enlightened person on the planet." When UG heard this he started teasing Mohan from the couch, congratulating him with great enthusiasm: "You are the only one I've ever met in my entire life!"

He hopped off the couch and sat on the floor next to Mohan; before we knew it he was taking the dust of Mohan's feet. Mohan tried to back away, terrified. When UG dropped a little hard on the floor, The Major and I eyed each other with a worried look. He winced slightly when he did it and when he was finished with his demonstration he allowed me to help him stand up again.

On the afternoon of the 26th UG read some passages about JK out loud from Mukunda Rao's book, condemning JK, insisting that there was nothing to get from him, repeating the man's name over and over. I was listening to all this with his words from a 1968 recording running through my mind: "I wonder if

Krishnamurti's abstractions have thrown anyone else into this state?" What he was doing was anybody's guess.

In the tapes of 1967 he gave detailed descriptions of the final talks he attended in the tent. JK was talking about the comparative mind and silence. UG described 'the strange *samadhi*' he was in while sitting in the tent. All this tumbled through my mind while he dismissed the influence of a man whose name he repeated for the next forty years. Once again it hit me that almost my entire adult life had been spent under the influence of these two Krishnamurtis, first from a distance, then up close.

In the evening some light singing went on, while UG sat on the couch looking wasted, propping his head up with his hand. Nagesh sang one song after another under the pale green fluorescent light of the living room. In my exhaustion, the harsh light of the room full of dark silhouettes was transformed into a blank theatre of infinity and finality. There was a sting of death, a brittle shell of appearances over a bottomless darkness full of energy. We focused on one presence that never focused on anything. He was the sparkling nectar of death, stroking his jaw absently while Nagesh sang another song, lulling us further into the pale dream. At a physical level, anyone could see his body was exhausted, but it seemed as if whatever was driving the thing before us was just a slender flame on the surface of a sun hovering just beyond the range of our limited sight. A thin paper was suspended over the unbearable beauty of nothingness.

CHAPTER 44

'I don't know what to do, I am helpless, totally
helpless'—as long as you think you are totally helpless,
you will depend on some outside agency.

The Sunday morning before we left, Yogini was depressed. "You
get used to everything I guess," she said softly.

We were picking our way through a trash pile on a shortcut
through a vacant lot, mounded with scattered piles of dirt, old
bits of clothing, food wrappers, plastic bottles, worn shoes and
shit, both human and animal.

Arriving at the house, we were served the usual coffee in
metal cups. The big smiling banker came in with his wife and
an enormous bundle of rupees for UG. Just then he started
teasing Yogini again about her 'share' of the money. She was
visibly upset, shaken up. Months before she'd handed over a sizable sum to him. He rarely said a word about her contributions.

When I asked her how it felt she said, "Now I feel like I
can leave."

She didn't though. He was playing around, but she gave him
a withering look and a cold comment so he moved right along,
unaffected.

She was like a cloud wisping around all the time. At times
it was smog, at other times a twinkling of fairy dust. She was
always dressed to kill. We had our little breaks for lunch. They
were pleasant interludes where we got along fine. We could have
so much fun on our own in public. It's strange how the whole
thing imploded in private.

Around UG there was too much intensity to manage communication. A local told me that in Tiruvannamalai, where Ramana lived, married couples often separated and those who went for serious *sadhana* had a tendency to fall in love.

UG's phrase about chocolate was: "Chocolate produces the same chemical reaction as falling in love. It's better to eat chocolate than fall in love and mess up your life!"

Yogini loved chocolate.

Suguna was anticipating the arrival of her second grandchild on Chandrasekhar's birthday. UG took advantage of this joyous event to tell the story of how he forced his wife to have an abortion in Chicago when she was 6 months pregnant:

"That was the only time in my life when I felt really bad. I had to throw the fully formed baby into the trashbin." It was his most grisly story.

Much, much later I would hear another confession second-hand, from Suguna herself. When he made his usual comment about never crying even once in his life, she asked, "UG, you never cried even once?"

Suguna was not a questioning person, but very sincere. Unable to resist sincerity he thought a minute and said: "Yes, when I was in London, and saw what had become of me, the people I was surrounded by, all criminals, I wept."

He was speaking of the period of wandering destitute in 1960. He would have been eligible for the dole but UG never took handouts. He obviously preferred to steal. Douglas told me there were hints at a night spent in jail for shoplifting food at that time. Similarly, when Mahesh asked if he really never felt fear in his life, he said: "When it was all collapsing around me," just before the calamity, "I was afraid."

Sitting next to him that afternoon, I had a vision of the sound of his voice as a vessel of emptiness that displaced the contents of the collective mind with its vibration. What was needed for the body to survive was left intact around the edges.

Outside, the Major told me UG offered two things to his audience: *Nirasha*, desirelessness, and *Nirmoha*, non-attachment.

Back inside, UG summarily addressed this claim:

"I am asserting with all my emphasis that wanting desirelessness is no different from the desire to run away with your next door neighbor's prettiest girlfriend. You must give up the sunsets and sunrises, then you don't have to give up staring at the bouncing breasts."

Then again: "You have to lose consciousness before the physical death can happen, then you won't know what is happening."

JK's line about how we were, 'sharpening the very instrument which is the problem' had a new voice: "There is no such thing as fear of the unknown. You are afraid of losing what you know."

There is no relationship between the two, another echo of JK's teaching. When I read this back to UG seconds after writing it, it seemed as if he was monitoring my progress more than anything, and he didn't correct me, or add any comment, which was itself comment enough.

One question that inevitably came up in my mind while I was around him was, *Why should we believe him if he tells us over and over that he never believed anybody else?* Obviously I couldn't let go of him while I was leaning on him. It was the classic dilemma of replacing one thorn with another. Logically there was no way out of it. Was there actually something in his company that was working on all of us? Was it really that we just didn't have the means to see it?

Hope springs eternal like a weed.

The more I investigated his life story, the more the exercise resembled a self-generated fiction based on hearsay, designed to fool myself out of my miserable circumstances, by searching for clues in a closed case.

In the relative world, what he said was rife with lies. He lived in the absolute, and from there everything was unknown, unknowable and unnamable.

"I am telling you, you cannot be interested in what I am talking about!"

Of course not. This is one thing that logically followed. So where did my interest come from? As always, my logical reasoning led to a dead end. It was a way of staying busy, occupying the mind.

"Round and round ran the ragged rascal."

He was too absolute. What he was saying amounted to physical death. His life story was evidence of his willingness to brush the whole thing aside.

"Can you throw in the towel and turn your back on the whole structure?"

"No. You are not ready to commit suicide!" was the answer.

Of course the great teacher, Gurdjieff, almost killed himself trying to get the same thing but he didn't seem to have made it. The fates will have their way.

"If there is any moral man, he will never talk of morals and he will never do anything immoral."

"The ego is nothing but the conflict between right and wrong, good and bad. It is an abstraction; it does not exist."

He could say that. Others were in no position to.

Mohan's questions were coming fast and furious as his departure loomed:

"UG, who is the listener?"

He was like a dog chasing its tail, digging a rut in the ground in the process. It seemed as if Mohan thought if he could ask his questions quickly enough, he would trip over his own answer and the whole thing would fall apart, but it never quite got to that point.

"How do you hear me when I ask this question?"

"You are talking to yourself."

"Who is answering the question if UG is not there?"

"No-one."

"How can I look without thought?"

"You cannot look for one second, if that happens you drop dead."

Exasperated, but not finished, Mohan demanded once more: "Can you not come clean once and for all and give it to me?"

"No."

A doctor from Mangalore called Dr Swami found a spiritual category for the beatings. The masters used beatings to accelerate the spiritual progress of their followers. UG immediately incorporated this into his talk while beating me.

"You see what that book said about JK beating David Bohm to accelerate his spiritual progress." He referred to some made-up passage in a non-existent book.

"I am hastening up his spiritual practice!"

Pow!

It seemed that any and all behavior was easily categorized in Indian spirituality. It was impressive and infuriating at the same time; another case of recognizing only what is already known; getting stuck in the honey of familiarity all over again, as the mind sharpened the pattern of recognition with clever inquiry. Each thing recognized is part of the insanity and the room was an insane asylum.

UG's presence made it seem so. Who was crazy and who was not was all a matter of learned perspective. The ineffectiveness of thinking was reflected in his absence and the glimpse of our ideas in the mirror of his life. Like a junkie, the knowledge inside demands another fix and another fix and another fix all the time. A withdrawal from questions is life-threatening, and in order to avoid cold turkey of waking up, we kept it going—or it kept us going.

"He was hitting Bohm all the time until he went crazy!"

I wasn't crazy yet. I used writing as a means of coping. It was my armor. It kept the wheels turning in a bloodbath of confusion. His beatings were harmless. I wasn't injured aside from a stinging sensation. It was the constant shock to my ego that got me. It was like of his curse words: Slap! = Fuck! Punch! = Shit!

As long as he saw or felt any shock registering in me or in the audience, he continued.

He made the absurd claim over and over again that his teeth were growing back: "My words have failed to bite you so I will have to bite you with my thirty-two teeth!"

Like the famous sage, Kabir, who said he'd wasted his life selling mirrors to blind people, UG was now repeating: "I am a complete and total failure!"

He said he had no idea how he had gotten himself into his state, so how could he advise us? He didn't know how he did it; all he knew was that he was 'thrown out': "This is the story of the body throwing UG out!"

No matter how I felt about what was going on, or how irritating things could and would get, the idea of going back to New York was depressing. The trip was coming to an end, I was tired of the constant abuse. Even if it was helping my 'spiritual growth', my new and very overpriced Swiss glasses were slightly bent; every time he swiped them off my face I was sure he'd break them. I had scratches on my face from where he was hitting me and my eyes were burning from air pollution.

Outside, under the green-tinted roof, I got to talking with a communist who had been an activist for years. I had noticed him sitting quietly with the others for weeks, a pleasant-looking man in his sixties with a youthful energy. I asked him how he met UG. Apparently a friend told him about UG but he was not interested. UG advised his friend: "Tell him I was married and had four children. I know what it is like to fondle a woman's breasts."

This, coming from a supposed holy man, brought him out of curiosity. He kept coming back for thirty years.

CHAPTER 45

The intelligent people are the dullest and dumbest people
(laughter)—they are the most gullible people.

March 30, 2006: UG was set to leave that night, it was cool out that morning, but inside it got hotter by the minute. He hit me three times—hard—as soon as I sat next to him, so I got up and went outside. I couldn't leave, because Yogini was there, but I was fed up to the teeth. Then mosquitoes started swarming around my head. It was a perfect metaphor. He just went on and on in there; it was insane. I wanted to get the hell out. I didn't have long to go, but aside from the fatigue and paranoia, Yogini was panicked about one of the women she was sure was angry with her for some reason. Everyone was tense and he was pushing us all right down to the wire.

People who had been waiting for six weeks to see him came in droves now that he was about to leave town.

"UG, are all aspirations the same?" a young man inside asked, with genuine curiosity. UG's answer was unrelated.

"He is expert in diverting us," the Major said.

"UG, is there any difference between choosing and an aspiration?" he tried again, trying to take it further.

"No." This brief answer was followed by an example of choosing chocolates and then another unrelated story about a young woman who committed suicide, and then:

"Sir, there is no difference between selectivity and pleasure. There is no such thing as pleasure and no such thing as pain. You want to be happy all the time. Your wanting to stretch it

277

LOUIS BRAWLEY

longer and longer is choking you."

His words were sharpened to a fine point, poking our addled brains with the shards of his unknowable wisdom, but, "Don't call it wisdom!"

One woman had been coming for years. Sensing it might well be the last time she ever saw him she was pressing him about how to approach what he was saying.

"UG, we are tired of trying, what can we do?"

"Your feet are so tired from running, running all the time!"

She didn't get what he meant, desperate for some clue from him before he left.

"Anyway it's not important! You are a sharpy, making lots of money," he comforted her with an uncomfortable diversion.

"What is the point then, UG?" she pleaded.

No answer.

"You got your answer anyway!" The Major stepped in and put a period on that sentence. He and Dr Swami were jumping in at the last moment, interpreting what had just transpired with UG for the others, encouraging hesitant people to speak up while they had the chance.

That afternoon we visited the young mother and her new baby for the last time. When UG left she was in tears again.

278

CHAPTER 46

*The continuity of life and the continuity of
thought are two different things.*

March 30, 2006 Bangalore. It was cool outside. The squirrels
in the street were chirping loudly. Inside it was getting hotter
by the minute. Some new guy wanted to talk about his death
experience. UG replied curtly that if there were anything to it,
he wouldn't be sitting there. Again, after three hearty slaps first
thing in the morning, I went away and, when I came back, he
immediately asked me to come sit on the couch again. I backed
off into the other room out of sight.

It was Indian New Year's Day and the 5-year-old niece of
a friend came and insisted UG come to her family's house for
a high tea. Her uncle later told me that a friend who lived
in the house was panicked, because if UG had not agreed to
attend the invitation, it meant their devotion was inadequate.
UG took the whole parade over in cars and there was a big
celebration and the father gave UG 1500 rupees in a show of
generosity. It was the height of hypocrisy. The same man was
doing everything in his power to destroy his son financially for
leaving a religious order.

Just as I was thinking of this we stepped out the front door
and UG took my arm, saying: "Why do they give it to me? I'll
just give it to him." (*The son.*)

As soon as we got back to Chandrasekhar's house, UG
came outside to give the boy money. He had to chase him
down the street to make him take it, even though he needed it

desperately. The kid was afraid he would be accused of getting special treatment.

By late morning people who couldn't fit inside watched from the window. It looked like a zoo turned inside out. And of course Mahesh came at the last minute on his orders.

UG called me over to the couch with the two of them and began knocking our heads together with the enthusiasm of a schoolboy. Then they went out to the front of the house to talk on the couch. Next door a crowd of young kids decked out in their finest clothes stood gaping, giggling at the famous film director Mahesh Bhatt. I'm sure they had no idea who UG was, nor did they probably care. They asked for photos with Mahesh who was happy to oblige.

Later Mahesh and I sat in the bedroom talking.

"UG basically said to me with that call: 'Come here, be beaten and go away.' I hear and I obey!"

UG's call was a rare occasion lately. He was pushing Mahesh out on his own. I asked what differences he saw in UG's methods in his later years.

"A farcical dimension is being introduced," he said with his usual flair. "It has become like a madhouse around UG. The lingo changes and a new vocabulary has erupted from the subterranean region, something incomprehensible."

"What about all this joking around?"

"UG was always funny in private but lately his humor is being displayed more openly. You've walked into a digital age of MTV jump-cutting and UG is right there, using it as a means to blast the spiritual foundations.

"On the way to the airport in Mumbai I spotted an image of Vivekananda on the back of a bus with the quote, 'Only those who live to serve are truly alive. Others are more than half dead'. Of course I thought of UG and as soon as I arrived UG started talking about Vivekananda visiting all the brothels of India and Sri Ramakrishna playing with his penis and fucking him from behind! All icons are demolished as you go. The means he employs may shift, but the position was the same from the beginning. Fire burns everything with the same heat."

UG started hollering for Mahesh, "Where is that bastard?" He was like a child who wanted his favorite toy.

"He's in there talking to the other bastard, UG!" someone said.

The room was packed to standing room only. UG called me out to take the remains of his coffee, "Is it your turn or hers?"

"Hers, UG."

"What are you doing?"

"We were talking."

"About what?"

"What else is there to talk about, UG? *You!*"

Those final hours in India saw him in fit and shining form, right up to the last minute. At lunch, he ate quickly, slipped into the kitchen and threw out his lunch. As he passed the door on his way back to the couch, like a lion entering the den, I heard him say under his breath, "What's happening?"

Gliding into the chaos of people packing the room to see him for the last time in India, he was flowing like lava from a volcano. Many different people blew through the house like leaves in a storm.

Uma was weeping inconsolably, convinced she would never see him again. As it turned out she was right. While she sat crying next to him at the dinner table he carried on eating. Turning to us when she left the room he asked, "Why is she crying? I never knew she was such a sentimental person." Uma was devoted to UG and had recorded the Money Maxims professionally at her own expense.

I couldn't believe it when he started giving an interview at eight o'clock. I just wanted to make sure I got the hell out of town. Now I pictured myself missing the flight and being left behind with my slightly grimy wardrobe.

Just as he brushed past me at the foot of the stairs, he told me to wait five minutes and then come get his bag. The woman with the premature baby showed up with her husband just then. Having been granted permission at the last possible minute to come and say goodbye, they asked to go up and see him. I worried that they might find him half-dressed. Following them up I saw him emerge from his room dressed in Western wear. He looked like a different person. I hadn't seen much of him since morning. I was worried about his physical body, another pointless concern. He was an expert at handling himself and looked as fresh as if he'd just arrived. She was lying on the floor before him in full prostration with her hands touching his feet, crying.

"Oh UG *garu*! We want to thank you so much for everything!"

"For what?" he said, as if confused, when the husband also dropped to the floor. "Hey! Why are you doing that?"

It would be impossible not to be moved by the sight of their unashamed devotion. Without sharing their religious background, I knew how they felt, although at the same time I could never have expressed myself like that. He never failed to ask people why they bothered with these gestures of devotion, imploring them not to, but they couldn't help themselves.

Descending into a chaotic sea of faces, shaking hands, with *pranams* to all, he glided gracefully through the crowd. With a final wave as he got into the car he took leave of Suguna and Chandrasekhar's house for the last time.

CHAPTER 47

You separate yourself from that awareness and
create an entity which is not there actually.

I woke up in the back bedroom of a friend's apartment in Brooklyn. A seedy grey light edged past the blinds as the radio alarm on the other side of the wall went off and my cell phone rang. It was Yogini calling from Gstaad. They were already looking for places to stay for the summer. It was March and summer seemed like a lifetime away. My cash reserves were running low. I thought of all the people who told me the money would come from somewhere. "He'll take care of you." All I could think was: *Where are they now? Where is he now?*

On the other hand, after being with him for extended periods, when you got away it was as though a heavy backpack were suddenly dropped. I had more energy. It was as if I could almost fly. I was being dragged kicking and screaming into a new existence. His influence washed through me like clean water gushing through a dirty pipe.

I spent the next two months listening to the first digital copies of UG's talks from recordings made as far back as 1967. There were interviews from within weeks of the calamity. They were a revelation. It was astonishing to hear him describe decades of struggle with Jiddu Krishnamurti and the degree to which he devoted himself to that man.

If you looked at the biographical facts of his life it was obvious, but he spent so much energy denying and making up stories about it that it was a shock to hear this version coming from him. The phrases were familiar, as if a deck of cards had been reshuffled, and the meaning shifted around. He described an English boy who insisted that UG was functioning differently than he was. He found UG more interesting than JK. UG goes on to describe how he used the boy as a mirror to understand what was happening with himself. It was a line word for word that he now attributed to JK: "That man (JK) was using me as a mirror for himself."

Something unraveled as I listened. Did it change the story? Was he saying something different? No, but what was on the earliest tapes was the story of his struggle. In those tapes there is the feeling that by then it was an empty story for him. Not once in all those hours of tape did I get a feeling that what he was communicating to us lately was different from what he'd been saying right from the beginning. The only difference was in the method. The words, the people and what they brought out of him were different in different circumstances at different times. It was a revelation about the irrelevance of facts.

I called Douglas Rosestone to find out what he remembered about the early days with UG before the calamity. He had seen the other side of UG's relationship with JK. I asked him about the before and after:

"Just before the calamity, UG was in what I would describe as a rage against his imprisonment in whatever it was he felt trapped by. UG was a very faithful person. It was not easy for him to brush aside the old man. There is a state before the final awakening of these people where they are very tenuously attached to the world. They are in a constant state of *samadhi*, which was the case with UG, even though he tried to conceal it. UG was torn between his loyalty to JK for helping him throw off a Theosophical background and wanting to be free of his influence. He was rough back then, with a supreme indifference and lack of concern for people's feelings."

It was like discovering old footage to talk to Douglas. Of

course it was also filtered through Douglas. No matter who I talked to, the version was slightly different.

I called Yogini in Europe. They were in the car and she turned the phone over to UG. I told him I'd just spoken to Douglas.

"Why do you want to talk to that guy?"

"I am investigating you, that's why!"

As an FBI agent I was just doing my job. UG laughed and hung up the phone.

A few days later I called Douglas again to ask about UG's reasons for being in Gstaad in the first place. UG said he discovered Gstaad in 1953, so it was a place already etched in his mind. It's pretty clear he was there because of JK. There is no record that I know of that JK was there before 1960 but he had traveled and lived all over Switzerland since the 1920's, and it was impossible to imagine UG was just there by coincidence.

Back in 1953 he was still hashing it out with JK one on one. It's interesting to note that the same year he had the death experience, he traveled to Gstaad, where he told us later he wanted even then to settle for the rest of his life. His wife was having none of that. It was too cold for her.

All this investigating just created new images. The more you know, the more information there is to overcome. I couldn't help it.

On one of the tapes the interviewer asked UG to recreate the events that lead up to the calamity. He carefully described the talks JK gave during the summer of 1967, starting with a discussion about education, shifting to the subject of the comparative mind. It was like unlocking the secrets of the universe.

"The talks on education were going on. The subject didn't interest me at all. When I set my feet in there, there was an awareness of the tent. I stepped into a peculiar state of awareness. There was a silence. I knew it was the mind... He (JK) said: 'If any of you have taken this journey with me you will find yourself in a state of great silence.'

"Then he stopped and he said, 'I got it. Anybody got it?'
Then he looked around, and said, 'What is, is a comparative
state of mind.' That hit me so hard! That means that was my
state of mind, the comparative state of mind. What have you
done? This chap has put you back 14 years! You have been kidding yourself! Otherwise you wouldn't know what it is."

The next day he started:

'There is this energy.' My body was vibrating...

'There is energy in this silence...'

"I became aware of some kind of movement inside me and
then he said: 'There is some kind of a movement...' I found
myself in a very peculiar movement, where the very movement
of a leaf was in me. That was the mind creating a state of movement inside. I asked myself, 'Why am I doing all this?' Before
he supplied the word I would find myself in this state, then
finally on the last day he said:

'In this silence there is an action.'

"When he said action I sat there in a peculiar state of *samadhi*. There was neither the observer nor the observed. The eyes
were fixed. No movement of any kind. He ended and got up and
I got up and left the tent. Three days later these things started
to happen. That action destroyed the mind. This action takes
place in an area which is not in the scope of awareness. There is
a tightening of the whole body. All you are aware of is tightness
when you lose awareness. Then you are dead.

"I knew him for 40 years. Why is he throwing these abstractions at me? Then why am I listening? I brushed aside everything but I replaced it all with him. Why am I listening to
him? Just by listening you are not going to get it. This made me
miserable so I still continued thinking in terms of the religious
experience. I could never conceive of this bliss without mind.

"When once you step into that you don't need to ask anyone. Whatever he has is only an idea, why should I listen to
him? It's only because I have an idea of what he has. I would go

to this precipice and see the valley there and want to jump. He takes me there and says: 'Boy, you have to jump!' He has hinted so many times that there is nothing there. I still imagined that there was a peak there. I thought I jumped over and I didn't go anywhere at all! The peak is my imagination. There is nothing...

"Oh we talk every day..."

It was the most detailed description of his big bang experience I'd ever heard. I could picture the scene, having seen JK myself. He said whatever happened to him was different from what happened to JK, and if anything like that happens to another person it will be totally different as well. Life comes in unrelated events expressed one after the other in different ways. Life is not of the memory. "Understanding is not the way." Understanding is a mental process. Mental processes are memory based, therefore understanding is a dead thing.

And then came that beautiful dismissive comment at the end of the tape describing all this. It was priceless. "Oh we talk every day..."

Later UG insisted that listening to JK had been a mistake. It may well have been that once things had taken their course for him this was obvious. I had a very distinct sense he used JK as a means of wedging himself out of his own dilemma. Why else would he give JK credit for pushing him to stand on his own two feet? Up until that point had he been leaning on the image of that man that he'd built inside himself? It was exactly the same way I was building an image of him.

I called Yogini in Switzerland and talked to UG to keep my spirits up. As a joke I asked to speak to 'Mr Krishnamurti,' to which he would answer,

"He died in 1986! He's not here!"

In the earliest tapes he seemed to be stumbling around in new-found excitement, as if he'd fallen through the mirror to the other side; he was trying to figure out what was happening with his body. At one point when a man asked him: "UG, Can

you put me into that state?", he said quietly, almost to himself:
"Look, sir, I have worked on this thing for twenty years."

It helped to hear that at least he'd struggled. Lately he
claimed never to have struggled with anything in his life. Guha
said he had to have suffered more than he let on. Leaving a young
family behind like that was no joke. His wife died, desolate and
mad, after he abandoned her. It was a heavy price that must
have weighed on him, not to mention his children left hanging
in the wind. At some point he was wandering around penniless
and yet he said he never looked back, but when Suguna asked
him, he conceded that it was during this time he'd cried at his
lot, at where he'd ended up.

Undeniably all this indicated a man who would stop at
nothing to get what he wanted. It made me wonder, what was
holding me back? "You are all frightened chickens!"

I believed him when he said that to imitate him was just
another idea: "Any movement in any direction only strengthens
the problem."

There was nothing to do but hang in there desperately.

I got the feeling from his description of the events leading
up to the calamity that, when he was able to step back and see
what his relationship to that man Jiddu Krishnamurti really was,
that was the moment when he walked out on himself. Walking
out on yourself is a trick no one can perform; there has to be
some kind of a breakdown. You have to drive yourself down
to the wire and even then there is no guarantee that it would
happen. "You will drop dead on the spot." Not suicide. It's the
kind of drop that is out of your hands, the horrible grace that
strips you naked and leaves you standing in the street, like that
quote I later found out was attributed to the renunciate Shiva:

*On whomsoever my grace falls, he will be robbed and
stripped naked and left standing in the streets.*

GONER

There was a flat dust in the air from the meat factory down the street. The brick and barbed wire neighborhood was a stark contrast to the Swiss countryside I imagined spending another summer in. A fly buzzing around in the room felt like my nausea. I was spending too much time alone. Pretty soon there would be no time for myself. From the concrete enclosure of the back yard I watched planes from La Guardia trace contrails across the sky overhead at twilight. Soon I'd be up there on the way back to the rolling green meadows.

CHAPTER 48

This cannot reproduce another one, physiologically or otherwise—
that's why I say this is the end-product of human evolution.

The basement studio was dark and damp with no kitchen and a window that opened into a cement stairwell. For the first month of the summer I was down there crouching over a notebook listening to CDs of his old talks, sifting through evidence thirty years old, while he sat upstairs talking.

In one tape he described looking at a clock across the room through the body of Valentine before he realized what he was doing. As a result of this condition, where he was not separate from anything anymore, strange things happened to him all the time. These were things no one would be able to measure or test. He was completely alone in his perceptions. It sounded like science-fiction.

He kept saying he didn't think this was the same state JK was in. He was connected to everything in a position of total vulnerability. I could see what he meant when he said it was useless to society, useless to us as individuals. He also said it was the only way to be at peace. It wasn't hard to see that it was the closest thing to death in life. For him life and death were as close as breathing in and out.

The idea that I am a separate existence interacting with 'the outside' is a fundamental mistake of identity. According to him, I am a collection of ideas strung together one after the other. I have been taught and carefully trained this way in order to survive and function in society. Seeing, hearing and feeling are as much a product of the social ideology as words.

Upstairs, UG was looking fantastic. He was eating well. In the mornings he teased the German astrologer with coffee, forcing it on him relentlessly. He insulted him, then patted him on the arm softly. Smiling playfully, he carried on and the atmosphere was very sweet.

Yogini was getting ready to go back to the States for the first time in a long while. Even though things were pretty calm with us, I was grateful not to be waiting around for a bomb to drop. From the balcony the sky looked like another one of those Maxfield Parrish illustrations. Billowing clouds foamed out around the silhouette of a birch tree with a cerulean blue patch of sky beyond. The mountains were losing snow quickly as the heat grew more intense earlier each year. You could see orange building cranes everywhere around town.

At the beginning of June I went for the usual work in Basel at the fair. On the last night of the fair I got into a conversation about what was happening in Gstaad. One of the managers wondered what I was doing up there.

"What do you do all summer?"

I told him I was writing a book and talked vaguely about UG.

"How long are you going to be doing this?"

"I don't know really, probably until he dies."

"Is it a spiritual thing?"

"I suppose for lack of a better term I would have to say yes."

He gave me a long silent look. It bothered me that I couldn't find a better way of describing what was going on. I thought about that conversation for the next year. How could I make myself clear?

When we were leaving the fairgrounds I watched a group of men walking on a level below me. They reminded me of a pack of animals. Lately I sensed a primal element in the people around me. The most dangerous behavioral trait in an animal is territorialism and humans are the most territorial of all animals.

There was a complete lack of territoriality in UG. He owned nothing but the clothes on his back, and gave these away easily as well as the money in his pocket.

While waiting for the train, I watched a bird riding thermal currents. Considering the assertion that the physical eye sees things as flat, I wondered about how I was piecing all this together all the time. What I was looking at as well as how I was looking at it was already an interpretation. Even my feelings were a learned response to outside stimulus; and it all came from 'those bastards',

How could I explain all this in the simplest terms when people asked about him? The simplicity of his comments was deceptive. I didn't have the certainty he spoke of. Out of context, what he said was invisible. I had no authority. I was a copy made of copies, parroting words, while his actions contextualized his words. Without his presence it was impossible to convey what he was getting at. I barely understood him while I was sitting with him.

A friend put me in touch with the editor of a new art magazine who wanted an account of the Basel Art Fair. It was an opportunity to publish and the editor liked my writing. Giving in to superstition, I handed over my first $100 paycheck as a writer to thank him for setting me on that path. He immediately demanded another hundred in euros and in Swiss francs. "It's a tradition!" I sidestepped the rest of the payment out of self-preservation. *I hope it doesn't ruin me!*

'Masterful inactivity and watchful expectation.' was the phrase he used to describe the state of mind he was in during that summer of 1967. He was determined once and for all to get to the bottom of JK's talks.

In the earliest tapes he spoke in a sort of vulnerable wonderment, but within one year of that there was an unmistakable change in his tone. The vulnerability turned into a harsh and exacting tone, leaving one with the impression that JK was finished for him; having provided him grounds to leap, his function as a diving board was finished. UG jumped or fell, plunging off the grid of thought into his natural state and, after that, the whole thing was over.

If JK didn't know what he was doing, and UG didn't know what he was doing, there was no way to know what I was doing. The flowering and burning on the vine of expectations, the dashing of hopes, the crushing of logic all took place at an accelerated rate. He was a particle accelerator of the human condition.

Nevertheless, my friend's question left me inventing answers.

"What do you do there for three months?"

"Working a reconstruction. Actually it's a demolition job."

"What are you demolishing?"

"Myself."

"You know those gurus destroy your personality!"

"If only it were that easy!"

I was stuck. I believed in UG so I was stuck with that subject. That's probably why he told me I had chosen the wrong subject for my book. I couldn't have maintained the interest to write a book about anything else. I decided that by calling me a saint he was implying that I was some sort of crook. This may have been a hint that I would profit from the book with the crookery of money.

CHAPTER 49

*All my talking is totally unrelated, just like a
maniac's—the difference is only a hair's breadth—that
is why I say you either flip of fly at that moment.*

When I came into 609 for breakfast, he was listening to a
recording of a radio show with him talking in a reggae-techno
hip-hop track mix. The four-letter words were bleeped out,
creating yet another rhythm:

"Just *bleep don't talk of love!" "You are listening to all
this *bleep!" His words worked well with the music, his statements echoed the frustration and anger of young people. The
recording in the background was from a video of an encounter
between UG, Mahesh and Mario from years before. He was
shouting that he saw no despair in him, despite Mahesh's claim
to be suffering.

"Who is that talking?" UG asked us when he recognized
another voice in the recording.

"It's X, the palmist."

"He's crazy!"

Someone in the back of the room piped up: "He was a little
fuzzy to begin with."

"How else did he end up here?" I asked.

UG brought us back to the centerpiece of the morning:

"Hey! I'm on the radio! You heard it?"

"Yes, UG. You are out of control!"

Curled up in the chair listening to his voice, he looked like a
little kid, making fun of and imitating himself. The tape went on:

"How do you translate those vibrations? You are interested in meditation. You want to prove to the world that this machine is registering the silence. You are translating that into the framework of that bastard! You are not looking! Why you are repeating all that nonsense? You have never in your life looked at anything! No! Don't say something!"

In the background George Harrison's sitar was wrapping around his voice like a breeze in the background with UG cursing in the foreground.

"Mary was a bitch and Jesus was a bastard!" UG shouted over the sound of his voice.

Then in the recording:

"I tell you it's all a theory. Some bastard comes along and fools us and he gets a Nobel Prize for it. They are all fooling themselves and fooling us. What they are saying is no better than what they are putting in those garbage cans!"

Back in real time he asked no-one in particular,

"Hey, what is he talking about?"

The recorded voice continued: "What I found was about thought but not thought! How do you look at it?"

A Doors song, *Riders on the Storm*, came in, mixed over a Blondie tune with wedding chimes mingled with the rhythm, while UG was screaming at the others in the recording about the barking of a dog and the grunting of a pig.

He hollered to me happily, "Hey, mister!' You hear it?"

Then, in the recording: "*How?* means you want to add more and more."

He went from animated to meditative, seeming to lose interest at intervals. Then he'd charge up again, pointing to the computer, while the rest of us carried on, eating the remnants of morning breakfast.

I asked a German lady from Cologne to explain something about my horoscope. I still couldn't get all this stuff about the twelve houses. Astrology was one topic of conversation I could never make head nor tail of. Toward the end of her explanation UG asked her about my chart.

"How is the chart, Madame?"

"Very good, UG!"

"Is he going to make lots of money?"

"He will make money through others."

How else does a person make money I wondered?

It was UG's Indian birthday, according to the Indian calendar, so we went up into the mountains toward Le Diableret to Lac du Rateau for an early dinner. There was a little lake, a pond really, with a boat moored on its banks, surrounded by meadows and mountain peaks. He was fooling around, hitting me with spoons, threatening me with packets of sugar. The children were there again and there was a lot of youthful energy in the air. Yogini and I sat facing him with a couple between him and me so he couldn't get too wild, but he spent the meal tearing up my placemat and threatening me with spoons and water.

After dinner I was telling one of the Osho people about UG's relationship to JK. UG was listening in but said nothing. I told her it seemed to me that the fact that JK cast aside the traditional approach to enlightenment was significant to UG when he was young. Given his background, despite the fact that now UG claimed his talk was old-fashioned, JK represented something quite radical in his time. There is no doubt JK was a remarkable spiritual leader. The fact that he was able to walk out of the Theosophical Society the way he did must have been a major influence on UG.

Eventually JK set himself up as a model. UG's insistence that we follow him around in the car, take no exercise, all the rituals of giving him money, having constant high tea, sitting day after day in that room, was almost a mockery of a model. It was almost as if he was out to destroy us by using our tendency to follow anyone. I really don't think he was out to destroy anything, it was simply his nature to attack the falsehood of these attempts.

Ellen decided to leave at the end of the month and go back to New York after almost a year of traveling with him. The Money Maxim 'Take the dough and hit the road!' gave her the push a year before. She increasingly struggled with the feeling of being out of sorts with others, agitated about living under what she felt was his total control.

I knew how she felt. For me there was nowhere else to go. Maybe I was just too desperate to leave. UG's seeming lack of concern for the comfort of those around him was an assurance that he was not going to let the pressure up for one second as long as you wanted to hang around. I was projecting dark feelings as I wondered how I would avoid going on those bizarre and infuriating rides when the Reverend arrived.

The American friend gave me a numerological reading one afternoon as we approached Saanen toward the end of a ride. According to the system I was a classic 7. That meant a tendency toward inwardness, spending a lot of time alone reading and thinking about how things work. It was an isolated life but I was on the cusp of a big change that year. Someone added from the back seat that it was also a big year for me astrologically. Pluto would be in Saturn in the 12th house that year, whatever that meant. It seemed like there was always some big thing happening in the astrological department, despite the fact that things went on much the way they always had.

Despite a rough patch with the apartment situation, Yogini and I were getting along. Things were quieter when I gave up the idea of having things my way. UG always talked about how essential it was to give up trying. It is impossible until it just happens. Meanwhile he was so attentive to me it was embarrassing. He would come over while I was on the couch or walking in a store and hold my hand while pretending to throw me around. I felt acutely aware of the quality of his touch. It was uncommonly soft and encouraging but I felt awkward, clumsy. Aside from that, there was the uncomfortable dynamic that even though he looked like a woman at times he was a man. I was constantly paranoid about taking too much of his time.

CHAPTER 50

You are always in a state of Samadhi; there is no question of going in and out of it; you are always there. I don't want to use that word; so I say it is a state of not knowing.

When Yogini returned, I moved back over to 601. It was a ground floor apartment across the street from where we were meeting. The wood-paneled apartment was musty, with décor and furnishings dating back to the seventies. It poured with rain all afternoon. Mario's girlfriend took the front room. He was sharing an apartment with a couple of guys in town. Lately couples were taking separate quarters. Relationships subject to a beating under normal circumstances had it no easier around him.

UG was about to move up from the basement to the ground floor apartment in Chalet Birkwild. The young man who occupied it before him liked to party. There were porn magazines stacked in the bathroom with liquor bottles all over the place. It was funny to think UG would be living there. Mario was painting, while the girls cleaned up. He and I went out for pizza that night. He seemed as confused as me: "I have no idea what is going on! Nothing makes sense." I couldn't have agreed more. Nothing was particularly wrong, but there was always some underlying chaos in life around UG.

An Indian guru from Zurich came after a long time. He was there for the afternoon with a few nutty followers and twenty shopping bags of lunch. It was a pretty wild scene. He was sitting next to UG screaming at everyone in the room again, including UG at times. He reminded me of Rasputin and acted as crazy as he looked. As usual, UG was unaffected but I sat in the room grinding my teeth for about ten minutes before Lakshmi turned to me and said softly: "Louis, there is no need for you to stay here." The way this mad man was hanging over UG, yelling in his face, shaking his arm, was extremely uncomfortable to watch. I took her advice and went back to 601 for the rest of the day to listen to tapes.

The next day, in the afternoon, UG commented that when he woke up the body was shaking, vibrating with energy. "I sleep maximum 20 minutes and when I wake up this body vibrates. What is that?" he asked Sharon, the only doctor in the room. Her silence, accompanied by raised eyebrows and beatific smiles, said, *I have no idea!* In the tapes from just after the calamity he used to say he believed more in what the yogis had to say about the body than the doctors. He reversed these statements according to the audience:

"The only advice I would take is from those medical people, all the spiritual bastards I would not even shit on!"

With the rain continuing day after day, I was going stir crazy in my new rooms, painting and writing, listening to tapes and playing endless games of solitaire. I avoided the scene in 609, dipping in for a few minutes or an hour around mealtimes, and then disappearing again. Eat and run! The feeling of choking inside was literally giving me a sore throat.

Play solitaire.
Read a book.
Eat chocolate.
Drink coffee.
Write.
Paint.
Think, think, think…

I did these things rather than sit up there and do nothing except maybe obsess about what Yogini was doing, how hopelessly delicious she looked that day.

"If you want only one thing in this world, you will get it. The problem is you want ten different things."

If I had stopped thinking of other things, she and I would have been having a wild time.

Frenchie and Dean, long-time friends, were visiting UG for a few days. Frenchie had a pain in her leg that doctors hadn't been able to treat. It had been bothering her for weeks and got so bad she stopped going for walks. She was sitting opposite UG one morning when he 'threw' me across the floor during a fake fight. Spinning around to catch his balance he fell forward, his hands landing firmly on her thighs. For a second his eyes locked with hers then he jumped back and apologized profusely.

"I'm very sorry, Madame! It's his fault!" he joked, blaming me.

Meanwhile, she felt a burning sensation in the injured leg. It was strong and persistent. She whispered to Dean what was happening. The burning sensation went on for a while and after that the pain in her leg was gone.

The next afternoon UG insisted she ride in his car. It turned out to be her last ride with him. In the car she casually told him what happened. He asked her, "Does it hurt now?"

"No."

"What happened?"

"When you fell on my leg, it burned, and now it doesn't hurt anymore."

"Yes, that's how it should be."

The next day he told everyone about the healing of her leg. Of course he twisted it around, making a joke out of the whole thing.

"Hey! It's a miracle! St Louis healed her!"

We all knew better.

Two years later she told me the look in his eyes when he landed on her leg never left her and the pain never returned.

I interviewed Robert Geissemann about the early years with

UG. He organized the only public talks in Saanen back in 1967 and rented a tent for him outside Chalet Piffening for another talk that was rained out.

His wife had been a close friend of Madame Scaravalli, JK's first organizer in the Saanen Valley. When they arrived at her door for a luncheon one afternoon Madame Scaravalli said to his wife, her old friend: "I cannot tell you not to come in, but I would appreciate if you didn't." Scaravelli may have felt bad about banishing her friends but Robert Geissman's wife was devastated and Geissman himself never forgave the affront. The pressure 'from above' was too much. After this the JK people invited him in no uncertain terms not to return.

"These people were like Nazis!" he said angrily.

I asked him what it was that attracted him to UG when they first met:

"I had the sense that he was a man living something."

He said that just before the calamity Valentine was concerned for UG's mental stability. She suggested he see a psychiatrist but he refused. Unlike JK, who was a frail man in a lot of ways, UG was strong as a bull and very stubborn mentally. That may have explained how he survived such a shock to his system, 'flying' instead of 'flipping', in his words. Many of the people who knew him during the year of his calamity said he was in pain, his face flushed red, running a fever with chronic headaches and body aches. More than once he thought he was finished.

After the interview with Geissman, another Italian friend described his experiences with JK as we stood at the dining table. As a young man he'd met JK and dropped a promising career as an engineer in Milan. Since the old man's death he'd become increasingly interested in UG. Describing a basic difference between the character and presence of the two men, he said JK was a bright light whose teachings you could explain to people. He was graceful and handsome, elegant and charming.

UG was also handsome and elegant, but in a different way; his teaching or what he said was a black hole, completely unknowable. With UG there was no one behind the words. The nothingness he embodied was devastating compared to the glowing and hopeful discourse of J Krishnamurti. By living with the people, UG's life made an immediate impact on his friends. JK's whole style was public and theatrical.

Geissman was more blunt and controversial in the second interview. He didn't like Valentine, she was too *rajasic*, Sanskrit for fiery and aggressive. He felt more comfortable with a 'meditative' woman, like his wife.

During their walks UG discussed with him what he should do with 'this thing' that had happened to him. Geissman was a writer so UG asked him if he could write the book that eventually became *The Mystique of Enlightenment*. Geissman declined, saying he was not the writer for the kind of book UG was suggesting.

He described the effect of UG's speech as 'extremely violent' during those years. I heard this from more than one person. Other people insisted he was sweet as honey with them, but Geissmann said many people became deeply depressed after listening to him. The tapes from '67—71 indicate an intensity that, while it is more within the scope of reason and logic than the way he talked while I knew him, was still pure UG. Cutting to the bone, as he put it, all the time.

Geissmann also pointed out that UG was a product of a tradition that specifies that when you come into something of your own it is your duty to destroy what has gone before you.

As soon as I got back UG asked me how it went. I could feel the tension in my chest when I started telling Geissmann's story about how UG refused to allow Valentine to be interviewed. I made a joke of it, talking with a heavy French accent, but Ray came alive at this piece of information. Krim, another long-time friend, also said that at one point Valentine was having all sorts of experiences, and UG told her to shut up about them. I stopped after telling Geissmann's story about Valentine falling in the JK tent and UG laughing at her. He twisted this immediately into a version where JK laughed at her and refused to help her. Sometimes the information about his behavior was blunt and cruel.

An Indian couple who had known him for years came to visit him. It was *Gurupurnima*, a full moon day auspicious for worship of the guru. They said UG would have lots of energy. I tended to brush these things aside but for the first time in a long time I sat with him all day without wanting to leave.

There was an unmistakable intensity in the air. More Indians showed up that day from France and he talked seriously all day. He had me sing some of the songs. One man asked about the meaning and purpose of life. Normally this would be met with a brush-off but he talked seriously for the rest of the day and into the evening. I noticed an unusual degree of warmth around him and a yellowish light in the atmosphere. I had seen it before while talking to him on a number of occasions. It was not anything necessarily coming from him as much as it enveloped everything around him.

That afternoon he was joking around making me sit 'at the feet of the master,' as he put it. So I sat at his feet and stared at him googly-eyed while he gave me an exaggerated stare right back. In the middle of this little comedy he said with an edge in his voice,

"You ain't got a chance!"

I felt a catch of hopelessness in my throat. The offhand dismissal seemed cruelly inserted into a playact. I couldn't help a comeback question, also falsely kidding...

"What exactly do you mean?"

He paused.

"You will never be famous as a painter," he went on. "If you want to, you can continue with that and perhaps in posterity you will be appreciated, but you are a very good writer!"

I was relieved, but at the same time he'd always tell me, right after praising the writing thing, that it took a long time to establish yourself as a writer. Much as I love reading, I'd never imagined becoming a writer. I still don't.

UG was teasing me about saving his life when he 'almost broke his legs.' Then to balance the picture he claimed that I was trying to play with his penis when I was taking care of him. I said I would have liked to but there was nothing left to play with. I made a joke comment, with serious over or undertones that he liked.

"UG, the light inside of you was so intense that your essential organ went within to worship."

He liked it so much he came over and sat next to me on the couch and made me repeat it and write it down.

UG suggested I interview Denise Desjardins, a French woman who knew him for decades.

"She has known me for such a long time! She also spent a lot of time with that Anandamayi Ma. You should talk to her," he said, with a light touch of his hand on my elbow while I sat at the dinner table. This kind of approach with a request was rare for him. His touch was angelic, like a cool breeze (when he wasn't hitting me).

Denise always brought him a beautiful cashmere sweater, which traditionally he wore for a day and then gave away. It was one of his stories:

"She was so hurt! She gave me a very expensive sweater from Scotland and I immediately gave it away."

She accepted his strange behavior. It never stopped her from coming or from bringing him expensive sweaters.

In the interview she talked mostly about Anandamayi and her travels to India. Later UG wanted to know all about it. He listened carefully, even though it was not about him. Since she was hesitant to speak of UG in response to the questions I wrote out for her she described UG on paper, since French was her first language and she was a perfectionist.

Her notes were as follows:

The first time I met UG I was stricken/impressed, first by his eyes, so sharp and penetrating, and then by the simplicity of his behavior and the smartness, the elegance, the harmony of his gestures. It was in Switzerland, and everybody around him was relaxed and seemed at ease. There was respect and care of course, but no idolatry. So my slight fear to meet him vanished and I could hear what he was saying with the deepest attention possible. As he often says, nobody can really listen, but what I could perceive was enough to impress me. I was able to feel the tremendous energy emanating from his presence—an energy equally able to comfort you or destroy what was necessary to destroy, such as is the case with beliefs, judgments or incessant search for perfection (as was my case), as well as the mask most of us were wearing. He reminded me of Rudra the destroyer, another name of Shiva. I told myself he is not a master, he is a phenomenon, a very rare phenomenon, beyond the ordinary structure of human beings. In him, the rose had flowered, while we remained as buds.

It is difficult to conceive someone who is functioning without knowing, without naming, without forming images. His memory is perfectly there when it is necessary to answer a question or recognize his friends. (He is) a man who is never separate from nature nor those who are near him. Non-separation, advaita, one could feel a little of what that is, that unitary process of which he spoke. He never speaks of love, but this process is much more than love. Even, in some cases, he says his body can feel the same pain that occurs in another body.

Can I imagine or conceive and, even more, talk, of a human being no longer directed by thoughts, but by the "incredible intelligence of the body"?

She went on to say a few words about Valentine, UG's companion of 28 years:

Valentine was a strong, courageous and even bold person. Straightforward, very frank, not conventional at all, saying what she had to say without hesitation, she did everything for UG without showing off or taking advantage.

These stories about the past were interesting, but people all had their stories. In each telling there is a reflection of the storyteller. UG was a chronic liar. He lied all the time but his lies were empty. He was a man who died before he died, then managed not to be in a position to pay taxes for his entire life by having a non-resident status in India, and living continuously on the road. Offered the possibility of residency in the United States, his reply to some official or another was: "You think I would live as a second-class citizen in this filthy country?"

But what a genius move! Without succumbing to the usual criminal motives, either religious or financial, he sidestepped taxes without breaking the law. That has to be a phenomenon as rare as enlightenment.

He never allowed anything with his name attached to it to be established. There was a story about the 'Goners Club' he started in the Black Forest, pulling together about ten thousand euros from all his friends, and disbanding the whole thing within an hour.

CHAPTER 51

I am all the time trying to knock off the reference point.

The Greek woman brought the entire set of original Geissmann reel-to-reel tapes of the early talks with the original tape recorder.

When UG asked what was on there she said: "Oh nothing much. It's all the same stuff you are saying now."

Once Geissmann gave her permission, she brought me the original tape player and the whole collection. I ate this new material up, filling notebooks with his statements. It was a gold-mine that had been buried for decades, an extraordinary story of an extraordinary man. Here he was decades later, an old man with a handful of people around him. He'd done a good job of keeping a low profile. Maybe there was something to what Western astrologers said about his Cancerian traits. He was a family man, managing life from living rooms around the world.

In a conversation with David Bohm from 1968, UG's voice cut through all the intellectual mush like a knife. Bohm's Krishnamurtian lines, those old familiar words and phrases, seemed hopelessly antiquated.

"Can we talk about intentionality…?" Bohm asked.

"Thought is completely useless in this area," UG blocked.

So many came and went away because 'nothing was hap-pening'. Yet in thousands of tiny moments, the unrelated events he always talked about, life peeked through the torn veil of thought under his constant blasting the bottom line.

Nisargadatta had a brilliant way of putting it: "Spirituality is nothing more than understanding this play of consciousness—try and find out what this fraud is by seeking its source."

I imagine UG's response to this sort of statement: *There is no consciousness, there is no source and there is no spirituality! The word 'spirit' means breath, that's all there is!*

He was constantly asking, "What are we doing here?"

Mahesh's description of him as a 'story buster' was perfect. As a film director, he knew the essential requirement for pleasing the public was to stick to the story of the hero who overcomes adversity and triumphs in the end. Take that away and you'll have no audience. It's a perfect metaphor for the functioning of the personality. This simple equation holds together the fabric of society, our reality. No wonder history repeats itself, it doesn't know what else to do. If it didn't repeat, it wouldn't exist. As he put it, if we had no problems we'd invent them to reassure ourselves that we exist.

There was more and more testimony in his early discussions about the old man: "The experience of what is being said there by (*Jiddu*) Krishnamurti within the field of thought has a tremendous effect, that is a beginning, you know, it is a beginning. And so your outlook, your way of life changes, that is the effect."

The tapes were full of apparent reversals of his current lines as well as comments that hadn't changed in forty years. Still it would be impossible to say he'd changed his line one inch. "They come year after year to listen to JK because it is a pleasure movement for them. That is not going to help them."

What about him then? He talked of the 'mentally induced states of *samadhi*' he'd experienced in the tent and the mystical experiences before that he rejected. There was some discussion of his life 'before wash.'

"People thought that I was a very frivolous person. But still inside me was this question, you know, 'What is this all about?'"

It was burning in him all the time until it burned him out.

"You see for most people this is an intellectual thing."

As Geissemann put it when I asked him what attracted him

to UG, "He was a man who was living something." When a woman pointed out, in another discussion, what a unique life he had had, he played it down saying it was not that unique in India. There were so many others who had been exposed to the same religious influence but it had no effect on them. Was it the intensity of his questioning that set him apart? Was it just luck? In any case, as he said to me once, "It was luck, not the luck of the gambler."

An English lady asked him boldly: "But UG, don't you have any powers? Couldn't you give someone a push in some way?"

Her question reminded me of UG's question to Ramana Maharshi, "What you have, can you give it to me?" His answer was actually not so different:

"Yes I have, but this is a very violent thing. I'm telling you, you wouldn't want this thing!" Then a pause: "It is not like a dove descending on your head!"

"Nature is a violent thing! It does not care about your comfort. Nobody can give it to you. Nobody! This talk encases you and there can't be any communication between me and you! 'Then why talk?' you may ask. Because this is the way to live! And talk destroys it!"

No matter what he said, I had a feeling the words were just a device rather than indicators of anything significant in themselves. That was the way I experienced his use of language. He had become more outrageous and still the relationship between what he was saying and the thing he was indicating was non-existent.

"If something happened to some monk in the Ramakrishna Math, they would have to leave there! It has nothing to do with that."

The evidence of this was clear already. Even Ramakrishna's behavior caused a lot of trouble in Dakshineswar Temple.

There was more discussion about how Western religions destroyed the possibility of a person coming into this state because there was no room for it in the belief system. In India they tend to leave these people more to themselves, treating them as madcaps for some time before turning around and enshrining them, instead of hanging them or burning them as heretics. Even in India, the survival of such a person could only be by luck or by chance. There are plenty of stories of the great sages of India being abused and ignored, but the story usually ends with someone stepping forward to testify to the greatness of the apparently crazy one as a saint, instead of a priest stepping forward to condemn them as a devil incarnate.

Watching how UG handled himself, it was clear that he'd gone out of his way to see to it that the enshrining could not happen at least physically, but in a video Bob shot the year before, he said it had already happened a long time ago. The enshrining is a way of putting him into a religious or spiritual frame and bypassing the content of what he was saying. No matter how he lived, his words will have to be twisted to suit the needs of the traditions. Enough people told me: "UG is saying what they all say." Listening to him was a different experience, but he always said, "You listen because you think I am saying what the others said."

Addressing that 'frame' of spirituality, he said to Bob, "Are you ready to throw away the frame?" I think he meant the death it would entail to do so. For me the company of UG was a benefit to enhance my life. I wouldn't have hung around if I wasn't convinced I was getting something. The thing is, what I came for I didn't get, and what I didn't know I wanted or needed, I got.

The way UG spoke out against politics would have landed him in jail or at least in trouble if he'd been a bigger public figure. Since the earliest days in the Theosophical Society, UG avoided power positions, sensing the compromise involved. Later he was able to speak freely, precisely because no one took him seriously; if they had, who knows what would have happened.

He never allowed people to criticize others in his defense unless it was so silly it didn't matter. When Mahesh started laying into Sai Baba, UG shouted at him: "Why do you bother about others? I am not competing with that fellow! The more followers he has the happier I will be!" He wasn't interested in converting anyone; he didn't need any promotion from anyone. He was right, what he had was free for the taking, but to remain so, it had to remain free in every area. He was not invested in his own words, and when someone showed a heavy investment in them he was equally dismissive of them.

The weather was getting colder but it was a perfect, clear day. The dark green silhouettes of Eggli and Wispile folded over each other with a purple layer of mountains beyond. All this was burned forever into the visual memory banks. After hours of staring at them through the window, pine tree forests and sparkling green meadows spotted with tiny, barely moving cows under a perfect blue sky burned into the cell structures. The sawtooth edges of the mountains went from light to dark as the shadows shifted. Clouds pulled spotlight openings across the mountains. Early morning mist seeped up the valley like fallen clouds crawling back to the sky as the earth rotated into a fall orbit, chilling the air.

The postcard view outside enhanced the feeling of a dream. The green of the grass was that perfect unreal green of Switzerland.

CHAPTER 52

*I am happy with misery, poverty and death; I am also
happy with wealth and psychological fulfillment.*

As soon as Lakshmi and the girls left, UG took on a fierce
mood, ordering the kitchen absolutely cleared of all food and
cooking supplies. By ten o'clock there was nothing left in the
kitchen. There were still a few days to go before major players
were scheduled to depart so the exercise was a preliminary, if
not total shutdown.

"I am not going to see people any more. No more eyeballing
and no more cooking here."

He wanted to know the dates of every departure.

"I don't want an ashram here! You people are restricting my
freedom of movement!"

The apartment was suddenly back in the condition we found
it in when we arrived. The summer was erased and he refused
to eat there anymore. A flurry of panicked looks circulated.

"I am finished with this place! Come on let's getoutofhere."

There was another scrambling in the kitchen as the cook for
the day heated up his rice sticks and someone else packed the
hot water and Leonidas, all under the threat of expulsion. It was
all he would eat but if he caught them in the kitchen he might
refuse to eat anything. Then, of course, he would ask for it later
in the car. The task was completed just as we filed out of 609,
grabbing bags, purses and passports along the way.

At the Cora coffee shop at Evian he declined his usual cream
with coffee. Everyone wondered, "What's he doing?"

UG's frailty was on all of our minds. It couldn't be helped, with little else to occupy us, the minds went straight to the usual channel: fear.

"The desire for permanence in every area is the cause of human misery."

This applied also to our feelings about him. We wanted him to last forever. His energy was amazing, but the body was subject to the laws of nature. He never wavered in this pronouncement, another unacceptable utterance to those with religious frames, that he was no more important than a common garden slug. We felt responsible—at least I know I did—for keeping him going as long as possible, which made us more uncomfortable.

We were ordered to drive along Lake Geneva, touring for a visiting Indian couple and their son. UG made sure they saw Geneva in a couple of hours without any unnecessary stopping. I was feeling remarkably light that day despite the driving. In a traffic jam in Geneva I jumped out of the driver's seat and ran up to his car. Sticking my pad of paper and pen into the window I asked for the autograph of the great Indian philosopher, UG Krishnamurti. Taking the pen with a smile he wrote, "You are the worst dunderhead I have come across in the world!" At the bottom instead of his name he wrote, 'Geneva'. I still have it tucked away somewhere.

We headed back on secondary roads next to farmland along the lake glistening like a sheet of aquamarine glass. Sunlight raked warmth across the fields under a yellow filter. The way the light hit the cows they looked like transparent plastic toys. The sky was full of variously full, puffy and stretched clouds in ornate flowery bursts.

Eventually his talk came around to the plan for September. He suggested a visit to the Black Forest. Picking Yogini out of the back of the room, he asked her if she approved.

"I hate Freiburg!"

The shrill tone of anger said it all. She associated the place with his fall two years before and the horrible time they spent watching him recover. He must have known she hated it. The place represented a horrible memory and a dark cloud of concern hovering in the edges of everyone's mind. The shrill response was a bolt of lightning illuminating that cloud. We all knew about those days in the Black Forest where it looked like he very nearly died. The unusual outburst from the one who usually sat quietly in the background brought a pause and nervous giggles went around the room. He even stopped talking for a second, cracked a grin, then went on with the idea for a few minutes, then dropping the idea as if it had lost its appeal, or done the job, whichever it was.

After coffee we drove to Launen for dinner. It was raining and we couldn't take the usual stroll to the lake. Instead, Ray circled the lake on a one-lane dirt road full of signs forbidding cars. We joked about the ticket we were in for if we were caught by local police. At the restaurant he was happy to find his favorite waitress on duty. She immediately brought his hot water and soup. Once that was done she began serving the rest of us. Seated at the head of the table, he was stone-faced until the Reverend gave me his seat next to UG. Straight away he was putting napkins on my head, splashing me with water for the rest of the meal, stuffing my mouth with bread. He took the candle and passed it in front of me in a circle three times with a smile. It is what the Indians call *Arathi*, a blessing with fire.

CHAPTER 53

What I usually do is restructure the question, rephrase it in such a way that the question appears senseless to you.

It was almost five years since I'd first met him. The leash was so tight around my neck that any little spark ignited my rage. He was threatening to drag us all over Europe in the coming months and the weather was rain, rain and more rain. There was no escape and the next day he got up fresh as a daisy, ready for more. I was worn out. I went for a long walk in the mountains on my last day of freedom from cars and chairs.

We headed for Cologne on the first day of fall to celebrate a birthday. Yogini and I stayed in different houses. She suggested we could share a room but I didn't trust that I would be able to sleep. I was so paranoid about another outburst. Sure enough, when we met on the street we ended up in a fight.

That afternoon there was a very expensive and mostly inedible lunch at a famous restaurant in a castle for the birthday celebration. The food was so marinated with vodka I couldn't eat it. We stayed on in Cologne for about a week.

I was in the front room of the house two days later when UG pulled me up from a nap. Grabbing my collar he dragged me into the other room and pulled my glasses off, hiding them under his leg. I was so pissed off I was shaking. Our host looked nervous.

"UG, I think he is getting angry..."

"Getting? He is already angry", he said with an uninterested wave of the hand.

Furious, I turned and punched the wall behind me as hard

as I could and walked out. I was able to find the apartment through a very blurry Cologne. Why did the little bastard have to be so incredibly annoying? Why did I have to react to him, to her? Why did I need to hang around and how pathetic I was to do it?

I lay on a bench by the canal in the sunlight. My arm was numb. Usually it was Yogini who brought on a good wall punching. At this point I thought I would be lucky to just go insane.

My bone-tired exhaustion and a slight fever gave the surroundings a primal presence. The surroundings were under an enhanced clarity. Every tree, every pile of trash, every traffic light, the movements of vehicles and the surge of crowds in the street became an organic whole. Every visual detail expressed a piece of a continuous monster movement, millions of bits of consciousness weaving a pattern without significance in an emptiness filled with civilized noise. Inside the building sat a tiny man, dwarfed by vaulted prewar ceilings, breathing the beast in and out. It was as if he was that beast watching itself in a state of unknowing wonder.

CHAPTER 53

Since there is nobody who uses this thought as a
self-protective mechanism, it burns itself up.

After Cologne, UG wanted to see some old friends in Rome. Unable to find rooms, we ended up in a town south of the city for a couple of days, making trips to Salvatore's in Rome for lunch. Yogini and I went to the Vatican while the others wandered in the city. After a couple of days UG wanted to go back to Vallecrosia. Once there, we sat in the garden between meals and rides. Yogini and I shared an apartment. I hung back, hanging out on the couch in there, reading detective books and killing time.

Yogini was fed up running up for me all the time to 'drag that fellow down here!' She said the only time UG talked to her was when he wanted me. "Where is that guy?"

During those days he made an observation I hadn't heard before:

"Love is a forced element in life."

I appreciated this dismissal of sentimentality, and yet when the Greek woman sang her gushy love songs to him, he smiled with genuine warmth.

He read my palm again, telling me I had lots of money and, like him, I didn't have to work. It gave me a pleasant feeling of being worry-free. Of course when Yogini asked me, immediately after that, what I was going to do when we finally left him, this pleasant feeling was shattered.

He kept the temperature high in the cave so eventually

318

everyone would wander out into the garden to cool off. He would saunter out with the usual question, "What's happening?"

The old cat came by and sat next to him.

"Hey, Cattie! I don't like you! Go away! They all like me, all the animals. When once I was in Rome with Mahesh, there was a panther...." telling the story we'd already heard so many times about the wild panther Mahesh was scouting to use in a movie. "Then he was jumping and dancing and I said *'Sit down!'* and it sat down! When the animal trainer noticed all this he asked them, 'Is he an animal trainer or what?' That fellow wanted to know. I was telling it to sit down in English, probably it didn't understand what I was saying."

Even though we knew the story upside down, right side up and in a fourth dimension if there is such a thing, it was still funny.

I asked UG to clarify a comment he'd made about his 'awareness' while sleeping.

He said: "Don't call it awareness, it is wakefulness."

No matter what idea I had about what he was saying, he gave it a new twist, undermining what I thought I understood.

California and I sat in the kitchen talking about him after lunch. After about an hour a barefooted elderly gentleman appeared in the door. Shuffling lightly into the room with a smile and a glint in his eyes, his brown trousers dangling around his ankles, sweater hanging gracefully off boney shoulders. He was munching on a breadstick with a non-look that indicated he knew we were talking about him. Taking a seat, he munched away as if nothing was happening and gradually the others came in and joined us. His hammy act of the toothless old man took the steam out of our discussion, evaporating the conversation while he ate his cheese stick. He injected so much life into the room, any conversation became unimportant, impotent. Making funny faces with his toothless grin while munching on the cheese stick, lately he was poking more and more fun at himself, at life, shrugging his shoulders while we laughed at this imitation of himself as an old man with no teeth eating a bread stick.

"What are you laughing at?" he asked with a shrug.

"UG, you are really something!"

"What took you so long to realize that?"

He sat there looking like the cat that ate the canary.

When I stayed back from a ride, the character of a place would come up a few notches in volume. As long as UG was around, the world was obscured by his white noise. With him gone, the scent of the garden and the sea rose up in the senses, shimmering in the late afternoon. The sound of heavy equipment and local workers cleaning up after a flood echoed among the buildings surrounding the garden. It was the time of year when kids are back in school and everyone is back at work after summer vacation. While he was around, yelling at Mario or shouting at 'Bitchie' for hot water, the sound of his voice in the background or foreground put a spell on things. I lost sight of it often enough since I was so immersed in it all the time. The world became a backdrop, a cardboard cutout. It meant nothing to him. His way of life was only possible when 'the body is a solidified imagination', as it was for him. We imagined we were in the world and he was putting in an appearance with no attachment to the reality we imagined shaking its foundations. He was the hint of something unknown, but there all the time. Being around him was a limbo, you could sense heaven, but you couldn't touch it, and you sensed that you were slightly dead because he was so completely alive.

Giovanni was there—an Italian engineer and the partner of Lucia, who owned the villa where UG spent his last days. He didn't say much, he was busy watching UG playing with the New Yorker's wallet again, removing all the paper money. He left the coins.

"Idon'tlikethejinglingofcoins!"hesaid,quotingRamakrishna.

Giovanni turned to me. Laughing he threw up his hands and said with a shrug: "He is doing something all the time!"

When the New Yorker discovered what he'd done, she happily played along. For all his abuse, there was a deep care in operation there. She had the good sense to hang in there with him, despite the difficulties, despite the warnings of all her friends, her family, and his nastiness. She was happiest when she was around him, that was clear. She may also have been the most miserable.

Back in Gstaad there were seven of us left. We met in his new apartment each morning where he was settled in his stuffed striped armchair like a little white monkey, fiddling with his fingers, yelling at Mario, giving orders or taking phone calls. He was almost always shifting slightly, flickering in the chair that embraced him like a throne. Even if you entered and he appeared to be asleep, the tiny frame seemed to be hovering weightless on a microthin layer above the chair.

Once someone said about Ramana Maharshi that meeting him was like meeting a tiger. He ate you whole and only the bones were spit out. UG commented without pause, "Here not even the bones are left!" He was a superconductor of infinite movement pulsing through a thin, agile body. He gave the impression of a ghostly puppet activated by unseen strings. "I don't even know what I am saying!"

If the audience disappeared he would have vanished into space.

"Nighty night." When that big wooden door clicked shut at night I was sure he was dissolving into thin air.

By this point everything seemed unreasonable. Yogini was back in the States for a brief visit, the New Yorker was either falling asleep on the couch under threat of expulsion, or racing around town shopping.

"Hey! If you want to sleep you go home and do it there!"

"UG, I'm not sleeping!"

"Don't try to be clever."

One woman came and sat quietly. Another sat with her eyes closed wearing the knit Osho brow. She replied to his occasional comments with a silent grin. California was slumped against the closet door with his hand to his forehead nursing a constant headache. Mario was on the floor trying to catch up on sleep. Cheapie, Bitchie, Shitty, whatever her name was that day, stared ahead like a doll with broken eyelids, and the deaf Australian musician sat there in a trance. I was relieved not to have the lady around to set off an explosion on the domestic front. The vacuum of the others left me as his target. I don't know if I was the most agitated person around but he teased me untiringly whenever I entered the room.

"Hey you bastard! What is going on?"

"Got me, UG. I'm just taking in the sights of Switzerland."

"Ohh, ho, ho, ho!"

I felt like I was suffocating; at the same time the air I came up for was his nectar. It was powerful beyond belief.

I got lost in his face. Watching the empty grey eyes, the fluttering movement of his hands as he spoke, the shifting of his legs. The implications of silly words glistened and flashed, disappearing into oblivion. In that body I had a glimpse of something just beyond reach. The carelessness was addictive, it made me think I had some of it, then I'd step outside and act like an asshole all over again. I was becoming more desperate by the minute. I knew I was a lucky son of a bitch to be sitting there. I was also damn lucky he didn't have much time left. The only way out of there was death to one or the other party. He was like a saintly Dracula: when he looked, there was no one in the mirror.

Taking a break from the inferno, I went up and stood in the kitchen watching the cows outside. In the bright fall morning the chalets looked smaller, a little like toys, with the big animals around them.

I knew I wouldn't go for the ride that day.

322

CHAPTER 54

*This kind of a thing must have happened to so many
people. I say this happens to one in a billion,
and you are that one in a billion.*

He had spent twenty years following JK, left his family, his wife
died, leaving his children in the care of relatives. He'd gone
broke, been arrested for vagrancy, possibly shoplifting, and
ended up on the streets after experimenting with every possible
form of spiritual practice. It sure looked like he lost everything
he had except his mind, and nearly that too. So when he said,
"Don't take my word for it! You will find out for yourself and by
yourself that there is nothing to it!", there was an authority that
left everything else in the dust.

If you took his words for granted, it was your problem. I
wouldn't have put up with all this if it were a matter of words
alone. I knew better. It was my choice to sit there, it was my
choice to stay there and it was my choice to suffer through all
this because, despite the pain of it, there was a certainty that
this was the only show in town.

I went upstairs and listened to a tape labeled '1970. Tape #7
Track #1 Part #1', A woman was comparing what he was saying
to what 'that other chap' was saying:

"You must rationalize to yourself why you are listening to
some other chap. Through that rationalization this structure
continues… You must damn both of them and walk out. You
don't have the guts to do that, you understand? You just don't
have the guts to damn the thing which you hold on to.

'You are saying the same thing that is being said elsewhere!'

"That's right, right through centuries. And some damn fool comes along and says 'You must preserve the teachings in their pristine purity'. What the hell has anybody discovered? I haven't discovered anything new! That's all that I'm saying!"

The next day we drove to Cologne.

The day after that we went back to Switzerland.

After another two days we went back to Italy. Collecting Yogini from Nice airport, where we'd dropped her off two weeks before, we returned to Vallecrosia for a couple of days. Then we went back to Gstaad for over a week.

Twice that week he partially lost consciousness on his way to the kitchen in his tiny apartment to throw up, and nearly fell. Yogini caught him once without his realizing it. We were sharing the apartment upstairs. He left us the key to his place in case he didn't answer the door. That spoke volumes. He came up and shared a meal with us since there was a small enough group to cook meals in the cramped apartment with a sloped ceiling. He was always warning people not to hit their heads. I had the feeling we were hitting his. Yogini was panicked that it would turn into a crowd but it worked out fine. Even after hanging around for almost five years it felt amazing to look in the other room and realize who we were entertaining under the same roof we lived in. He had me cook for him once or twice. It was as if I had learned a magic trick, making edible rice sticks for him. When I was most nervous about it, he loved them; when I got overconfident, I messed them up. Luckily Yogini and Cheapie coached me and no-one died from eating my food.

Yogini and I got along well for longer stretches. It was peaceful.

We stayed longer as people came and went from Cologne. There were rides to Evian, Montreux, Avry, Neuchatel, for coffee or little shopping outings. At every stop he got ice to shove in the back of my shirt, water to splash on me, and sugar packets to press into my hands.

The pass to L'Aigle was splashed with autumn colors. Out the window of the little attic apartment a birch tree was in movement all day. Cobalt green leaves flickered with crisp light. Layer upon layer of foliage was spread out among the chalet rooftops, with the mountains in the distance changing color all day and into the night. No matter what time of year it was, the place was spectacular, a visual orgy.

We started meeting in 609 again. It gave me an excuse for some exercise. Mornings and evenings I walked over on back roads and across fields.

The moon grew in the night sky over Saanen and Gstaad. Out the windows I watched the trees go gradually bare. The clear sky in the evening was spotted with stars.

We stayed in Gstaad far longer than anyone expected. There was constant speculation about his travel plans. His schedule of travel to India had shifted over recent years. At one point he expressed surprise that the body seemed to be lasting longer than he expected: "It seems I may even make another trip to America."

It sounded as if he were talking about a gas tank that was fuller than the fuel indicator showed. It was hard to accept the frailty in front of us. He was so lively despite his fragility and there was always that wild card up his sleeve.

He started talking about having his family visit him in Switzerland. He was getting calls from the wife of his grandson, who had just given birth to twin girls. Great-granddaughter was also calling, 'threatening to show up', as he put it. He prepared all the paperwork to give the twins money for their education, 'to make them very rich girls, so they can throw their parents out!'

They came during the Thanksgiving holidays.

As soon as they arrived he made sure I was 'attacked' by

the babies and his great-granddaughter. He brought them on in force, ignoring the tears and howling. The parents trusted him. We knew he wouldn't hurt them but his gleeful indifference to their tears was nerve-wracking. There really was something devilish about it. Once he slapped one of babies, a little tap really, just enough to make her cry while making her 'dance', as he called it, jiggling her little arms around. No one said anything but it was shocking even to me. Later, when a therapist friend asked him why he did it, he said, "To see what would come out." Another time, he demanded a fifty-euro note from the same guy and immediately passed it on to one of the babies. Looking at him with a shrug he said, "See, all gone."

The therapist said if you trusted him you could learn a lot from these games. If you didn't trust him, he didn't play them. He said he was driving UG along Lake Geneva one time and commented that they were across the lake from Montreux. UG turned on him and screamed that they were not across from Montreux at all, it was Mont Blanc or some place it obviously wasn't, and everybody including UG knew it. No one dared to say anything. UG was too busy hollering at him.

"Look with your eyes! Not your non-existent head!"

He said this went on until he was ready to throw UG out of the car. The minute he had that thought UG turned to him with a big grin and dropped the whole thing.

The California crowd came at the same time the Italian friends showed up. UG started talking about staying for Christmas. It was the most expensive time of the year to stay in the most expensive place in the world for high season. Typically absurd economics were set in motion.

He came with us to see the newly renovated Co-op store in town on his way to the bank and the post office with Yogini. It was freezing cold yet he wore a sweater, refusing his coat. Repeatedly someone or other asked if he wanted his jacket, his response was always the same:

GONER

"You are all frightened chickens! There is no such thing as cold, no such thing as heat for the body. Look at the animals in the fields!"

He strolled along wearing slip-on summer shoes on the snow-banked street, a white tangle of hair sticking up on the back of his head. We called it a 'sky-hook'. He was an odd sight among conservatively dressed tourists and locals bundled against the cold. People stared. By the time the two of them checked their boxes his body was shivering. He kept stopping to make a point, talking the whole way, reading from a letter some woman wrote him.

"'UG, you are the most amazing discovery of my life.' What? What is she talking about?"

We inched along to the bank. I didn't bother to point out that the cows were in the barn for the winter and anyway they have fur. I tried to herd him forward by playing the idiot sheep dog, making a clown of myself to distract him, falling in the snow, walking like I was retarded.

Laughing, he asked Yogini, "What's the matter with that guy?"

"I don't know, UG."

CHAPTER 55

All we can do is be ourselves, and no one can help you be that.

I called Douglas again. "Did he ever talk normally?"

"Well, before the calamity he was like anybody else in that sense. Afterwards that was all burned out."

When they first met, UG insisted that he had to meet JK. Douglas said he drove with him to the chalet where JK lived and forced the nervous 19-year-old to knock at the door. Sure enough, JK answered.

"Did he say anything about UG?"

"No! In fact UG told me not to mention his name."

"How was it to meet him?"

"Well it's funny because he actually came to the door and it was a bright sunny day and he asked me: 'Look, sir, do you ever see the clouds, look at the sky?'"

"No, you're kidding!" We laughed. It was like the start of a typical JK talk.

"I'm serious. He actually said that. He was really like that! But a very charming man. Amazing man really, but UG went far beyond whatever JK was. UG became a sage, something Krishnaji was not."

Douglas asked me about UG's health and whether he had mentioned any travel plans. I could only repeat what I'd gotten used to repeating lately, that I didn't have a clue: "I really don't think he knows either. I think he waits for his marching orders and then just goes."

Someone was playing videos from the last trip to India for

him. Chandrasekhar sang his songs about UG. There was a profound sadness and longing for clarity. UG translated the song.

"You say that there is no mind, there is no religion. You tell us that you yourself are Shiva. You go on saying that *moksha* and enlightenment is bunkum. 'How am I to get into that state?' I ask you. You just look at me and smile with pity in your face. I dedicate myself to you. Please accept."

"Not a chance!" UG muttered to the video.

Then we watched some JK videos on YouTube while UG sat across from us, absently picking at his fingernails, a thousand miles away.

"He's so intellectual," Ellen said.

"I don't get it? What is he talking about?" someone else piped in.

To the others it was new information, but to me the voice was a flashback to years of examining the implications of every word. Now they were all irrelevant, since across from me sat a man who had unhinged the steel grip of that voice and opened up a space of wonder and frustration.

UG sat in his chair, indifferent to the video.

"What is that?" he asked.

"It's your old pal," I said.

"Oh," he mumbled. "All nonsense."

It was an odd sensation to sit with one Krishnamurti in the room and another one in cyberspace. In a video of UG from YouTube the contrast was bold and harsh. He chopped away like an ax at all the tools JK used to communicate. He was certain and JK so hesitant. It was amazing to consider that UG had listened to the man for years, yet somehow he didn't end up stuck there. He chopped it to pieces and burned it up. I thought of the guts or the explosiveness it must have taken to get this guy out of his system. Reminded again and again of the analogy given in the spiritual texts where you use one thorn to remove another thorn. If you don't throw away the second thorn, what has changed?

UG was my new thorn. Could I throw him out?

For all the ideation, dramatics, sex scandal and whatever else I found problematic about JK, I was beginning to reconsider his formidable presence. I really didn't know what to make of him, of UG or the relationship between them. I knew I was finished with him but the rest was unclear. What to make of this guy?

UG was on his own, out to sea, clear as a bell, devastating, charismatic, right up to the edge of unbearable. Lately it didn't mean JK was a total phony. There was the fact that meeting JK made meeting UG easier.

He once told Mahesh about telling the old man, "I feel like a blind man in a pitch-dark room looking for a black cat that is not there!"

The reply was, "The cat is there."

"He was lying," Mahesh said. "Feeding people on hope."

The pain in a back molar was getting worse. I was waiting to have the work done in India where it would be cheaper. When I was there I never did anything about it. The New Yorker offered me her scheduled appointment at the local dentist. I took the plunge. The young Italian dentist turned out to be a seeker. He was curious about UG after hearing the New Yorker talk. Later that evening he came over to meet UG and heard all about his dental theories: "My thirty-two teeth are growing back, sir!"

He even agreed to have his mouth x-rayed. It never happened but the dentist enjoyed his visit. UG told him he wanted to get all his teeth back so he could bite people with his teeth since so far his words had failed.

The dentist assured him his words were quite biting, particularly the ones he was directing at the New Yorker.

CHAPTER 56

*I knew that something really fantastic had happened inside—
what it was, I didn't know, but that didn't bother me.*

On Christmas Day UG was shouting to the rafters with particular vehemence about the usual array of filthy bastards. It seemed crazy. Was it any crazier than before? I don't know. Shilpa came in bright as a ray of sunshine, completely recovered from a little family drama the night before; presents were opened behind UG's back and breakfast proceeded as usual. Sumedha put a bow on the telephone next to UG. He smiled as she did it.

He got up to show off a newly dyed, slightly splotchy shirt. Someone asked how the job went. As he pulled his sweater up over his head to show off his work from the night before, his hair was standing on end. He looked like a rumpled baby chick. "Pearl grey!" he proudly declared to the room. The sunlight from the window turned the bush of hair around his head into a flame of white. The stick figure looked funny and sweet. He looked strikingly different, with a new sweater and dark slacks. There was a youthful energy in him that morning.

Once the big day was over I launched a few questions at him about his education. His first subject was Advaita Vedanta and second subject was psychology. He studied these for three years. As he said before, he had studied Eastern and Western approaches to the mind before rejecting them both. I asked him what the Advaita Vedanta studies included and he said they studied Gaudapada among others. Shankaracharya had reinterpreted the main texts in a new way.

"Shankaracharya, Madhavacharya, Ramanujacharya—three great scholars created three systems of thought."

This was probably the wording of the lecture he attended. He rattled off answers like a machine as little details I had heard a thousand times before came after long pauses. He sat silent, eyes closed, then he would open his eyes and a sentence or two came out. The details led nowhere. I looked into his eyes with two little pinpricks of light in them wondering, *What is it in there that informs the mouth?* Some disengaged piece of information was uttered in response, with no relevance to the machine uttering it.

Staring into the fire I had the feeling I could sit there forever and still not 'get it'. Like he said, the thing trying to get it was a barrier. I was a monkey jumping around on hot coals, drunk with ideas. Sitting next to him, trapped by the belief that he was going to free me, was futile. What to do about that? I imagined he freed himself by hashing it out with JK. Wasn't the hashing out just in his head? If he was a projection of my imagination, wasn't JK a projection of his imagination?

No, that wasn't it.

The fire burned on. These thoughts churned around in my head. Nothing came of any of them but hot air. And that's not it either.

"Inaction is action, that is your Gita."

After the holidays, we moved around a lot. On January 11th we were in Gstaad again for a day. As it turned out it was his last day there. He occupied the last place for less than six months.

I came in early. The curtains were pulled and it was hot. He sat in his chair, his thin frame outlined by pale green-grey stripes. There was a powerful energy radiating in the room extending in all directions. The pleated curtains behind him went on and on into infinity. His neatly pressed pants draped over thin legs. The feet were side by side on the wooden table in front of him, hands clasped around one knee. One hand habitually folded the crease in the pant leg while the other clasped it.

He was silent, a rarity those days. There were waves of something pulsing through him, beneath him, expanding gently in all directions. Was that the pollen of a human flower? What ever it was, it was swirling around the physical form while he sat with a blank stare. His head sat firmly on narrow shoulders like a ramrod. An indefinable, almost liquid energy was permeating every fiber of the atmosphere around him. He was immersed in it at the same time he generated it. His eyes were hooded and when he closed them it appeared as though he was bathing in a warm embrace. His head drifted back ever so slightly, as if he was picking up a scent in a breeze from another dimension. I could feel the infinity of it breathing into the room.

My God, it was something that day! He was stillness itself and the infinity of it breathed into the room.

All the hollering at us was designed to cover the tracks of this beatific perfume. I had a glimpse of that place he inhabited while sitting next to him at times. Sitting there feeling the impending surrender to it beyond the limits of consciousness, I resisted these sensations as sensations but they were overwhelming. The evidence was overwhelming. At such moments my body and everything I perceived were a red herring, a false note, a distraction from that. It was an unbearable totality that would finish me off if I let go. Anyway, that's what my fear told me. It was just exactly as he said, if you see anything for once, you are finished. No matter how people denigrated his riddles, jokes and outrageous statements it was obvious to me that he was absolutely literal. I am the riddler, the joker, the squatter in this body, the filthy bastard Louis. He lived in the fire of life, while socialized beings sit shivering around orange-colored Halloween paper decorations pretending to be warm.

One day later he left Gstaad for the last time. No one knew it then, but that was it. I remember a discussion in the van

behind his lead car about what would happen when he finally
died. It seemed almost gauche to bring it up, but the others
acknowledged similar thoughts. We headed to Vallecrosia.

Thus began a final whirlwind tour of the Italian coast and the
French Riviera. Every day we drove to Nice, Monaco, Imperia,
then back to his cave at Vallecrosia. We went for day trips into
little medieval towns in the surrounding Italian mountains.

There was one town where we stopped for lunch on the
coast. It was a little harbor, featuring a grotto about which
Lord Byron once wrote a poem. UG sat in the car while we
explored the place. At the restaurant he joked with the waiter.
He was having a good time. When he got up and went off to
the bathroom I followed. There was a tricky stairway involved.
I stood waiting outside for an unusually long time. When he
emerged he looked disheveled. There was water all over him
and his clothes weren't tucked in properly. It was becoming
increasingly difficult for him to move around. It seemed like
an indignity to him to put this appearance in the world, but
that was my problem, he didn't care. He was a withering leaf
in autumn getting ready to drop in the wind. The perfume had
lasted a long time. The shell was crumbling, revealing perfect
light inside, bursting and faint as a breeze.

One day later we went to the airport to pick up some visitors. As he disappeared at the far end of the waiting area with
them to see about some problem with the rental car, he was
limping. It felt like a riptide going out. I stood watching helplessly from the shore. He was favoring one leg more than usual.
They were gone far too long. When they got back, we loaded up
the cars and got lost on his last drive.

CHAPTER 57

Your teacher must go, it doesn't matter who the teacher is.

The next morning, Yogini woke me up with the news.

"UG fell again! Avner was there first and helped him up. He's asking for you!"

When I entered the room that morning he was sitting in the chair.

"Sir, I need your help again!"

I helped him dress and immediately he described again how he'd fallen while washing his clothes and had to crawl to the door. He'd passed out while picking up a bucket of water.

"It's been warning me." He said later, "The wobbling at the sink in the morning happened a few times."

He sat in the chair dressed and ready to go, but he would never walk across the room again without help. Again he got down to business. This time he wanted to dictate his swan song. The time had come to put his final expression down in black and white.

I spent the nights with him again, bringing him water and tending the fire. He slept on the couch, and soon after he fell, we realized it was impossible for him to stay upright in the chair. He kept sliding down, so we moved him to the couch the next day, and he stayed there until he died. He never showered after that day and there was no smell of body odor. In the mornings he was not interested in eating breakfast before the others came.

"Forget it, sir! I'll eat later."

After the long nights, I tried to get to my room before I

had to start answering questions in the kitchen as the others arrived. Had he eaten in the night? Did he sit up? How was the constipation? I had no good news. I had the impression he was trying to figure it out himself. Occasionally he drank water but it was the beginning of an ordeal with food and water. The cardiospasms, his 'plumbing problem', grew increasingly worse. The body was weakening, fading out. He already threw out most of the food he ate anyway.

Months before, as we were walking to the bank in Gstaad, he commented as we passed an old man with a cane,

"I don't want to become in-valid." The pronunciation was unmistakable. If he couldn't stand on his own two feet, forget it! Mario once bought him a cane as a joke. UG used it to hit him.

At night when they left, I heard them talking outside as it rained softly on the glass roof. I sat with him in silence for a few minutes, letting the dust of the day settle, then rearranged the furniture in preparation for the night. I took a seat in the chair opposite him and averted my eyes from where he lay on the couch. He looked so bad during the first few nights I was afraid he would slip into a coma and die. His breath became labored and then stopped. Then it would catch again. I wondered what I would do if it suddenly stopped for good while I was alone in there with him. A doctor friend calmly assured me that it would take some time for that to happen. His vital signs were strong. Since the first fall, he'd have his friends who were nurses and doctors check on his pulse. The right wrist was 'the bastard', the left was 'the bitch'.

"How is the bastard today?"

"Oh, he is bossing her around, UG."

He used to talk about the split down the middle of his body, one side male, one side female. During the days when 'the saints went marching out' the two sides were making love to each other. Later I found a passage in the St Thomas Gospel, "When the man becomes a woman, and the woman becomes a man, then you will enter the kingdom of heaven."

Each day I was caught up in an emotional reaction to something or another. After a few days he refused to remove his clothing. "What for?" He talked about the legality of euthanasia in Switzerland. "What is it called? Sodium pentothal?" He joked about using the poison as an option for 'getting rid of this body' instead of having me 'pack him up' for 400,000 dollars. It should have been morbid but it wasn't.

"Don't call it suicide. You had no choice about your birth, but you have some control over your death. If I am sure of anything it is that I will fall again and I don't want to suffer like this. Don't tell me about your sacredness of life! What about all your own soldiers you are killing in Iraq and Afghanistan? There is no meaning and significance to suffering, sir! Don't tell me all that rubbish. Some ideas for you to preach in the church!"

When I was alone with him at night, I waited and watched until morning, feeding the fire in the stove until I sweated. He played with this one too: "It's too cold." I put in more wood. "It's too hot in here, I am sweating." Horrified, I waited for the room to cool down. What was too hot? What was too cold? Meanwhile the plastic wall clock ticked on through the silence and a distant church bell marked the hours. At five in the morning a blackbird sang in the dark, heralding another dawn. I longed for a good night's sleep, escaping to the rooms upstairs as soon as someone showed up.

Once again, constipation was a problem, but his attitude about it was the usual: "Don't call it constipation, sir! This body will take care of itself!" If he agreed to an intravenous drip, he would have recovered his strength. "Not a chance!" As ever, with nothing else to do, thinking was far worse than what was happening. Not to worry or show concern is taken as a sign that people don't care. It was nearly impossible to internalize a lack of concern for results. After two weeks there was a day when he didn't eat at all. He was still constipated, demanding I hang around all the time in case he needed my help to move. I escaped sometimes, running out for a few minutes to the oasis of the supermarket. By evening he still hadn't eaten.

"Why are you forcing me all the time? I am *not* going to eat!"

That day I was more wasted than usual. I slumped into the corner behind him, and the next time he needed to be pulled up I hesitated long enough that he asked Avner to lift him. Avner was a quiet young Israeli man who was relaxed and easy with UG. After praising Avner, UG complained that I was hurting him. To offset a feeling of guilt, I joked with Avner, asking what he was doing for the rest of the evening. I flushed knowing he must have felt my frustration. It was shameful.

I felt like the last person fit to nurse an old man. It would have been appropriate for him to ask me to leave at any moment. We would all be better off. But I wasn't finished just yet. He wasn't about to let me off the hook. Difficult as it was, I would have been devastated if he had.

That previous fall, when I told UG I couldn't afford to go to London to visit his old friends Ed and Lulu, it was one of the few times I fished for advice. We were sitting alone in his apartment in a rare moment while the others were out running errands. "Let's finish the job, sir," he said. I asked because I sensed the end could be close and I didn't want to go away for some stupid reason. I'd have spent the money, that wasn't the concern, I just didn't know at the moment what to do. His gentle statement reassured me. No matter how hard it was emotionally, I knew the only thing I wanted to do was be of some service, I just didn't want to cling. He let me off the hook by keeping me on the hook.

Mahesh called to tell UG he could not die without seeing him. UG told us he was not ready to leave yet, which was little comfort since Mahesh was one person who had the means to fly in at the last minute if it came to that. I figured UG would at least wait until his daughter came but that was weeks away. It was only February 10th.

GONER

On the eleventh he was able to drink water and eat again. The next morning around 3:30am he asked for some water and spilled it on his lap. As I was cleaning it up, he said the body hadn't eaten in days and he hadn't shit in a week and still it was going. Cursing medical technology one more time he said: "Your whole way of living is the cause of human misery! This body can take care of itself. It just goes gracefully and you dump it in a cave somewhere!"

Facing him alone in those early hours, the impact of his words was especially potent. He was addressing the presence of thought before him, no matter where it originated. It was an interesting sensation to be talked to like that.

One grey morning he seemed to be dying for sure. I was feeling inept, useless and hopeless when I finally left and went to my room to rest. I bathed and went to bed by seven. When I awoke from bad dreams it was silent outside. I was gripped by racing thoughts and anxiety about what I was doing in there with him. I made a point of talking to the doctor again. She assured me it would take much longer for a coma to set in.

Then she said in a soothing Southern drawl: "He has such vast stores of energy. That last meditation was... whew! He's not ready to die. He is orchestrating this whole thing in complete control."

I told her I felt completely helpless and way in over my head. She smiled and said there is a myth that sages draw people to them in their last years, and clearly he had drawn Yogini and me close in these past couple of years. Whatever these fragments meant, her words were a comfort and of course flattering. It was curious to hear her speak of meditation. No one really talked about it, but being in his presence was a meditation all its own.

Just after our conversation, Lucia brought him some gnocchi. He ate and then he drank water for the first time in hours, looking over at me without a word as if to say, "You see ... you know nothing!"

I hugged her and thanked her profusely.
"Why? I didn't do anything."

CHAPTER 58

*I can't do anything about it, there is no question of
going back or anything; it is all finished—it is operating
and functioning in a different way. (I have to use the
words 'different way' to give you a feel about it.)*

Weeks went by and not much changed. When Bulbul, his daughter, arrived she anticipated his recovery. He looked bad, but not that bad. He allowed her to give him a foot massage. When Mahesh arrived shortly after Bulbul he was not convinced it was the last scene yet. She was anticipating his recovery. Mahesh and Dr Lynn discussed the possibility of this being the end.

"I don't think the old man is dying yet," Mahesh asserted in the kitchen. Lynn thought the illness could be cancer related. Having witnessed his last recovery he was skeptical as well. "He could recover, he's capable of anything."

At night I sat watching tiny ants streaming into the room, up the couch, along the floorboards, performing intricate tasks. When we killed them by crushing or poisoning them without concern he reminded us they had as much right to be there as we did. I never saw him kill an ant, a mosquito or a fly. He would swat at them, yell at them, but he never touched them.

Fourteen people showed up in one day. He made a show of offering me the Robot Fund in front of everyone. I ignored or refused it again, but in the back of my mind I was inventing elaborate scenarios where I gave the lion's share to his family, making sure to split off enough for myself of course. How much would I take? Hmmm.

In the night his breathing was like a kite disappearing into the clouds. Each time it gradually reappeared, slowly descending again into his wasted body.

During the day, he implored the Reverend over and over: "I need your help! What is the future going to be?" I had the feeling he was calculating the possibilities for his return to Gstaad. There was the impending issue of what would become of his accounts there.

He constantly brushed aside the concern about food with a wave of his skeletal hand: "This body can take care of itself, I have never listened to those filthy ideas and I am not going to start now! Ten days I haven't eaten a thing and I am fine."

Each day he sat or lay on the couch and held forth like always, bringing people together who had known each other for decades. Old stories were reviewed and new ones were hatched.

I read the 'Swan Song' to Moorthy, a retired philosophy professor, so he could edit it properly after I'd 'ruined' it.

"He is a very good editor, sir!"

Here is the final version...

[U.G. Krishnamurti ... mid-February 2007.]

What I have found of and by myself runs counter to everything anyone has said in any field of human thought. They have misled themselves and misguided everybody. You still fall for all that because if, for instance, you were to change your diet you would die of starvation. But I want to live forever! Can you keep me alive and healthy, the way I have lived for ninety years of my life? No? But that's all that interests me!

When once it throws out everything that has been put in there by your filthy culture, this body will function in an extraordinarily intelligent way. It can take care of everything.

If at any time I accept anything, it is not what the religious people have told me about the way the body functions, but what the medical doctors have found. Yet, what they do not know is immense; and they will never know how this body functions.

I have never taken any medicine nor have I ever seen a doctor. All the doctors who have advised me not to live the kind of life I had been living are now dead and gone. There is one exception—once, I had typhoid fever when I lived in Madras. My wife's brother was a top doctor in the General Hospital in Madras. The British had a wing in the hospital for themselves and nobody else was allowed to stay in the rooms in that wing. That year, however, they opened the wing to the general public. So my brother-in-law got me one room in it and another for my family members. In that room my wife and grandmother stayed. Three nurses took care of me taking turns every eight hours for a whole month, after which I walked out.

Although I assert that all doctors should be shot, I don't advise others not to see a doctor. I don't know what I will do if I am in a situation where I want to prolong my life a little longer. So I would never tell others not to see a doctor.

I brushed aside everything born out of human thought. Everything they told me falsified me. And what you are trying to get you can never get, because there is nothing to get.

What you are is a belief; if you let one belief go, you must replace it with another; otherwise, you will drop dead. I am telling you, a clinical death will occur. It is not the near-death experience of those 'near-death' scoundrels.

So you better go and make money and enjoy the fruits thereof.

All those filthy religious people are fooling themselves and fooling everybody, living on the gullibility and credulity of people, making an easy living, selling shoddy pieces of goods and promising you some goodies that they can never deliver. But you want to believe all that nonsense. It's a reflection on your intelligence that you fall for all that crap to which you are exposed.

Nobody has given me the mandate to save you people or save the world. The human species should be wiped out for what it has done to every other species on this planet! It has no place on this planet. If I am sure of one thing, it is that. If it were not for your destructive weapons, you would have been wiped out a long time ago. And you are going to be wiped out, because now others have the means to wipe you out. But you are not going to go gracefully without taking every form of life on this planet with you.

With minimum means you can wipe out the maximum power.

The body knows what it needs to do to survive. If it does not have the means to survive, it goes gracefully. The only reason for this organism to exist is to give continuity to the human species. Sex is only for reproduction, but you have turned that into a pleasure movement. What else is sex for than reproduction?

The human kind appeared on this planet and it thinks all this has been created for its use. You think you were created for a grander and nobler purpose. The human being is a more despicable thing than all the other forms of life on this planet.

You are just an animal, but you are not ready to accept that. You are not more intelligent than the other animals.

The native intelligence of the human body is amazing. That is all it needs to survive in any dangerous situation in life.

The native intelligence is what you are born with; the intellect is acquired from what they teach you. So, you don't have any words or phrases, or even experiences, which you can call your own. You have to use that knowledge that has been put in there in order to experience anything.

There is nothing to your love: if you don't get what you want, what happens to your, 'I love you darling, dearie, honey bunch, shnookie putsie, sugar britches, petite shu-shu, sugar booger?' If you don't get what you want out of all that, what happens to your lovey-dovey?

The only test for me is money. How free you are with your money? I don't mean, "How wasteful you are with your money?"

I have nothing to lose if the whole thing is wiped out. I have nothing to gain if it remains the same.

The only relationship you have with anybody in this world is "What do I get out of it?" That's all you care about. Other than that, there is nothing to it!

You all fool yourselves thinking that you are going to get some-thing by hanging around me… ho ho ho! You're not going to get a thing because there is no need to get anything from anybody.

You can't fit me into any religious frame. I don't need to fool people and thrive on their gullibility and credulity. Why should I? I'm telling you, you will lose everything! You are not going to get anything from anybody. There is no need for me to say you're not going to get what you want from anyone else either. That you will find out by yourself. But that you can't do either by your own effort or by your volition or by anything you do or do not do. That is not something that happens in the field of cause and effect.

Everything was thrown out of my system. I don't know how I was thrown off the merry-go-round. I went round and round and round. I was lucky—luck, not in the sense that when you go to a gambling place and win if you're lucky. They put me on a merry-go-round; I went on and on and on. I didn't have the guts to jump off. I was just thrown off like an animal thrown from the top of a tree. The animal just gets up and runs off.

Fear makes your body stiff and then you will certainly break your limbs. My body is never stiff.

The demand for permanence—permanent relationships, per-manent happiness, and permanent bliss—in any field and in any area of human existence is the cause of human misery. There is nothing to permanence.

So don't be a damned fool! Go and make money. That's the only thing that impresses me—cash on the barrel! I told my grand-parents this even as a little boy.

I am in perfect harmony with this world, exactly the way it is.

I will never break the laws, no matter how ridiculous the laws are.

I told Bertrand Russell, "The H-bomb is an extension of your policeman; are you willing to do away with the policeman?"

"You have to draw the line somewhere!" he said. I just said

goodbye and walked out.

There is no need to change this world at all; and there is no need to change yourself either.

I am not a sociable man; yet I am not anti-social.

What I am trying to emphasize over and over again is that what has happened to me has nothing to do with the spiritual nonsense they preach; it doesn't have even a teeny weenie bit of spiritual content. It is a physical phenomenon pure and simple. Once this body is freed from the stranglehold of whatever is put in there either by spiritual teachers or secular teachers, or by those scientists and medical technology, it functions in a very efficient way.

At the time I was born, when my mother introduced herself to me as "I am your mommy" and hugged me and kissed me, I apparently kicked her; and she died seven days after I was born. When they put me into the frame of an enlightened man, they said that the mother of such a child can never have any more children or sex, and that she would die. Actually she died of puerperal fever, but not because she gave birth to an enlightened man. They have to put such people into that frame of giving birth to an enlightened man.

An enlightened man can never have sex because he cannot reproduce another one like him. Once an interviewer on television asked me, "Can't we take your sperm and make a woman pregnant?" I answered, "There is no sperm anymore." Anandamayi stopped having her periods when she was twenty-one, after whatever had happened to her. She was a nice lady. She was a genuine article.

Your birth is not in your hands. You're here because your parents had sex. But I can say now that your death is in your hands.

There is no meaning in and no purpose to suffering.

If a body is lucky enough to stumble into its natural way of functioning, it happens not through your effort, not through your volition; it just happens, but not by what you do or do not do. It is not even a happening within the field of cause and effect. 'Acausal' is the most appropriate word for it, because a happening can never be outside the field of cause and effect.

346

If it stumbles into this of and by itself, such a body will be so unique that it will be unparalleled in this world and will function in an extraordinary way. Such a body has never existed before on this planet.

You don't have to take my word for it. Be miserable and die in your misery.

And such a man will be more spiritual than all the other claimants, but not in the ordinary sense of 'spiritual'—that nonsense must never be used. Spirit is only the breath as in 'he breathed his last'; the word has nothing to do with the spiritual crap.

The End.

CHAPTER 59

Such a flower, you can put it in a museum
and look at it—that's all you can do.

On *Mahashivaratri*, the new moon of Shiva, he rolled over and slept for 6 hours. It was the longest stretch of sleep he'd had. Sleeping on his side had been a turning point in the recovery two years before. In the morning he ate a hearty breakfast of *idlis* and *ghee*, taking coffee with cream during the day. The family reunion was gaining momentum and seemed to fuel him. Lucia handled the growing crowds graciously, coming into the room whenever her busy schedule permitted to sit at UG's feet and gaze into the face of the celestial flower in her garden.

"They spent eighty-five thousand Euro to build this for me!" he would remind us. "Nice people." Turning to me: "Not like you! You have become a very cheap bastard!"

I thanked him for the compliment.

When the gang from New Jersey came, Guha sat at his feet, occasionally stroking his knee or arm. Lakshmi talked to him in Telugu. The girls caught up with Cindy and studied amidst the chaos. The New Yorker was calling from New Jersey every few minutes. Just before his fall, she was forced to go back to the states because of a family emergency which prevented her from returning to be by his side. Her 'brother' Guha pleaded the case for her return, suggesting she could deliver some items for UG and leave again. She was shopping for him from two thousand miles away. He covered his ears, shouting: "I don't want that bitch anywhere near me!" Of course he asked after her

348

immediately upon their arrival. She'd had a car accident right after getting back and was pretty banged up. "Is she alright?" he wanted to know. Mostly she was distraught to be away from him at such a crucial time.

I spent most of that day on the floor next to the couch out of sight. The light playing over the walls and furniture was so beautiful. For once I didn't want to leave since, with all the others around absorbing his attention, I was in a unique position to relax.

Mahesh went back to India. Lynn left to California, certain there was plenty of time before UG went.

One night I heard him talking out loud in his sleep. He lay with his arms out nearly shouting: "What are you doing? It's too big!" It looked like he was directing the placement of some object.

The next night I awoke in a state of dreamlike awareness. A blue light was glowing on the ceiling and objects around him. In my dreams things always happened in an imaginary space, but this time it was clearly the same room.

At night he would gesture with his hands the way he did sometimes during drives or during the day in quiet moments. It looked as if he were directing people. One night I was sitting opposite him after everyone left. He was lying on the couch with his hands on his chest when he started gesturing with his eyes closed, pointing to me and then touching himself on the chest. I could make nothing out of what I saw. I was an ignorant onlooker in a conference between himself and some unseen party. It looked as if he were saying, "Never mind him, he's just here looking after me."

The others said that when he fell in the Black Forest three years before he told them he could see things happening all around the world in places as far away as Australia. Sometimes he said he was out in the stars or could see things on other planets. When I asked if UG was mentally 'out of it', they said he was definitely not. UG himself didn't seem to understand how he could see these things.

There was one other incident that reminded me of my Catholic roots. I was sitting across from him listening to his breathing. Just as I was drifting off to sleep I felt a sphere of breath turning inwards gently eased into my mouth. I some-times wonder if he was giving me the strength to 'finish the job'.

Guha and Lakshmi came early one morning. They sat on the floor in front of UG. He was lying with his eyes closed and patted the air in their direction saying quietly, "Good." For the first time I saw Guha break down and cry, doubled over on the floor with his head in his hands. His beloved was on the way down the river. I barely looked over at Lakshmi who also had tears streaming down her face. She moved to cover them with her sari. I couldn't help crying myself at the sight of it.

Before dawn a wind was up, banging the lemon tree against the roof like a spirit in the dark. An agitated wind persisted throughout the day. Yogini was extremely highly strung and a woman fainted in the kitchen, falling flat on her back on the floor. It was odd because she didn't even bruise her head. All day I had anxiety in my stomach.

UG was talking about a voice in his head: "It is all the time telling me it has been long enough and now it is time to pack up and go! It is a little song: *Time to goo-o. Time to goo-o.* What does it mean?" he asked innocently. No one wanted to answer that question.

When two old friends from Venice arrived in the afternoon he greeted them warmly. He had a lengthy conversation, think-ing they were someone else. He kept asking where their daugh-ter was. He made a joke of it, when he realized his mistake, but a swell of concern went through the room. His face looked ashen and swollen, the eyes were more vacant than usual.

In the afternoon I was talking to Mario on the second floor by a window. I couldn't make sense of what he was saying for the life of me. Suddenly there was a racket out the window as hundreds of swallows flew into the courtyard under grey windy skies, filling the air with flapping wings and sharp cries. Someone shrieked in the courtyard. It was like a scene out of Hitchcock's *The Birds*. After swooping around in crazy confusion for a few minutes, they flew off, leaving bird shit everywhere. When I went to take a bath for the night I had to walk under a ladder where someone was washing bird shit off the walls. The day was filled with bad omens right out of a horror story but nothing happened.

All day people came up to tell me UG was looking for me: "Ah Luigi, there you are! He's been asking for you!" I felt like a zombie, barely holding it together. The heaviness mixed with mental fatigue resonated in my guts whenever he shouted at me not to run off. There was nowhere to go anyway! I was sitting around so much I could hardly bear to sit any more, let alone in that greenhouse cave with him all day and night. It felt like my chest cavity was being dragged into the floor. I didn't leave the grounds for two days at one point. I felt like an inmate in a fancy asylum.

By seven o'clock there were about fifty people in the room. It was beginning to look a lot like India. He looked weak and slept a lot. Still his hands were waving around with those mysterious gestures, waving at things no one could see.

I tried to be as quiet as possible in the mornings, making breakfast in the kitchen next door. Every little sound reverberated in the stone house. Yogini would slip in next to me at the stove and ask how I'd slept. Usually the only sleep I had was in the earliest hours of the morning when the end of my shift was in sight. When he awoke I would help him with his few needs and then leave the room as soon as she was there. On a rare occasion he would say something to me. She was so quiet that he said little to her during the early hours. After so much time with him, there was nothing else to talk about. Once the others arrived he would start talking. I would go up to the apartment, climb into bed and lie there with the shutters drawn. The faint light grew stronger against the wall until I drifted off to sleep. It was as if my life was drifting away. There was a total loss of control, an uncertainty about the future like I'd never known before.

One morning after I was gone he spoke of a dream where a goddess appeared to him and said she would be taking care of him from now on. The name Bhuvaneshwari came from Guha later. Later, when we were alone in the room, I asked him what had happened.

"It's all just empty words and empty phrases. Image without content," he explained, brushing it aside with one of those sweeping gestures.

Each day he talked more about the song in his head. *Time to go. Time to go!*

One morning he said: "If it is saying that, it means in fact that it doesn't want to go." He was a disinterested witness to what was unfolding around him and within him. Sometimes it looked like he was uncertain about what he should do, but not eager to find out, maybe impatient? I don't know. The only effort he made was to share the mechanics of that body as it faded out.

He tore in half and tossed big checks from the New Yorker and the Reverend. Into the fire they went. The Reverend's check for 364 thousand dollars was postdated to 2008. It was his way of teasing UG into hanging around but it wasn't working.

That afternoon he said, "It's very strange, the breath is blocking the speech." Then he laughed to himself. He hadn't moved from the couch. "There is an urge for movement here," he said, indicating his legs.

Aside from a few trips in as many weeks, once to pee and twice unsuccessfully to shit, he hadn't moved from the couch at all. The second time he passed out twice without realizing what had happened. His eyes rolled back and he went limp. I quickly put him back in the chair before he realized what had happened.

Was he trying to starve himself? Was he trying to eat and unable? If the blockage opened, didn't that mean that he was going to improve? Was he waiting for Mahesh to show up and to straighten out legal matters, before he would go? Was he getting ready to starve himself to death once he got to Switzerland? Whenever they checked his vital signs they were so strong it was hard to imagine him dying any time soon. It was also hard to believe anything he said about the future since he was so unconcerned about it. Any discussion he started about it was doomed to speculation. I wondered at times whether he could will himself out of that body, but that would mean there was a will there, something that ran counter to everything he said. As he said to us in Menton weeks before, he was accustomed to being in the dark, something the rest of us dreaded.

On another day he said: "I close my eyes and I see millions and millions of faces of people. I don't even know them."

Then again: "It's strange: when I close my eyes I see a baby. Every time I close my eyes I see a baby."

The Reverend said, "I also see a baby."

"Of course. You are a holy man, sir."

A friend bought some paintings from me, after some months of hinting that he was interested. The purchase was an unexpected and very timely windfall. The way UG was bashing my paintings, I didn't want him to find out about it, but at that point it was as if he orchestrated it. I was getting anxious about everything, money, the future. And there was the question: what the hell was going to happen with me and Yogini after this? What the hell was I going to do?

Another life-saving windfall was the gift of a computer as thanks for taking care of him. Ray and Sharon went shopping for it online. Dr Lynn's daughter picked it up in the States and delivered it. UG presented it as a gift from the Reverend. I was beyond lucky to receive it and in no position to refuse such a gift. My old computer was dying and he was right, it was my lifeline.

Thanking him for the gift felt completely inadequate and awkward. I was so choked up I had to leave the room in a hurry or start crying in front of everybody. I went back to the apartment and sobbed like a baby.

CHAPTER 60

Nature in its own way throws out, from time to time,
some flower, the end-product of human evolution.

Chandrasekhar and Suguna finally arrived after countless delays. She entered the room and fell to her knees in front of him. With her head in his lap she cried in Telugu:

"Why is this thing happening to you! Oh UG!"

He looked at her with the tenderness of a mother, unaware of his own tears. Covering his face with his hand, he looked at the wetness on his hands with surprise, "Look! Crying! Oh my God!"

It was as if someone pulled aside the veil of his gruff exterior, revealing the essence that was usually hidden, an untarnished mirror of all of us. The room was swept with emotion. They had come expecting him to make a full recovery, imagining a trip to Switzerland and Germany once he was on his feet again. His condition was a rude awakening.

The little dining room opposite the kitchen turned into a media center. People were informing parties around the world, tapping away on computers and Skyping. Mario and the New Yorker had arranged the installation of a hotspot before she left, making it possible to communicate with the outside world about what was happening. Every time I went in Avner was trying to Skype someone: "*Hello... Hello...can you hear me?*"

We got the word that Ajja, the Indian sage, had died. People were talking about the loss of masters in the world and the disastrous consequences of it.

UG changed his line every day or so about whether that 'UG' was even still there. It wasn't a new line but he was more focused on the topic than usual. Nothing I heard from him contradicted his basic message. In fact, as his death approached, his determination to communicate the specifics of his state without distortion was his main focus.

"This is a functional being and you are all ideational beings!"

He had the Reverend repeat this line all day.

On a tape from 1969 he said the exact same thing about 'functionality'. Since the calamity he'd been repeating the same thing over and over. Had anyone 'gotten' it? If so, not one of us would have been able to say. The effects were continuing to unfold.

I spoke to Chandrasekhar outside in the garden. I'd been re-reading his *Stopped in Our Tracks*, and we were talking about the frustrating persistence of thought, in all its tenacity. It was constantly interfering with everything in my life, even at a time like this. I asked what would happen with UG's body once he died. He asked me if it would be possible to cremate the body in Italy. I had no idea.

On the evening of March 11th I half expected to be let go of my duties as night watchman. UG didn't urinate all day. What was I there for? He could have had anyone sit with him at that point since he didn't move anyway. Once the others left, he peed and drank water again. He contradicted not just everything he said, but everything he did, canceling the need for conclusions.

He made it clear over and over that life itself is something you can never understand.

It was very potent to listen to all this. The repetition came in handy later when I was out in the world, so easily distracted by the repetition of the usual nonsense.

CHAPTER 61

What is necessary is for man to free himself from the entire past of mankind, not only his individual past.

UG gave Mahesh the signal to return. That night he said he would wait for Mahesh to arrive and then I would go.

"You have two days left, buster!" he said to me. "And then I say 'bye, bye.'"

After almost exactly five years, I was being given my walking papers. I didn't know what to say. After weeks of the routine, with little sleep and a sensation of claustrophobia mounting, I felt nothing. He wasn't joking anymore. During the days leading to that final message I'd spent a lot of time on the new computer, avoiding the room. I simply could not sit still any more. *What the hell am I going to do now?*

All I could think of was I needed a root canal. That gave me something to do in Gstaad. It was as if he'd erased the hard drive in my thinking. I was completely scrambled. That afternoon Yogini called her father who said he would help her get a job with the government. She was in tears.

Calls came in from friends around the world. When the yoga teacher Desikachar called, UG didn't have the energy to take the phone. Desikachar's father was Krishnamacharya, who had offered UG some yoga and pranayama exercises to help with the painful energy outbursts after the calamity. I relayed his thanks to UG for the delicious lunches he'd prepared in Gstaad in years gone by.

UG was lying quietly on the couch, saying almost nothing.

He spoke in short bursts, describing how the breathing was 'cutting off' with what he called a 'locking mechanism' when he tried to talk. Then he said his breath was coming from the opposite corner of the room. After about five minutes of sitting up and talking he would collapse back onto the couch.

Guha noted that since he'd arrived the angle of the pillows that held UG's head were gradually getting lower and lower.

In the morning UG ate some rice flakes and drank water, saying it was enough to sustain him until Mahesh got there. The day was calm. I had the thought that a windy day made it hard for him to hang on to his body. He was like a barometer for nature as well as people. On a calm day he was calm. Everyone was silent, waiting and watching him intently. It was a deathwatch now. All pretext of a recovery was off. While Moorty was still there, I had helped him stand up and take some steps around the room. Pretending to do a little dance, he was barely standing for a minute when he signaled me to let him go and he fell back on the couch. Everyone applauded but no one was fooled.

The end was clearly in sight and the grieving looks and sad stares were getting to me; it was all too much. I couldn't stand it. It felt like we were all breathing down his neck. He didn't seem to care, but all I could think was how he described going off to die in a cave alone, not a room full of people staring at him with sad faces. The atmosphere felt heavy and I wondered if this was how it would end.

At one point he was staring at the ceiling, pointing and laughing. Guha, sitting in a chair at the foot of the couch, asked him what was so funny. He pointed to a line of light leaking through the ceiling insulation. "It is a line," he said and laughed. It was like watching a newborn discover things with the senses. He was delighting in them. There was no indication that he was in pain. Over and over he emphasized all that the body was was a vehicle for breath and that was all.

"This is a light body. I don't mean 'light' in that sense, I mean it weighs very little."

When I showed up after a morning rest, he said to me: "This is the last day, buster! You have become a web maniac."

The message to stay there all day was clear. I cannot explain how impossible it was to do it. I felt like a bucket that was full of that room. One more drop and it would burst.

I drifted in and out.

Suddenly Mahesh burst into the grieving room, like a broken dam, thundering fresh air into the room with a big splash. He fell to the floor and kissed UG's feet for a long, long time, and then patted his knees with an intensity that was unusual even for him. Just as he had the first time I met him, Mahesh swept life and humor into the room, shaking the dust of sentimentality out of the atmosphere.

I still remember how he grabbed the leg of UG's chair in Pareek's apartment in Mumbai the first time I saw him, shaking it around and growling at UG like a playful tiger while his eyes darted around the room to measure the effect on his audience. His lack of decorum was the very reason UG loved him so much. He was full of life, the very thing that was now ebbing out of UG's body. Then as now, his solid physicality seemed almost dangerous next to UG's frailty, his lightness.

Sitting on the floor in front of UG, who was now barely moving on the couch, he delivered all his messages from the friends who were unable to come. Then he put himself at his disposal. UG explained faintly that he was having trouble breathing.

"Of course you are!" bellowed Mahesh. "There are too many fucking people in this room!"

Everyone laughed. UG started giving him instructions. He should be moved to a place where people could not find him and allowed to die. The words came in halting breaths with all of us leaning forward to hear.

"Even that St Louis should not know where I am. Or be

allowed to come anywhere near me."

Mahesh should keep all the money left in his account. Then he named a figure of four thousand dollars, tossing this mistakenly reduced figure at him with a little gesture.

Mahesh laughed: "What a fall it was, my countrymen! Add a few zeros, UG!"

Everyone laughed again, clearing the smoke of grief for a moment. Then the room went quiet. People leaned forward or sank back with tears in their eyes. I sat at the kitchen table behind him, waiting for a cue. He said nothing. The air was heavy with expectation, I had the feeling he was trying to figure out what to do if he wasn't going to die right away. Maybe he wanted to get rid of us all so that he could die in peace. It seemed to be too late for that. In the silence a recording of Indian chants drifted in softly from the bedroom. The place was starting to feel religious with the music going and the devout vibe hovering around. The situation began to seem awkward and predictable.

UG started breathlessly telling Mahesh he wanted to get out of this place and be alone. Then there was another pause. In the awkward silence I thought, *This is too much, he wants us out of here.* It was as if we were smothering him. So I got up, swept the computer under my arm and walked out. The others followed close behind me. Maybe the time had come for Mahesh and Ray to put him in a car and drive him back to Switzerland.

Once we were all outside I had the feeling we should all go away so he could die in peace. It was as if everyone had the same idea at the same time. Just as we were talking about it Mahesh came out and made the final announcement. UG ordered him to tell us that we should all leave and go back where we came from so that he could die.

CHAPTER 62

It is like water finding its own level, that's all– that is its nature.

There was a brief pause, and then everyone moved. He'd trained us well; when he said it was time to go, people went. Suddenly it occurred to me that of course Yogini and I had no car.

For Chandrasekhar, Suguna and Bulbul the news was devastating. They had no idea of the extreme frailty of his condition before they arrived. Now they were hoping at least to stay on, but all hopes were shattered as the hours passed. At first he conceded that the three of them could stay in the house next door.

Soon, however, this option was abruptly removed: "Tell them all to go back where they came from!"

They had to vacate the house. They were heartbroken. Suguna tearfully told Yogini: "He always treated me with such dignity and now it is all over."

It seemed so brutal, so indifferent. After all those years of hosting him in Bangalore, in a house he'd bought for them after presiding over their marriage, watching the children grow up, tending to the finances, they were banished. The fact was, during his last visit to India, Chandrasekhar told UG that he did not want to see him die. He made the request with great feeling and his wish was granted with absolute finality.

The crowd broke up. I went up to the apartment and sat there in a daze. I didn't know what to do. Yogini and I had the feeling that it was ok to stay in the apartment until we arranged for transportation.

Mahesh told us not to leave just yet. He was overwhelmed,

361

in a bit of a panic about the whole situation. It was just him and UG now and UG yelled at him to go and rent a wheelchair, take him out and dump him somewhere! UG had the idea that Mahesh could accompany him to Switzerland, but he was clearly in no condition to be moved.

"He wants me to get a fucking wheelchair and take him out and dump him somewhere! I can't drive, I don't speak Italian and I don't have a visa for Switzerland! What the fuck am I supposed to do?

"He is telling me to go out and ask a stranger to help!"

Yogini offered to rent a wheelchair from the medical supply store down the street, but eventually things calmed down. Later, Mahesh came over to us in the garden.

"Forget about the wheelchair, my dear," he said. "He's calmed down. But now he's talking about going to France. I don't know what is going to happen but don't leave yet!"

A plan was made to have dinner with the others. Mario and Shorty were instructed to stay in the area but off the compound. Mario was there to deal with the Italian authorities and Shorty was in charge of the funds to pay for the disposal of the body when the time came.

At sunset we were walking toward the restaurant, when Mahesh called on Yogini's cell phone. UG wanted me to come back in a hurry. He needed help getting to the toilet. I ran back immediately. Was this another last minute reversal? Would I be there until the end?

By the time I got back, the crisis had passed. The Reverend was back, crouched in front of the stove with UG yelling at him. Yogini was hovering just inside the doorway. I thought maybe he wanted me to help with the fire but when I moved in that direction he snapped, "Not you!"

Nobody said anything. I suddenly felt like the guest who came back after the party was over. We left wordlessly. UG told Mahesh to call Ray and Sharon back when he saw that he would need help dealing with the situation. They were the most obvious pair for the job, she was after all a doctor and he a minister, so they were experienced with the comings and goings of life.

Mahesh followed us outside. We stood in the gravel driveway and he said: "It's not over yet! I don't get the feeling that you are finished."

I was relieved and took his word for it. We went back upstairs. At that point I didn't know what feeling to have. The call really threw me off once again. Yogini was already talking about what to do next, while I was sitting there wondering if I'd just blown my opportunity to stay to the end because of a goddamned dinner plan.

Then she reminded me of his offer of money 'to start a new life'. I had dropped the idea of taking money but I was feeling dark. All I could think was, *What now?* While playing with the idea of having all that cash, I caught myself thinking that at least I wouldn't have to go back to the life I was leading. The thing about taking it was that it seemed like an act of fear. I knew where it came from. Why should I take money others had given him for doing something any one of them would have eagerly done? It was a disgusting feeling. The other unspoken running commentary in my head was that living with Yogini was not going to work. My life in New York was not going to work. I was fucked. *Stand on your own indeed*, was all I could think; the shelter I'd been living under was gone.

The last thing he said to me was: "It's time for you to go and start your new life."

What was that going to look like? I didn't have a clue.

We went back and met the others in an apartment by the sea. Sitting on the balcony absorbing the shock, we talked things over before going down for dinner. The sun was setting. The coast of France to the West was purple with a necklace of dotted lights glittering at the edges.

After dinner we went back to the apartment. Smoke was

rising in a column like a straight line up from the chimney of his cave, slowly dispersing in the night sky. The curtains were glowing like red coals. For the first time since meeting him five years before, I felt as if I was out of place.

The next morning Yogini reminded me about the money. Mahesh was standing in the driveway so I went over and poured out my worst fears. This was it, I didn't want to leave any stone unturned before I left. I didn't know what my job prospects were anymore, I was nearly broke with no medical coverage. In light of these fears about money, the issue was obviously not resolved. Walking away from it seemed on the one hand stupid, but I knew damn well I didn't come to UG for money. His talk of giving it to me planted a vile obsession that nagged at me. By the time I was finished talking to Mahesh I was emotionally broken, slobbering all over the place.

"I don't even trust my fucking emotions!" I cried.

Mahesh thought this was great!

"Finally, my dear! You are having feelings about all this! That's it, man! You are not finished yet. Leave all that spiritual shit out, what is it you want? You have to finish this! I told him you wanted to see him one last time, he said you can come in, but no talking…"

So in I went to see him for the last time.

CHAPTER 63

*You haven't even taken one step. There is
no need for you to take any step.*

UG was lying on the couch, eyes closed, hands clasped across his chest. Everything was the same. Ray and Sharon sat opposite him. I wasn't sure if he was sleeping, but it didn't seem like it and it didn't matter. I went over and sat on the floor in front of him. The barest movement of his chest indicated breath. I had nothing to say. There was nothing to ask. I wanted to resolve this money obsession and the only thing to do was sit there and let it be burned. I knew he knew. It was in the air.

Looking at him lying there in a relaxed splendor, all I could think was: *I came here because he had what I wanted and it wasn't money.* For all his talk of money he had a complete disregard for it. Now he was dying and he still wasn't bothered by anything. That's what I came for and that's what I wanted.

Just then a spider crawled across the rug in front of me. The thought came to me: *That spider doesn't need money.* Of course spiders have no economy, they haven't messed up their way of living by imposing values on things (at least as far as we know). If something that simple doesn't need money, why did I need to worry so much about it? My fears evaporated. I sat a little longer, looking at him. *Is there anything more?* I wondered.

Thinking that it was all over, it didn't feel like anything was over. I was leaving the room, I was leaving that body lying there, but what was going anywhere? Who went? Who stayed? I couldn't think of a reason to keep sitting there, the job was done.

That was it. I got up quietly, turned and gave a *namaste* to Ray and Sharon and walked to the door. When I turned to look at him one last time, his eyes were open. I was just at the threshold of the door. It was too late even to pause, so after five years in the company of the most amazing living creature I had ever met, I gave him a little wave goodbye, and he smiled and waved from the couch and I walked out.

CHAPTER 64

But whatever you experience is worthless—it is not it—because this is a thing which cannot be experienced; it is not an experience.

The invisible thread was severed. I went back up to the apartment and sat waiting for a ride out of there, while UG lay across the garden in the cave with the curtains drawn. The property was silent.

That night I dreamt that his daughter, Bulbul, was calling me from the yard. I woke up and looked outside the window, but no one was there. Unable to sleep, I wandered around the rooms with moonlight coming in the windows from above the palm tree. I could see the windows down there glowing blood red. A column of smoke rose straight up into the stars.

I went out to check my email from the hotspot in the courtyard and Mahesh walked out, a black figure wrapped in a shawl. He gestured to me but I didn't want to approach and, after a beat, he disappeared into the house. A few minutes later Ray emerged from the house and walked over to the cave where Mahesh had emerged without looking up. It was a change of shifts.

I felt desolate. Something was heating up, burning before exploding and disappearing into space. I thought about the year before, when I found myself standing on a street corner in Brooklyn in the dead of winter after months in Europe with him. There I was in that horrible freezing limbo again, wondering what the hell happened. How could it be so easy to go from the warmth of his presence to the nightmare of civilization?

Looking across the terrace at the glow from those windows it seemed like the whole world was coming to an end.

For the next twenty-four hours we both got endless text messages, emails and phone calls, all with the same question, "What is happening?"

I felt foolish and angry and helpless and hurt all at the same time. There was a feeling of despair, grief, in my guts. I was on the verge of tears but if I let it go I would have fallen apart. What happened to the certainty I'd felt while I was sitting with him the last time? I walked away feeling light and confident and suddenly was in the clutches of a grief more awful than when my father died. Everything I looked at, the streets, the stores, the landscape and the sky, were soaked with wrenching emotion. My throat was sore from choking back tears. Every time I looked across the garden it was as if I was violating something sacred, really sacred, a natural force coming to an end, dissipating, eroding, erupting?

The smoke coming from the chimney reminded me of night after night sitting in front of the stove, feeding the fire as he lay there. Now that the leash was off my neck the command was clear, "Get out! Go!"

I went from being as close as I'd ever been to another human being to as far as you could get.

When we finally drove off, a day later, every kilometer we covered felt like more weight dropping away inside me. It was a beautiful sunny day and the ride over the Italian Alps was beautiful and light. When we finally reached Gstaad we went up to Yogini's apartment to wait. The apartment below us sat empty like an echo.

CHAPTER 65

What is behind all this is life.

Each morning I woke up with a dull ache and the worrying started. All I could think about was money. We sat watching the clouds go by in the skylight on the sloped ceiling. Yogini tended the garden on her balcony. I bought crates to make a work table. I wanted to use a quote from Mukunda Rao's book and there was a copy in UG's closet. We went down to look for it. The door whooshed open like a carpeted vault. Everything was exactly as he'd left it. Dim light sat in the room like a fog filtered brown by the heavy curtains. Yogini sat on the couch, while I found the book in the closet and had a quick look around the apartment. Two boxes of cream sat side by side in the otherwise empty refrigerator. His suitcase was on the table at the foot of his bed. It was spooky. We left in a hurry.

Shorty finally called while Yogini was out. As soon as I heard her voice I knew it was over.

UG died in the afternoon of March 22, 2007, somewhere around three o'clock. The body was taken away the following day.

I didn't ask what they did with the ashes. I didn't ask where he'd been cremated. Much later I asked for details but in that moment I just listened and felt surprisingly little. Later I learned that it took some days before the body was cremated. His body waited in line for a week at the crematorium, just like everybody else. "I am just an ordinary guy. You people are afraid to be ordinary, that's your misery."

Misha came and emptied out the apartment. The place upstairs was too small for the two of us so I decided to rent it. Yogini went back to the States and was gone for four weeks. I wondered if we would survive each other when she got back. With UG's words ringing in my head, I wandered around in the mountains. Each afternoon I went in a different direction. "This body is a solidified imagination."

A couple of times I went down and sat in his apartment around dusk. There were disembodied presences floating through the place, as if looking for him. I'm not prone to sensing that sort of thing but it was undeniable. They were just there and then after a couple of days it stopped. "Just because you don't see them, doesn't mean they aren't there."

As I sat on the couch, the high-pitched whine of the refrigerator penetrated the otherwise hushed room like the humming sound of the dehumidifier in his cave. Any place was suitable for him but the murky light affected my mood. For a second, in my own body, I felt the severity of the way he lived. "You wouldn't touch this with a ten-foot pole. You can't ask for a thing you don't know!"

After a few days it became clear that I had to move down there, the other place was too small for both of us. I moved my things in and opened all the windows, sleeping on the couch. I couldn't bring myself to sleep on his bed.

As soon as Yogini got back, we had a huge fight and I went up to Cologne to cool off and decide whether or not to stay on for the rest of the summer. Shorty told me about his last days. He was in a coma for four days before he finally died. Once he was gone, she and Mario went in to help clean up and take care of final arrangements.

"Did he look different?"

"His color was a bit different, but he looked pretty much the same."

"How did they remove him from the room?"

"Two men lifted him from the couch to carry him out. I was worried that his head would flop back since they picked him up from under the torso and the legs, but the body was stiff."

"Were they respectful?"

"They were very professional."

Mario said just looking at the body it was clear that whatever UG was, was gone. When the men from the crematorium asked if anyone wanted to accompany the body none of them felt the need to go. Shorty, who was the most emotional person of the lot, had no feelings whatsoever.

"It was clear he was absolutely gone. That was the amazing thing. There was nothing left."

And so, the box with the remains, the carbon contents of UG Krishnamurti, born 1918, died 2007, was loaded into the van and driven away to be burned. I had never seen a dead person outside a funeral home, so with those images I tried to find some closure, but it was just information.

At times the enormity of it all hit me. It was usually while I was walking through the streets of Gstaad, thinking about how strange my life was now, living in Switzerland, having spent five years with UG in the most amazing intimacy imaginable. It brought tears to my eyes. Talking about it was embarrassing at times; it was hard to contain myself.

"The only thing that will happen around me is that people's burden will be lightened a little, that is all."

That was an understatement.

"What ever you do with that book, you cannot put me into the frame of a religious man!"

CHAPTER 66

*Is there any difference between going to a church
and coming here?
Basically the motivation is the same: you are
looking for a new teacher, a new Bible, a new
order, a new church—that is all you can do.*

I left Chalet Birkenwild for good in November. Yogini left the
month before, eager to find a base in the States and get a fresh
start. I was in no hurry to go anywhere, but there was work
in the States that December and the idea of being there alone
was not appealing. After working fairs in London and Paris, I
headed back to Gstaad to pack up my belongings. Sitting in
front of the open door leading out to the yard, I was alone with
my luggage and an open road. There was enough cash to get
me around for the remainder of the year. It was cold out the
back door. I knew every floor in the building by then. The first
summer I spent two weeks in the basement. The next summer,
we walked UG home for three and a half months, meeting in
the basement cave. I spent almost two months in there taking
care of him day and night. After that, we shared the apartment
above him and finally I lived in his last apartment. I could never
have imagined spending that much time under those circumstances in the small cow town nestled in the valley of the Alps.
It was the last base I had.

When I met him I had hopes, to attain what he'd achieved
or, barring that, for some break to pull me out of the mess of my
life. Now I was on my own in the world with nowhere to land.

What had I learned?

Yogini and I drifted apart. There didn't seem to be much point in hanging on to the relationship, yet the habit of being in one had a life of its own. We stayed in touch, but whatever was going on between us was even more nebulous than ever. It was the resting place of a familiar voice on the other end of a phone line. So much for finding 'love'.

In an interview with a woman radio show host from the 1980's UG states the case about love quite eloquently.

(The questions are in italics, UG's replies are in plain text)

I wanted to ask about love.

Oh my god, oh my god.

People talk about love...

What do you think? What do you think?

I don't know.

I don't know then...

Is that another...

There must be two. "I love somebody and somebody else loves me." Wherever there is a division there can't be any love. You see (*laughs*), you see we are trying to bridge this gap, which is horrible for us. Which has no meaning. Which is demanding something from us with this fancy idea that there must be love between these two individuals.

So is there...?

What is the difference between 'I love my wife' and 'I love my country' and 'I love my dog.'? (*Both laugh*) It may sound very cynical to you. The fact of the matter is that there is no difference. You love your country; I love my country; so there is war.

So there is no love? Love is another one of these thought things?

Yes. Created by thought.

How about the body? Can the body know love?

It does not love itself. (*laughs*) There is no separateness here.

So there is no love? (laughing)

You want me to give a positive answer? (*Laughter*) I don't want to give any clever answers, any diplomatic answers. Why we are asking about that... about love?

Human beings are consumed with it.

Obviously our relationships are not so loving, so we want to somehow make that into a loving affair. And what amount of energy you are putting into making that relationship a loving thing! It's a battle! It's a war! It's like all the time preparing yourself for war, hoping that there will be peace, eternal peace. So you are tired of this battle, so you settle for that horrible non-living, non-loving relationship and hope and dream, one day, it will be nothing but love.

'Love thy neighbor as thyself', and in that name how many millions have been killed?

There is no relation between love and sex?

No. The moment there is a pleasurable sensation the demand to extend it longer and longer is there.

It would be easy to miss the other bits, where he was telling us all we have all we need to thrive and live. It's easy to miss in a transcription, the amount of joy and laughter his words produced despite the reaction of ideas to such blasphemy against the false god of hope. On that note:

So what about all the other spiritual ideas, the religious ideas? Is there any tradition that you know of...?

I can say one thing. All that is false as far as I am concerned, and falsified me. So don't ask me the question, 'How can all of them be false?' No, that's not the point. I don't want to be falsified because that's not the way I am functioning. I wanted to relate all that to the way I was functioning and struggled and struggled and struggled, so hard...

You struggled?

It got me nowhere. So there is no way you can reject it, because that created you.

Which created me?

The value system has created you. So there is no way you can free yourself from that. Anything you do to free yourself from that value system is adding momentum to that. This is the one thing that never occurred to me at that time.

This is pretty bleak! (Laughs)

It's not bleak! How can you say it is bleak! That's the only thing! It's the real thing...

It just is...

It is!

It is. It's not bleak. It's not anything, it just is.

Not at all, not at all bleak. You would like to use that word, fancy phrase 'bleak'. Is it bleak? Look at that, at this moment. Wonderful! I don't write poetry. The next moment I look at you as beautiful as the ocean there. Probably more beautiful if I am free from all the ideas that I have about beauty, you see. It's something, you know, extraordinary! That's all that I am interested in, you know; nothing needs to be done to change anything.

That about wraps up why Yogini and I drifted apart. Some couples are lucky enough to have sufficient common ground to maintain the exchange rate. Ours lacked that essential ingredient. There was also the basic ingredient missing in my case —money. The words of the face reader in Madras rang in my head, "He's useless to women." I never had much more than a few dimes to rub together anyway. It was a blessing and a curse all rolled into one. When I felt sad about it, a quick review made my demands to have things my way overwhelmingly obvious. There was nothing I could do about that. I worked with enough rich people to know the money wouldn't solve my problems. It was as much work to stay with a beautiful woman as it was to leave her.

The only thing left was to write, so the central focus of my life was writing about UG. It was my base and travel was a way of life. Work and shelter came my way in New York,

London, Paris, Venice, Miami, Basel, Los Angeles, San Diego, Bangalore, Delhi, Mumbai, Kathmandu. Without my planning it, a life of total stasis had been transformed into one of constant movement. Places were interchangeable. After a while it didn't matter much to me where I was. UG used to say every time he landed somewhere, "What am I doing in this place?" I started to feel that way. It was strange to have the words echo in my head.

In Paris I saw a vagrant woman sitting in a doorway. When I looked into her eyes they were like his. It was that same blank uncomprehending stare without anything behind it.

Walking around a mountain in South India, I came across a pile of ash in a field. At first it looked like a burnt broom, then I noticed a very simple clay ceremonial vessel and some bits of bone in the grey heap, indicating a cremation site. It was the remains of a poor villager, too poor even to afford the announcement sheets I saw around all the other cremation sites. After a few days the site was swept clear.

Life came and went, but what remained? What was there before... and what about after? No one knows. Life, having dropped another set of ideas into oblivion, went about its business of reshuffling the atoms. So actually, did it go at all? UG called it a 'reshuffling of atoms'. The energy that was animating that form went somewhere. He used to say, "Be careful what you say, it goes out there and never disappears." I guess we pick it up with new antennae, that was the reincarnation, thoughts being reanimated by other antennae. What does this have to do with anything? I don't know.

I spent days listening to taped discussions from UG's early years after the calamity. It was like oxygen at a high altitude. UG wiped the slate so clean there was not much left of the slate, but no matter how many hours I spent listening to it, nothing happened. The measuring sticks were all gone, in the sense, now he was gone, I was alone, and there was no company to monitor myself against.

At times there was a pleasant sensation that nothing really mattered anymore. Life was all that mattered. The same fears and anxieties were all there, but their grip was weaker, they fell off without as much struggle. Who knows if that was a result of age or his influence?

When I met other people who spent years with him, the impact he had on their lives was more obvious to me than it was to them. He was an invisible virus acting on the mechanism of understanding. You never really knew what was happening or had happened when it came to him. It was more felt than known. When I met a friend in London after two years, he asked what had changed in me. I said it was as if I was more myself than I'd ever been. If it's true that what I think I am is a borrowed idea, why that should be such a relief is beyond me.

"You separate yourself from that awareness and create an entity which is not there actually."

In the front of my calendar book I carried two photographs of him. In one he is a fierce looking young man with longish hair standing on a balcony in Madras with a thousand-yard stare. In the other he is a thin old man sitting cross-legged on the floor, playing cards with two children. I am left with the memory of five years spent with the old man and the voice of the young man from the audio files of my computer. The recordings are full of clarity, coming from nowhere, going nowhere. It stands alone, cutting through the other voices like a knife.

"I don't even hear what I am saying."

When I met him, he burst the narrative thread of my life like a bomb blast, uprooted me, and threw me out into the world.

"JK prepared the ground for what I have to say."

The mystery of that relationship will never be clear to me. What it looks like changes from day to day.

"You cannot experience a fact. You can only experience an abstraction."

In a video clip on YouTube from an interview in Australia

he compares himself to a common sewer rat, going on to say: "We are not honest, decent or decorous to admit that nothing there is mine. Everything is taken from outside."

It doesn't really matter how I got into that hotel room in February of 2001, all that matters is that I got there.

"Go and live a new life."

That already happened. His words cleared the net, disappearing into nothingness, while all my words bounced back and hit me in the face like tennis balls. Doesn't matter, I cannot see a way forward or back. There is no way anywhere. No wonder we scramble and make excuses to run from what we are. Habit is so strong it amounts to fate.

"Round and round ran the ragged rascal."

His mischievous poetry said it all.

When he was finished literally trying to drive us out of our minds, he died.

"Only when there is money can you dictate the terms of the relationship."

Following UG around was like being dragged through your own personal psychological ideological sewer pipe full of blockages, scrapes, clearings, and a final spewing forth of ugly bits that ended with a complete exhaustion that meant nothing to him. In the process you were subtly cleansed or clarified. For him there were no pipes, no sewage, no problems. He moved all the time like a breeze or a hurricane.

"You and I are in the same place. You are running away from the place and asking others where this place is."

I returned to India to work on the book with the excuse of researching. Moving gradually north, I ended up in Nepal, a country he refused ever to visit. To celebrate turning fifty I trekked up to Annapurna Base Camp but I didn't have a 'calamity'. The plane nearly crashed twice, attempting to land in a severe thunderstorm on April Fools Day. I almost fell off a glacier into a raging river out of sheer stupidity as I came down from the mountain, and the little row boat nearly capsized when I was caught in the middle of the lake at Pokhara, alone with a thundering storm pounding down on me. *Muchunga Mudu,* 'magic three' the Indians call it. Each time I smelled oblivion I said out loud: "Hey UG, I'm not finished with that book yet."

"A God is one who has no fear at all."

After two years and seven rewrites, I had a dream where he appeared on his death-bed. In it he stood up and threw himself forward on to the ground in full prostration. Then his face appeared in front of me, it was all I could see, eyes half-closed, murmuring, "I can't hear you." Who knows if that means anything, but it made finishing the book seem more urgent than ever.

He also repeatedly told us all, "Your job in life is to shut up."

I keep reaching out when I want to rest, but the world is so light now, it weighs about ten pounds. I am pulled along in the current with no control, waiting to see what is next; it's not an unpleasant feeling. Drifting aimlessly, with no home, no insurance, no property, I find myself waiting for the anxiety to flower, but instead it wilts and drops.

The trips back to India revealed more about Hinduism than I could have imagined, but UG seemed prior to everything spiritual, religious or philosophical. There was nothing in any of it that explained him but there were sacred texts that described what other people like him may have been like. He was outside everything thought could cook up and what that was in fact, as he always said, was impossible to articulate. After reading many of the *Upanishads* and books about Ramana, Nisargadatta, Anandamayi Ma, it hit me that the expression of UG Krishnamurti represents a radical departure. His way of living was unmistakably clean. Not once had he compromised by dishing out false hope or talking about things outside the realm of language. His use of language, foul as it was at times, was never less than precise yet simple enough for a child to comprehend.

I'm haunted by my inability to absorb the fact that everything I think is on the wrong track when it comes to him.He said when you are completely lost in the jungle you just stop! As lost as I am, I am not lost enough.

"Everything I did was irrelevant to this."

In the spring of 2009 I was staying in a garage apartment on the banks of the Hudson River. It rained every day while I was holed up in an apartment that resembled the one in Gstaad. Thunder murmured in the darkness at night, fireflies punctuating the spaces between inky black silhouettes of trees like senseless constellations. A light blinked on and off across the river. It occurred to me that I was finally living the enviable life of a lazy lout. Was writing just an excuse to avoid working a real job, struggling to make ends meet? Well, I had to do something. I had nearly nothing and it suited me fine. At times it hit me that I didn't learn a thing from UG. He took some things away from me, forcibly of course, that I really didn't need, just by being what he was.

"It's out of your hands. It's out of my hands. Just leave it alone, let it be."

Yogini came for a visit and we sat on the deck watching the river with thunder rumbling across the Catskills. It was a quiet visit, very amiable. We hung out for a couple of days. After she left I was having a philosophical afternoon. It occurred to me that if you drop love, happiness, and pleasure, you eliminate most of life's problems. When I sent a friend an email outlining this profundity, his wife asked,

"Can he do that?"

Of course I can't. It sounds good, though, doesn't it? What hanging around UG made possible, learning how to carry on with this way of living on the road, becomes its own corner. The ease of life I experience reminds me of what struggles he went through. My comforts are the limits of my knowledge. Knowing is my treasure and my trap. The idea of speaking the truth is ridiculous. 'Schoolboy's logic' is a perfect job description of philosophy. It provides jobs. All I have to do is think of UG asking that simple question,

"Does it operate in your life?"

That puts it all in perspective.

"If somebody asks you, 'What does UG say?' you won't be able to say."

I sat on the deck listening to the birds settle in for the night. Heavy rain made the lawn a deep green at twilight. Grey clouds drifted overhead. The days flew by, each one with its own little achievements and failures. The sounds of distant traffic were a vague mumbling of humanity. In the two-store town I was a stranger who came and went, forgotten soon enough. Big pastures sat empty, historical markers named sites of pre-Revolutionary buildings on the roads. Time was suspended among the fields and the stands of trees. Trucks and cars were for sale in lawns by the side of the road. The idea of buying one was immediately followed by that feeling of heaviness, the weight of ownership. The less you own, the more easily you can move.

"It takes enormous intelligence to be alone."

Despite living in the backwoods, I was never alone. Who was I kidding? He said in one sentence the job could be finished, could be finished if it were possible to listen. If only. Listening means dropping *me* but I am the one who is listening. It's impossible so why don't I give up? Because it's not even possible to give up, you have to be robbed, beaten and left naked in the streets of the unknown. Apparently that is only possible by some divine accident that distracts this *me* long enough to act.

"And in that silence there is an energy..." said JK, and at that moment UG said to himself, *What that is I could not know.*

And he presumably gave up, or was given up on by the collective consciousness. In that moment, as he told Mahesh, there was real fear, as his world was falling apart. But by then it was too late. As if seeing the whole thing go over the cliff, he gave up and fell into what he really was all along.

"I crossed over and found myself in the same spot. There was nowhere to go."

In the last line of *The Mystique of Enlightenment* he says,

"So, if you don't want to go anywhere, where is the need for you to look for a path?"

Damned if I know.

The taxi pulled into the driveway under the willow tree. The sunlight was disappearing over the river in the dusk. It was time to go. Pulling the door shut behind me, I lugged my bags out and said goodbye to no one.

I had a flight to catch out to the west coast.

Q: *Although everyone who is supposed to have undergone this 'explosion' is unique, in the sense that each one is expressing his own background, there do seem to be some common characteristics.*

A: *That is not my concern; it seems to be yours. I never compare myself to somebody else.*

Recent and Forthcoming Books
from
Non-Duality Press

I Am That I Am *by* Francis Bennett
A Christian perspective of the true Self

Emptiness and Joyful Freedom
Greg Goode & Tomas Sander

The Courage to Stand Alone
Conversations with UG Krishnamurti

Memories of Now *by* Han van den Boogaard

The Heavenly Backflip
by JC Amberchele

The World is My Mirror
by Richard Bates

The Sun Rises in the Evening *by* Gary Nixon

Nothing to Grasp *by* Joan Tollifson

Silence Heals *by* Yolande Duran-Serrano

The Direct Path *by* Greg Goode

A Flower in the Desert
by Richard lang

CONSCIOUS.TV is a TV channel which broadcasts on the Internet at www.conscious.tv. It also has programmes shown on several satellite and cable channels round the world including the Sky system in the UK where you can watch programmes at 9pm every evening on channel No 275. The channel aims to stimulate debate, question, enquire, inform, enlighten, encourage and inspire people in the areas of Consciousness, Non-Duality and Science. It also has a section called 'Life Stories' with many fascinating interviews.

There are over 200 interviews to watch including several with communicators on Non-Duality including Jeff Foster, Steve Ford, Suzanne Foxton, Gangaji, Greg Goode, Scott Kiloby, Richard Lang, Francis Lucille, Roger Linden, Wayne Liquorman, Jac O'Keefe, Mooji, Catherine Noyce, Tony Parsons, Halina Pytlasinska, Genpo Roshi, Satyananda, Richard Sylvester, Rupert Spira, Florian Schlosser, Mandi Solk, James Swartz, and Pamela Wilson. There is also an interview with UG Krishnamurti. Some of these interviewees also have books available from Non-Duality Press.

Do check out the channel as we are interested in your feedback and any ideas you may have for future programmes. Email us at info@conscious.tv with your ideas or if you would like to be on our email newsletter list.

WWW.CONSCIOUS.TV

CONSCIOUS.TV and NON-DUALITY PRESS
present two unique DVD releases

CONVERSATIONS ON NON-DUALITY – VOLUME 1
Tony Parsons – The Open Secret • Rupert Spira –
The Transparency of Things – Parts 1 & 2 • Richard Lang –
Seeing Who You Really Are

CONVERSATIONS ON NON-DUALITY – VOLUME 2
Jeff Foster – Life Without a Centre • Richard Sylvester –
I Hope You Die Soon • Roger Linden – The Elusive Obvious

Available to order from: www.non-dualitypress.org

CONVERSATIONS ON NON-DUALITY
Twenty-Six Awakenings

The book explores the nature of true happiness, awakening, enlightenment and the 'Self' to be realised. It features 26 expressions of liberation, each shaped by different life experiences and offering a unique perspective.

The collection explores the different ways 'liberation' happened and 'suffering' ended. Some started with therapy, self-help workshops or read books written by spiritual masters, while others travelled to exotic places and studied with gurus. Others leapt from the despair of addiction to drugs and alcohol to simply waking up unexpectedly to a new reality.

The 26 interviews included in the book are with: David Bingham, Daniel Brown, Sundance Burke, Katie Davis, Peter Fenner, Steve Ford, Jeff Foster, Suzanne Foxton, Gangaji, Richard Lang, Roger Linden, Wayne Liquorman, Francis Lucille, Mooji, Catherine Noyce, Jac O'Keeffe, Tony Parsons, Bernie Prior, Halina Pytlasinska, Genpo Roshi, Florian Schlosser, Mandi Solk, Rupert Spira, James Swartz, Richard Sylvester and Pamela Wilson.

CPSIA information can be obtained at www.ICGtesting.com
Printed in the USA
BVOW07s1033040914

365498BV00001B/48/P